AMERICAN SKINHEADS

**PRAEGER SERIES IN CRIMINOLOGY AND
CRIME CONTROL POLICY**

Steven A. Egger, Series Editor

American Skinheads
The Criminology and Control of Hate Crime

Mark S. Hamm

Foreword by William J. Chambliss

PRAEGER SERIES IN CRIMINOLOGY AND CRIME CONTROL POLICY
Steven A. Egger, *Series Editor*

PRAEGER

Westport, Connecticut
London

The Library of Congress has cataloged the hardcover edition as follows:

Hamm, Mark S.
    American skinheads : the criminology and control of hate crime /
Mark S. Hamm ; foreword by William J. Chambliss.
      p.   cm.—(Praeger series in criminology and crime control
policy)
    Includes bibliographical references and index.
    ISBN 0-275-94355-0 (alk. paper)
    1. Gangs—United States—Case studies. 2. Subculture—Case
studies. 3. White supremacy movements—United States—Case studies.
4. Terrorism—United States—Case studies. 5. Hate crimes—United
States—Case studies. I. Title. II. Series.
HV6439.U5H34   1993
364.1—dc20   92-23061

British Library Cataloguing in Publication Data is available.

A hardcover edition of *American Skinheads* is available
from the Praeger Publishers imprint of Greenwood Publishing Group, Inc.
(Praeger Series in Criminology and Crime Control Policy; ISBN
0-275-94355-0)

Library of Congress Catalog Card Number: 92-23061
ISBN: 0-275-94987-7

First published in 1993
Paperback edition 1994

Praeger Publishers, 88 Post Road West, Westport, CT 06881
An imprint of Greenwood Publishing Group, Inc.

Printed in the United States of America

∞™

The paper used in this book complies with the
Permanent Paper Standard issued by the National
Information Standards Organization (Z39.48-1984).

10 9 8 7 6 5 4

Dedicated to the memory of
Mulugeta Seraw, 1961–1988

Contents

Figures and Tables

FIGURES

TABLES

Foreword

The shameful ironies of history are sometimes extraordinarily revealing. In the city of Dresden, the target of America's most vicious firebombing in World War II and the setting for Kurt Vonnegut's masterpiece, *Slaughterhouse Five*, groups of shaved-headed youths gyrate and scream to music proclaiming racism, white power, and death to immigrants. Are we witnessing an aberration that will capture the imagination and devotion of a few angry youth or is this the first stages of a mass social movement with an ideology rooted in hatred and paranoia?

Americans for the most part live in a cocoon; they are oblivious to the consequences residing in changing political and economic forces beyond the shores of California or New York. The collapse of the Soviet empire and the destruction of the Berlin Wall proclaimed by left and right alike as a victory for democracy brings with it the most serious threat to democracy and world peace in sixty years. From today and into the next century, millions of poor immigrants from Eastern Europe will make their way across borders to the countries of Western Europe; Germany will suffer the burden most heavily, but all European nations will be affected. Symbolically closing the borders will not work; no state can provide the intensive surveillance of its borders that would be required to stem the human tide of desperate people.

It is absolutely certain that one reaction to the influx of immigrants competing for scarce jobs and even scarcer resources will be that segments of the middle and working classes of Europe will blame the victims of seventy years of Soviet economic failure. The middle and working classes' humiliation, shame, and rage at being unemployed or poorly paid will be directed against the immigrants. The music of the skinheads will appeal to their worst fears, and provide a rationale for their plight and a solution to their problems.

Ambitious and ruthless politicians will seize the opportunity to gain political power. What is today a relatively minor social movement has the potential to become the major social problem of the next century.

This outstanding book helps us to understand the social and pyschological dynamics that have led to the development of the skinheads in particular and of social movements based on hatred in general. It provides refreshing insights utilizing diverse sociological theories of crime and deviance. Mark Hamm's theory is refreshingly eclectic; he avoids the tendency of many writers to ignore the value of what are often seen as incompatible theories. He is at ease integrating reinforcement theory with Marxist dialectics, which in the end provides a multilevel analysis that is original and provocative.

Mark Hamm has delved into worlds where few sociologists dare to venture. In an era when social research is dominated by data gathered from the milking of government publications and the responses of faceless people to stilted questionnaires, he has risked interviewing people who are not exactly friendly to academics. He has endured listening to music that is more painful to the ears than were the Doc Marten boots that kicked his shins for his being seen with an Indonesian prostitute. By taking chances and using the best of sociological observational and interviewing methods, he has brought to life a world that most of us otherwise would not know.

And there is the music. The medium carries a message; and the message works to convert people to a belief system based on violence and hatred.

The skinheads are a world unto themselves. The more they are attacked, the stronger grow the internal ties.

Not content to hide behind the apron of the impartial observer, Mark Hamm makes an impassioned plea for developing strategies that would turn the tide of neo-Nazi terrorist groups. The research and imagination of the author provide a sound basis for developing these strategies.

In recent years we have seen a resurgence of outstanding ethnographies: Martin Jankowski's *Islands in the Streets*, Eleanor Miller's *Street Woman*, Terry William's *Cocaine Kids*, and Judith Rollins' *Between Women*, to name but a few. Mark Hamm's contribution takes its place at the top of sociological ethnographies along with this distinguished list. The book will serve not only to educate us, our students, and the public, it may well encourage other sociologists to leave the cloistered halls of their universities and discover what is happening in the real world.

Mark Hamm's fine work is social science at its best.

William J. Chambliss
George Washington University

Preface

The actions of Nazi Germany against Jews in Germany, Poland, Romania, Czechoslovakia, Holland, and France have been the object of countless reports and polemics, and of extensive research and scholarly interpretation. Although much has been agreed on, questions still remain about the legacy created by this horrid *lapsus* in European history.

For example, images of Nazism abound in our world today. They are frequently invoked in the media; university courses exploring World War II and national socialism seem to attract more students of history and political science than almost any other subject; and the burden of Germany's past shapes the forces that are coming to define the true power center of the emerging European Community. On the loftiest level, Nazism has become the topic of metaphysical speculation.

This book is about the relevance of Nazism to the understanding of modern developments in crime and delinquency. It appears that such research is necessary. Since the collapse of the Berlin Wall in 1989, a shadow of ethnic and racial violence has once again fallen on the land of Germany. Reminiscent of the brutal, wildcat method of Aryanization employed by youth under Hitler, these crimes have been committed not by an older generation of lost-cause Nazis, but by energetic teenagers with crewcuts, bomber jackets, and stormtrooper boots.

From the cities of Berlin, Bonn, Dresden, Leipzig, and Munich to the villages of Bruel, Cottbus, and Hockheim, German neo-Nazi skinheads have used clubs, knives, beer bottles, brass knuckles, ball bats, Oriental throwing stars, explosives, and guns to assault (and sometimes murder) an estimated 3,000 *Auslanders*—or foreigners—from the Third-World nations of Nigeria, Uganda, Mozambique, Vietnam, Pakistan, and Turkey (Bensinger, 1991; Jackson, 1991; Mücke, 1991; Seidelpielen, 1991; Ward, 1991).

The reemergence of such political crime is by no means limited to Germany—the birthplace (lest we forget) of national socialism. Today, swastikas appear in graffiti near the Holocaust Museum in Amsterdam and on Jim Morrison's tomb-stone in Paris. In London, Nazi graffiti is visible in Piccadilly Circus and Carnaby Street, as hundreds of young skinheads walk the streets unabashedly displaying Nazi regalia in visual terms for the general public to see.

During the 1980s, racial attacks in Britain reportedly increased to 70,000 a year, primarily because of skinhead violence. Included were the murder of seventy-four Asian and Pakistani men (Brown, 1984; Gordon, 1990; Hiro, 1991). This wave of violence began its surge in May of 1985 when skinheads from Britain, Belgium, Denmark, and France instigated the tragic Brussels soccer riot leaving 38 people of color dead, and another 200 wounded (Cooper, 1989). And it continues to this day. During the Persian Gulf War, for instance, British skinheads and other white extremists were implicated in the firebombing of some twenty mosques in the greater London area (Bowling, 1990).

Several years earlier, a shaven-headed sixteen-year-old white male from Plymouth, Massachusetts, jumped a security fence and spray painted a black swastika on the face of Plymouth Rock. In this place of historical significance, the skinheads received their symbolic welcome to the shores of North America. But this is more than a book about graffiti. Rather, it is an attempt to illustrate how times have changed; and once again, Nazism has something of a universal character about it.

I endeavor to explain how a modern form of Nazism has flourished in markedly different cultures — from the great industrial centers of Western Europe to the streets of Chicago, Dallas, San Francisco, Las Vegas, New York City, Detroit, and Milwaukee — and how it has appealed as much to intellectual youth of the day as it has to functionally illiterate factory workers and prisoners who cannot even spell Nazi or Hitler. As such, I attempt to delineate the reified beliefs, values, and norms used by these new adherents of Nazism to inveigh violently against the rationalistic individualism of democratic societies throughout the Western world.

Yet I bear only criminological witness to the emergence of neo-Nazism among today's youth. I leave to historians the task of judging the political effects of neo-Nazism in North America and elsewhere. Some historians have already set themselves to that task. If these pages can help them to accomplish their aim, I shall have accomplished mine.

I am pleased to engage in the custom of thanking those who have helped me complete this project. I am indebted to the encouragement, assistance, and inspiration of Freda Adler, Gregg Barak, Andrew Boberschmidt, M. A. Bortner, Benjamin Bowling, Bill Breeden, Thomas Castellano, William Chambliss, Susan Christopherson, Robert Clouse, James Conyers, Walter DeKeseredy, Marie Douglas, John Dunfee, Steven Egger, Milton Firestone, John Hewitt, Anne Kiefer, Pat Lauderdale, Christopher Perry, Hal Pepinsky, Richard Pierard, Robert Regoli, Jeffrey Ross, Lisa Roth, Marla Sandys, Jeff Schrink, David Skelton, Bob Shafer, Brenda Starkey, Peggy Strobel, Brian Tuley, Ralph Weisheit, Louis Weschler, and L. A. Wilson.

I owe an especial debt of gratitude to Richard G. Landini, president of Indiana State University, whose leadership has made ISU an outstanding institution for the academic study of racism.

The research publications of the Anti-Defamation League of B'nai B'rith proved to be indispensable in this research, and so have James Coates' *Armed and Dangerous*, Kevin Flynn and Gary Gerhardt's *The Silent Brotherhood*, Paul Fussell's *Bad, or The Dumbing of America*, John Hagedorn's *People and Folks*, Dick Hebdige's *Subculture*, Elinor Langer's "The American Neo-Nazi Movement Today," and Walter Laqueur's *Fascism*.

Finally, I acknowledge the American skinheads who came forth and agreed to participate in this research. After all, this is their story.

Part I

Idiots with Ideology

Every youth movement presents itself as a loan to the future, and tries to call in its lien in advance, but when there is no future all loans are cancelled.
—Greil Marcus
Lipstick Traces

1 _____

The Neo-Nazi Skinheads of
North America

It's about time in this country that we replace racism and bigotry with love
thy neighbor.

—George Bush
January 1990

If you can't eat it or fuck it, kill it!

—A New York City Skinhead
June 1989

Criminologists rarely describe crimes of violence in full detail. Violence that is
grounded in a morality of sheer hatred has never been depicted in the literature.
Therefore, a logical way to begin the *American Skinheads* is with a brief explanation of the crimes these youths are capable of committing.

There is no lack of information in this area. During the 1980s, according to
one source, the tally of skinhead violence included 121 murders of blacks and
gays in urban areas across the nation, 302 racial assaults, and 301 cross burnings
(Wooden, 1991). On one evening alone—November 10, 1988 (the fiftieth anniversary of the Nazi *Kristallnacht*)—American skinheads were reportedly involved in more than sixty incidences of anti-Semitic vandalism, assault, and
harassment (Marovitz, 1991). Yet one of these crimes stands as an exemplar of
ideologically motivated violence.

THE KILLING OF MULUGETA SERAW

At about 1:30 on the morning of November 13, 1988, Kenneth Murray Mieske
(aka Ken Death)—a stocky twenty-three-year-old singer in a heavy-metal band
called Machine—drove his car through the rainy streets of Portland, Oregon. At
his side were twenty-year-old Steven Strasser and nineteen-year-old Kyle Brewster. Mieske, Strasser, and Brewster were members of a skinhead gang called the

East Side White Pride and they were intoxicated on beer. Their hair was cut short and they wore jeans, bomber jackets, and black steel-toed boots.

Simultaneously, a young Ethiopian immigrant named Wondwosen Tesfaye double-parked his light brown Dodge sedan near the corner of 31st Avenue and Pine Street in the southwestern section of Portland. Tesfaye was accompanied by two other Ethiopian immigrants: Tilahun Antneh and Mulugeta Seraw, a slightly built twenty-seven-year-old employee of Avis Rent a Car. Seraw got out of the Dodge, leaned into the open window, and bid his friends good night.

At this point, Ken Death rounded the corner of 31st and Pine where he encountered the Ethiopians. Mieske had never seen the immigrants before, and vice versa. "Move your car!" roared the drunken Mieske. A moment passed and Mieske shouted, "Move your fuckin' car!" Another moment passed and again Mieske yelled, "Move your fuckin' car!"

Just as Seraw backed away, Mieske, Strasser, and Brewster approached Tesfaye's car. Mieske carried a baseball bat. He smashed the front window of the Dodge, spraying Tesfaye and Antneh with shattered glass. Then he turned on Seraw.

"No, please!" cried Seraw. "Please!"

Using all the power of his strong young body, Mieske then beat Seraw in the head with the ball bat as Strasser and Brewster kicked the 110-pound immigrant with their boots. When they were finished, Mieske had fractured Seraw's skull in two places, killing him.

Twenty-four hours later, Portland police searched the three-room apartment of Strasser and Brewster. In the first room, they discovered a collection of baseball bats and clubs. In the second, they found racist propaganda published by a Southern California organization known as the White Aryan Resistance (W.A.R.). And in the third room, they found a small library on the rise and fall of Nazi Germany (ABC News, January 15, 1991; Langer, 1990).

SOCIAL IMAGES OF THE AMERICAN SKINHEADS

Despite the horrifying nature of this sort of crime, little is really known about the American skinheads. Instead of careful, well-researched accounts of these young people, the American public has been inculcated with information that is often sensational, frequently sanitized, and highly contradictory. Nevertheless, this information has played an important role in communicating the imagery and symbols of the skinhead subculture.

Between 1988 and 1991, American skinheads were the subject of more than fifty national magazine articles, at least a dozen commissioned reports by anti-racist organizations, one Federal Bureau of Investigation (FBI) monograph, numerous television programs, and two Hollywood movies (*Skinheads* and *Hail the New Dawn*). The imagery emanating from this extraordinary coverage is that skinheads are an angry and demonic group of shaven-headed neo-Nazis who are often wild-eyed followers of Satan. They are depicted as physically fit young white men dressed in blue jeans, white power T-shirts, red suspenders, and Doc Martens, a heavy steel-toed boot of British make. They are said to range in age from about thirteen to twenty-five, and are thought to be aligned with a brand of rock and roll called speed metal, thrash metal, and/or death metal. The skinheads are fond of painting graffiti on sidewalks, buildings, and tombstones. Their mark is said to be the swastika, or sentiments such as "White Unity," "No Jews," and "Niggers Suck."

More than anything else, skinheads are depicted as vitriolic racists. In fact, many skinheads themselves cite racism as the primary reason for their violent behavior. For example, there is the case of Clark Reid Martell.

In 1984, twenty-five-year-old Martell started what is considered to be the first neo-Nazi skinhead gang in the United States—Chicago's Romantic Violence. Romantic Violence was composed of twelve other young white men recruited into the group by Martell after he had read Adolf Hitler's *Mein Kampf* (Leo, 1988). On January 25, 1988, Martell and six members of Romantic Violence were found guilty of breaking into a woman's apartment, beating her until she was unconscious, spraying her with Mace, and then drawing a swastika on the wall with her own blood. They did this because the woman had been seen talking to several black folks on the street (Anti-Defamation League of B'nai B'rith [ADL], 1988c). Said Martell at an assembly of white racist leaders shortly before his arrest: "I am a violent person. I love the white race, and if you love something, you're the most vicious person on earth" (quoted in Coplon, 1989:82).

Accordingly, the skinheads have been portrayed as youth who are profoundly alienated from mainstream society. Why else, we might ask, would they commit such atrocities? Leonard Zeskind, research director of the Center for Democratic Renewal, explains this alienation primarily in terms of economic disadvantage. About the skinheads, he argues that "We now have the first generation of young white kids who don't expect to live better than their parents and [they] are looking for scapegoats" (quoted in Cooper, 1989:271).

More to the point, Eva Sears of the Center for Democratic Renewal characterizes skinheads as "alienated and disaffected young whites who feel that the future has little to offer them" (1989:25). Others view skinheads as "impressionable young people" (Hackett, 1987:22) and "disenfranchised working-class youth" (Klanwatch, 1991:54) who "are mainly high school dropouts" (Came, 1989:44) that have "been abused by their parents" (Wooden, 1991:2). According to a recent FBI report: "Most skinheads come from broken families. The insecurity they felt as children developed into rage, and they relieve their rage by attacking others" (quoted in Anderson, 1990:A12).

Joan C. Weiss, former executive director of the National Institute Against Prejudice and Violence, explains the underlying cause of this profound alienation and rage not as a reaction to educational disadvantage or childhood insecurity; but rather, as a natural "backlash to major social changes such as the women's and gay rights movements, as well as to the institution of affirmative action programs" (1989:28). Similarly, a 1988 U.S. Justice Department report on hate crime attributes skinhead violence to "a perceived decrease in government efforts to prevent discrimination in education, housing, and unemployment" (quoted in Barrett, 1989:4). These reckonings on alienation are further echoed by Ralph Neas, executive director of the Leadership Conference on Civil Rights, who claims that "As a result of the Reagan administration's offensive against municipal affirmative action plans, one would think the white male had become the primary victim of discrimination in this country" (quoted in Barrett, 1989:4).

This perceived victimization has also been voiced by a number of skinheads. For instance, David Mazzella, former president of the Hollister, California, WAR Skins told a newspaper reporter in 1987: "These people [nonwhite immigrants] take our jobs and land and give us nothing in return. We're prepared to fight, to kill, whatever it takes for the preservation of the white race" (quoted in Klanwatch, 1989:8).

To demonstrate these strident beliefs, Mazzella became one of the leading skinhead recruiters on the West Coast during 1987, appearing several times on California television and radio talk shows. In August of 1988, Mazzella fled Southern California after a warrant was issued for his arrest following an incident where he attempted to strangle a teenage boy who tried to interfere with his recruitment efforts. Mazzella traveled to Portland where he took up residence in an apartment with Steven Strasser. At length, Mazzella indoctrinated Strasser and two friends into the skinhead way of thinking. These two friends were Kyle Brewster and Kenneth Mieske, who together with Strasser, would three months later bludgeon Mulugeta Seraw to death (Klanwatch, 1989:8; ADL, 1988c; Langer, 1990).

In sum, the social and political contentions of the Reagan era seemed to have produced conditions conducive to extreme alienation among white, working-class youth in the United States. In turn, this extreme alienation caused certain white kids to shave their heads, tattoo themselves with swastikas, espouse racist beliefs, and commit hate crimes; usually with baseball bats, work boots, guns, or knives. This is the social imagery of the American skinhead. It has become manifest in numerous articles and reports filed by experts on hate crime. Most influential among these expert opinions has been the research publications of the Anti-Defamation League of B'nai B'rith.

The ADL contends that skinheads commit their hate crimes "out of desperation and impatience" (1987a:2). "Skinheads," say these experts, "are undisciplined, violence-prone, and many are obvious misfits" (ADL, 1988c:28). Moreover, young whites become skinheads because "their anger at their plight has led them to identify with the most violent and offensive image they could imagine—Nazism, which most youngsters have seen on television, in the movies, in comic books" (ADL, 1989b:29).

Gang Structure

The social imagery of the skinheads is completed with a highly distorted picture of gang structure. On one hand, experts say that "the 'fraternity' of skinheads offers youth an identity and a support network, and its impact reaches children as young as 12 years old" (Sears, 1989:24). These experts have also found that "gay-bashing (random beatings of lesbians and gays) is an initiation rite for certain Nazi skinhead groups" (Sears, 1989:26). In fact, experts from the John Brown Anti-Klan Committee claim that "Today's Nazi skinheads . . . are [highly] schooled in Nazi philosophy and taught to kill, Green Beret style" (Gatewood, 1989:1). This remarkable discovery is confirmed by the experts at the Center for Democratic Renewal. They contend that "many racist skinheads have a straight-forward neo-Nazi political philosophy and a developed sense of political identity" (*Monitor,* April 1988:6), and by experts at the National Institute Against Preju-dice and Violence who argue that "The neo-Nazi [skinheads] are prepared to take up arms and overthrow the government to . . . defend their communities against [minorities]" (Terrell, 1989:3).

Standing in instructive contrast to these research findings, however, the FBI claims that "Skinheads in and of themselves are not necessarily organized, *nor do they share any common beliefs"* (quoted in Cooper, 1989:263, emphasis added). Likewise, the Southern Poverty Law Center has gone so far as to suggest that "There is no single national organization, [skinheads] frequently move in and out of gangs, and gangs themselves split and merge" (Klanwatch, 1989:5). But the most intriguing expert opinion has been filed by the ADL. Their research sug-gests that the skinheads, as a delinquent youth subculture, are falling apart right before our eyes. "The skinheads," according to the ADL, "have severe internal problems. There is substantial evidence of drug use, Satanism, intragang vio-lence, and all the other sociopathic tendencies to be found these days on the outer fringes of the youth culture" (1988c:28).

SOCIAL IMAGERY, PUBLIC POLICY, AND YOUTH CULTURE

The shaping of public opinion about the American skinheads has taken place within a generally hostile atmosphere. Indeed, the social imagery of the skin-heads is built on research that is often misinformed, typically incomplete and unbalanced, and invariably simplistic. These ill-derived stereotypic characteris-tics have, in turn, raised the threat potential of the skinheads to the point at which a sort of moral panic has ensued, leading to drastic actions taken by social control agents and community activists to send the skinheads into a tailspin of decline and disarray. Put simply, everybody loves to hate the skinheads, but nobody wants to spend the time, energy, or money to figure out why these youths have turned out to be so magnificently deviant to begin with.

The battle against the skinheads has been waged at the highest levels of the American legal order, the "outer fringes of the youth culture," and various points in between. In January 1990, President George Bush told the congregation of a black church in Washington, D.C.: "Americans must recommit ourselves to work for justice and for unity of all people. No more racism. Leave the entire baggage of bigotry behind."

Less than a week later, the president extolled his Congress and country to do something more than just talk about racial violence in America. "Everyone of us," said the president, "must confront and condemn racism, anti-Semitism, bigotry and hate. Not next week. Not tomorrow. But right now! Every single one of us."

These have not been idle words. Six months before this presidential address, then U.S. Attorney General Dick Thornburgh—a long-time crusader against racial violence in America—also decried "the shocking reemergence of hate group violence," and promised to track down members of such groups "no matter what" (quoted in Barrett, 1989:A12). After this, federal prosecutors trained their legal sights on the skinhead subculture, as the FBI initiated some forty investigations of skinhead gangs across the nation (Cooper, 1989).

On February 22, 1989, the confrontation with the skinheads moved to the halls of the U.S. Congress where Representative John Conyers (D-Michigan) and Senator Paul Simon (D-Illinois) introduced a bill entitled the Hate Crime Statistics Act. This act requires the FBI to begin categorizing acts of prejudicial violence as a means of publicizing the extent of skinhead activity throughout the United States. Testifying in support of the Hate Crime Statistics Act was former U.S. Senator Birch Bayh, now chairman of the board of the National Institute Against Prejudice and Violence. "Once the American people really know about it," said Bayh, "most of them will demand that this trash [the skinheads and other hate groups] be kept in the alley with the rest of the garbage" (Cooper, 1989:274). And on February 7, 1990, the U.S. Senate—responding to what it called, "a rising tide of hate crimes nationally"—voted 92–4 in favor of this new act, predicting that its implementation would cost taxpayers at least $10 million (Koch, 1990:1).

Such strong hate crime policies have also received support at the state level of government. During the 1980s, forty-three states passed some form of statute against institutional vandalism and thirty-one states enacted laws against bias or harassment, including interference with religious worship and cross burning laws (Finn and McNeil, 1988). Seventeen of these thirty-one state laws were based on a model hate crimes statute prepared by the Anti-Defamation League. This model legislation was, presumably, an outgrowth of ADL's research on hate groups such as the skinheads. Burton S. Levinson, ADL national chairman, explained the "necessary and crucial" importance of this model legislation in a recent ADL monograph: "Law enforcement authorities can deal more effectively with hate crime *if they know exactly what they're fighting*" (ADL, 1988b:2, emphasis added).

Presuming that they also "know exactly what they're fighting," other experts have called for broader changes to counteract what the ADL continues to call the "bewildering menace" of the skinheads (1989b:1). For example, the Center for Democratic Renewal has advocated "Long-term planning and sweeping changes . . . to alter social and economic conditions in which extreme right-wing influence flourishes" (Sears, 1989:26). Without these sweeping changes, the Center for Democratic Renewal predicts that "a new Hitler state [may] be built . . . on the backs of young people" (Sears, 1989:26).

Other experts have developed elaborate educational programs to counteract the skinhead movement. Based on their "original research on the causes and nature of [skinhead] incidents," the National Institute Against Prejudice and Violence publishes a newsletter and training materials, and provides "consultation and technical assistance on preventing and handling incidents and responding to activities of the . . . neo-Nazis" (Weiss, 1989:29). Based on their own research, the ADL also currently makes available four different educational publications on confronting strident forms of racism.

Together, these materials have been cited by the U.S. Congress and used by the U.S. Department of Housing and Urban Development, the U.S. Department of Justice, state and local human relations commissions, more than 200 colleges and universities in the United States, and have been the primary source material for media presentations on dealing with the skinheads (ADL, 1989a; Cooper, 1989; Nielsen, 1990; Weiss, 1989). We might, therefore, assume that these research materials were ultimately used by the president of the United States and the Congress to launch their new war on racism.

Community action groups have also ratcheted up their campaign against the skinheads through both nonviolent and violent means. On December 13, 1988, more than 200 residents of Seattle, Washington, peacefully protested a skinhead vigil commemorating the 1984 FBI killing of a well-known white extremist (Buursma, 1988). One week earlier, another 300 Portland residents marched in silent mourning for the skinhead killing of Mulugeta Seraw (Gatewood, 1989). And on November 22, 1987, Los Angeles police called out attack dogs and water cannons to disperse several hundred anti-skinhead activists who had gathered to protest a speech by Georgia-based white racist J. B. Stoner, who spoke to a handful of skinheads at a Ramada Inn in Glendale, California (Tricarice, 1987).

Perhaps the most dramatic display of community activism occurred on March 4, 1989, when more than 1,000 angry antiracist demonstrators surged up California Highway 12 to the town of Napa where they confronted some 100 skinheads who had been attracted to an event billed as the Aryan Woodstock. The skinhead security force for this event was armed with two automatic assault rifles and five shotguns (ADL 1989b; field notes). More than 450 California Highway Patrol and Napa County sheriff's deputies lined the highway to prevent a violent confrontation between the skinheads and their detractors (John Brown Anti-Klan Committee [JBAKC], 1989). Subsequently, this event gained nationwide media attention.

Yet, this community activism has led to an event that is potentially even more troublesome. On January 14, 1989, 150 antiracist youths with shaved heads (the antiracist skinheads) met in Minneapolis, Minnesota, and formed a coalition called the Syndicate. The Syndicate was composed of members of Minneapolis's Anti-Racist Action (ARA); Milwaukee's Brew City Skins; the Des Moines, Omaha, and Kansas City Mid-America Patriots; Chicago's ARA; Indianapolis's ARA; and two groups from Cincinnati—Skinheads Committed Against Racism, and the Anti-Racist League (JBAKC, 1989). These antiracist skinheads gave reports on local conditions and the status of their struggle against the racist skinheads (now officially referred to as Boneheads by a consensus of everyone at this meeting). Three major themes emerged from their reports.

First, in cities where there is a strong and organized antiracist street presence, it has often been difficult, if not impossible, for the Boneheads to get a foothold in the community. Where local antiracist skinheads were weak or disorganized, the Boneheads have been quick to exploit the situation on the street. Second, most Boneheads in the Midwest were being recruited by a Bonehead from New Orleans named Matthew Myer. Myer is a member of the National White Resistance and has a prison record for assault (ADL, 1989b). Since 1989, he has traveled throughout the Midwest recruiting white youths in coffee shops, bars, and high schools (field notes).

Finally, the Syndicate agreed that wherever the Boneheads do get a foothold in a local community, they destroy the counterculture/youth scene by their "violent, racist and disgusting acts" (quoted in JBAKC, 1989:6). To preserve their counterculture, the Syndicate took an uncompromising stance against the Boneheads: They vowed to use violence as a necessary means of defending the subcultural scene and its belief system from the racist skinheads. In other words, the battle against the neo-Nazi skinheads had evoked enough public wrath to warrant the development of vigilantism.

CONCLUSIONS

In 1988, *New York Times* correspondent Katherine Bishop reported that "Law enforcement and other groups concerned over racist violence . . . take some solace in the fact that the rebellious nature of the skinheads makes them difficult to organize into a mass movement" (1988:17). These same law enforcement officials and community groups would take little solace, however, in the research published by the Southern Poverty Law Center who write that "The emergence of Skinhead gangs represent a unique and frightening phenomenon in the history of white supremacism in America: for the first time, a nationwide racist movement is being initiated by teenagers who are not confined to any single geographic region" (Klanwatch, 1989:1).

These conflicting reports exemplify the problem of translating a moral panic — preserved by inconclusive research — into coherent public programs to control hate crime. Do the American skinheads represent spontaneous, rebellious, unorganized street gangs that lack a common belief system? Or, are they a highly organized, nationwide racist movement with a clear and well-developed political agenda? Are the skinheads falling apart because of internal problems, or are they truly a "frightening phenomenon in the history of white supremacism in America?" Are the skinheads profoundly alienated, disenfranchised, working-class, high school dropouts from broken homes? Are they drug users who listen to heavy metal and worship Satan? Lamentably, we don't really know the answers to any of these questions.

This lack of knowledge has serious implications for public policy and community action. To the extent that the public fails to understand the organizational and behavioral dynamics of hate groups like the American skinheads, the public will fail—in the words of President Bush—to responsibly "work for justice and for unity of all people." That is, if they don't know *exactly what they're fighting,* how can government officials and community activists ever win their struggle against hate crime?

Such a lack of knowledge carries even more severe implications for the American criminal justice system. Today some 4,000 white racists are locked away in state and federal prisons throughout the United States—many of whom have committed hate crimes (ADL, 1988a; Flynn and Gerhardt, 1989; Pelz et al., 1991; U.S. Department of Justice, 1985). In the absence of conclusive research on the causes of hate crime, how can correctional administrators ever design meaningful sentencing guidelines and effective rehabilitation programs for offenders who commit these crimes?

A logical place to begin answering these complex questions is with an untrammeled examination of the most rudimentary evidence as it exists today. On this basis, we are able to draw three tentative conclusions about the American skinheads:

First, although no one (including the U.S. Department of Justice) collects comprehensive statistics on hate group members in the United States, evidence suggests that the number of racist skinheads in the nation has been growing at a spectacular rate. Through reports issued by their thirty-one regional offices, the ADL counted several hundred racist skinheads (mostly in California) as of November, 1987. In February 1988, these same thirty-one offices reported that some 1,000 to 1,500 racist skinheads were active in twelve states. By October of 1988, the ADL indicated some 2,000 racist skinheads in twenty-one states (1988c, 1989b). By April of 1989, the ADL estimated that the number of racist skinheads in the United States was 3,000 and growing (Reed, 1989) and the Center for Democratic Renewal set their number at 3,500 and growing (Coplon, 1989). In the early days of 1990, the FBI issued a report saying there were now simply "thousands of 'skinheads' in America" (quoted in Anderson, 1990:A12). By a conservative estimate, then, we might conclude that the number of racist skinheads in America increased about 1000 percent over a twenty-four-month period.

The second conclusion we can draw (with absolute certainty) is that some American skinheads—such as Kenneth Mieske and Clark Martell—are capable of committing egregious acts of violence. We may also conclude that other skinheads are capable of committing other forms of hate crime. Between 1987 and 1988, the ADL reported a 41 percent rise in anti-Semitic acts, including arsons, bombings, and cemetery desecrations. The ADL notes that most of this increase was "either claimed by or attributed to Skinhead elements" (1989a:4). Fully two-thirds of the racial assaults reported to the Southern Poverty Law Center in 1988 were thought to be linked to skinheads (Klanwatch, 1989), and attacks by skinheads were reported to be the most numerous and violent against gays and lesbians during the late 1980s (Berrill, 1990).

The final conclusion we can draw is that the lack of social science research in the area of hate crime violence has produced its own set of problems. Most immediately, it seems to have created an intellectual deficiency that has undermined the coherence and effectiveness of public policy and community action. More important, this intellectual deficiency seems to have worked to misrepresent the scope and dimensions of hate crime in America; and for this mistake, still other individuals and communities may suffer the humiliation and pain of hate crime in the future.

The present analysis builds on these tentative conclusions and endeavors to answer three primary questions:

1. Why did the number of racist skinheads increase so dramatically in the United States during the late 1980s?
2. Why are racist skinheads so violent?
3. What is the most efficacious public response to this type of violence?

In answering these questions, the analysis also sheds light on skinhead gang structure and personal attributes of individual skinheads. In so doing, I attempt to answer two additional questions:

4. Do racist skinheads represent spontaneous and rebellious street gangs that lack a common belief system, or do they represent an organized, national movement with a clearly developed political consciousness?
5. Are racist skinheads truly alienated from mainstream society?

The analysis begins by tracing the history of this peculiar subculture.

RESEARCH NOTE

There are obvious limitations to the data I have used to draw conclusions about the American skinheads. Similar to the problems inherent in using Uniform Crime Reports, the data published by the ADL, the FBI, the Southern Poverty Law Center, and the Center for Democratic Renewal have all been collected for specific agency purposes and may not contain the degree of accuracy required for social science research. Furthermore, such data may have been deliberately tampered with to legitimize the goals of the various data-collecting agencies; and data collected over time, such as those of the ADL and the FBI, are subject not only to changes in record-keeping procedures but also to the vagaries of state and federal law.

Yet these limitations do not necessarily preclude our ability to use such data in an attempt to make sociological sense of the American skinheads. Indeed, a rich sociological tradition is built on this sort of methodology. Relying on data collected from such diverse sources as police, courts, and regulatory agencies to mortuaries, prisons, and governmental commissions, scholars have examined white-collar crime (Chambliss, 1978; Sutherland, 1949), shoplifting (Cameron,

1964), air pollution (Espisito and Silverman, 1970), food and drug regulatory activities (Turner, 1970), and occupational safety violations (Page and O'Brien, 1973). In fact, the classic sociological study of suicide (Durkheim, 1897/1951) was based on official agency records.

2

A History of the Skinhead Nation

Men travel side by side for years, each locked up in his own silence or ex-
changing those words which carry no freight—'til danger comes. Then they
stand shoulder to shoulder. They discover they belong to the same family.
They grow and bloom in the recognition of fellow beings. They look at one
another and smile.

— Antoine de Saint-Exupery

Q: Why did you become a skinhead?
A: I dunno, it's the way I've grown up I suppose.

— Conversation with a London Skinhead
July 1991

To understand how the skinheads became an international youth subculture, it is
necessary to look at the movement's history and then move forward to the
present. This exercise is important because youth subcultures, like the dominant
cultures they come from, are shaped by the historical context in which they
emerge. That is, each youth subculture is inflected by a specific ideological force
field transmitted from the past. This historical transmission, as we shall see, then
gives each subculture its own unique life and meaning. Our point of departure is
London, England, beginning sometime during the mid-1950s.

BEATS, HIPSTERS, AND TEDDY BOYS

Post–World War II London was a place of extraordinary social change for British youth. In the words of former Prime Minister Harold Macmillan, it was an
era when "some of our people never had it so good" (quoted in Bromberg,
1989:12). For the first time in history, British youth began to enjoy a modicum of
unrestricted and discretionary consumerism. Their wages rose twice as fast as
those of their parents whose young lives and social landscape had been ripped

apart a decade earlier by Hitler's unrelenting Luftwaffe. But these were brighter days for British youth. These were the days when compulsory military service was eliminated. They were the days of pinball arcades, coffee bars, night spots with French names, continental suits, jazz, and something new called rock and roll.

Amid these times, several tribal-like youth subcultures developed on the streets of London. There were, first of all, the beats (or beatniks) and the hipsters both based on information that trickled into the British youth scene about urban American blacks. This information took on almost mythical proportions among youth of the day. In his brilliant sociological treatise on postwar subcultures of Great Britain, Dick Hebdige has written that, "The Negro was [seen as] blowing free, untouched by the dreary conventions which tyrannized the more fortunate members of society, and although trapped in a cruel environment of mean streets and tenements, by a curious inversion he also emerged the ultimate victor" (1979:47).

Spurred by American writers Jack Kerouac, Allen Ginsberg, and Norman Mailer, this romantic idealization of the poverty-stricken black male came to serve as a paradigm of freedom-in-bondage for the mostly white population of British beatniks and hipsters. It was symbolized in jazz by such artists as Charlie "Bird" Parker, John Coltrane, and Miles Davis. The beat and hipster styles were uniquely American; in early postwar London, few young black men were to be found in working-class communities of the city. Hence, the British subcultural identity with the oppressed American Negro was utterly abstract—it had no concrete basis in reality whatsoever. And so, the beats and hipsters eventually slipped quietly into obscurity; their objects becoming the first of many great social artifacts to emerge from the postwar youth subcultures of Great Britain.

Into this void came an indigenous version of the hipster/beat subculture called the teddy boys. The "teds" took their name from King Edward VII (r. 1901–1910), a famously flamboyant dresser who simultaneously became King of England and Emperor of India at the age of 60 (Bromberg, 1989). Onto this fascination for aristocratic flamboyance, the teddy boys grafted a subcultural style stolen from the beats and hipsters—a penchant for urban American rhythm and blues.

The traditional teddy boy dress was a bright turquoise, pink, or green high collar shirt with white frilly cuffs, pegged trousers colored apricot or orange, a thin rayon tie, neon green striped socks, high-heeled "brothel creepers," and a brightly colored Edwardian jacket with a velvet collar. All of this was set off by hair cut in a DA (duck's arse), with a quiff (long forelock) slicked down by serious amounts of Brylcreem (Bromberg, 1989; Frith, 1978; Hebdige, 1979). Whenever they went into a London scene in those days, the teddy boys played records by Elvis Presley ("Heartbreak Hotel"), Little Richard ("Good Golly Miss Molly"), Gene Vincent ("Be Bop a Lula"), and Jerry Lee Lewis ("Great Balls of Fire"). It was part of their style and the first sign of the excitement that lay ahead in the 1960s.

Yet the subtle interplay between black and white musical forms (thoroughly recognized by the beats and hipsters) was altogether lost on the teddy boys. That is, the teds saw early rock and roll as an immediate expression of youthful energy, and nothing more. To the flamboyant teds, rock and roll meant revolt against everything and everybody — those drab routines of unskilled labor, school, family, prostitutes, police, and foreigners.

During this period, Britain had accepted its first wave of skilled and unskilled black Jamaican and other West Indian men who had come to London to find jobs, homes, and respectability for their families. For the most part, these immigrants assimilated well into British society (Hebdige, 1979). However, a small group of immigrants in the ghettos of West London presently became associated with racketeering and prostitution enterprises, and this attracted the hostility of the teddy boys (Jefferson, 1976).

In the spring of 1958, the teds became involved in numerous unprovoked attacks on young Afro-Caribbean men in the ghettos of West London. And in July of 1958, the teddy boys figured prominently in the bloody Notting Hill and Nottingham race riots (Jefferson, 1976; Clarke et al., 1976; Hebdige, 1979). Each of these outbreaks involved large gangs of white males targeting isolated black families and individuals. These events were important: They marked the introduction of racial violence as a postwar subcultural style among British youth.

MODS

By the early 1960s, two events sufficiently transformed the British youth scene to render the racist teddy boys an underworld anachronism. First, by 1962 the massive influx of Afro-Caribbean immigrants into London's working-class communities had been completed, and a social rapport between blacks and neighboring white groups had become possible (Hebdige, 1979). Second, by 1963 the British music scene had undergone a stunning artistic metamorphism. At the center of this development was a resurrection of the beatnik's strong emotional affinity with American blacks. This affinity converged with black gospel music, rhythm and blues, and white country/western music to produce a revolutionary form of rock and roll. The four Beatles from Liverpool (named in honor of the beats) were almost single-handedly responsible for this development. The rising tide of youthful consumerism continued into the early sixties, and in July of 1964 — just as Britain and the rest of the world were experiencing their first flush of excitement over Beatlemania — Harold Wilson was elected prime minister under a banner promising to bring Britain "the white heat of technology" (quoted in Bromberg, 1989:19).

It was within this context that London's second homegrown youth subculture, the mods, came about. Unlike the flamboyant and violent teddy boys, the mods were subtle and subdued in appearance and behavior. The mod style was grounded in what Craig Bromberg calls a "quiet, subversive, self-conscious code of coolness" (1989:19). The mods dressed in conservative French and British suits, black ties, and black crepe-soled shoes. Their hair was short, clean, and worn in a French crewcut with small amounts of clear lacquer. Basking in the white heat of technology, the mods were especially fond of their cool Vespa and Lambretta motorscooters (Bromberg, 1989:19; Frith, 1978; Hebdige, 1979). This style enabled the mods to smoothly navigate between students and teachers at school; siblings and parents at home; co-workers and bosses at the office, factory, or dock, and among other members of the mod subculture.

Yet beneath the surface of the cool mod style was something edgy and rebellious. Hebdige has noted that "the mods . . . concealed as much as they stated [and] undermined the conventional meaning of 'collar, suit and tie,' pushing neatness to the point of absurdity" (1979:52). And Dave Laing (1969:12) has mentioned "some intangible detail (the way the tie was knotted, the brand of cigarette smoked) which seemed strangely out of place in the workplace or classroom." In short, the mods were a bit too alert, too neat, and too cool. This was, moreover, the result of widespread amphetamine use among the mods—a trait they had inherited from the beats and hipsters (Bromberg, 1989; Frith, 1978; Jefferson, 1976; Hebdige, 1979).

Because their style included both a conservative appearance and the use of a highly euphoric drug, the mods developed a secret identity as they scootered between London's cellar clubs, discotheques, boutiques, and record shops; all the while maintaining a frantic schedule of work, school, and family activity. At the center of this secret identity, once again, stood the black male:

[For the mods] the Black Man was a constant, serving symbolically as a dark passage down into an imagined "underworld" . . . situated beneath the familiar surfaces of life where another order was disclosed: a beautifully intricate system in which values, norms and conventions of the "straight" world were inverted. (Hebdige, 1979:53–54)

Here, in this secret underworld, the mods celebrated black soul music. Throughout the early sixties, American artists such as James Brown, the Isley Brothers, Sam Cooke, the Miracles, Bobby "Blue" Bland, Jackie Wilson, Otis Redding, and Wilson Pickett provided the major inspirational stimulus for the amphetamine-driven mod subculture. Yet this British fascination with American black music soon extended far beyond the mods and the four beats from Liverpool who were quickly becoming the most successful entertainment act the world had ever seen.

By 1965, a literal army of white British rock bands had joined the mods and the Beatles in their celebration of American black music. These bands drew largely from the Delta Blues tradition established by such artists as Elmore James, Willie Dixon, Muddy Waters, Robert Johnson, Sonny Boy Williamson, and Leadbelly. They included the Animals, Yardbirds, Pretty Things, Kinks, and the ever-popular Rolling Stones. Yet among the mods, British groups like the Small Faces, the Who, Zoot Money, the Spencer Davis Group, Shakedown Sounds, and Georgie Fame and the Blue Flames became enormously popular because of their straightforward cover versions of American soul classics like "Bare Footin'," "Don't Lie to Me," "Roadrunner," "Papa's Got a Brand New Bag," and "(I'm in with) The In Crowd" (Hebdige, 1979:53–54; Davis, 1985).

Yet the nervous, amphetamine-edged, secret style of the mods also was short-lived. In the ceaseless flux of British fad and fashion, the mods were soon swept away by a remarkable new scene.

HIPPIES

By 1966, London youth had been deluged by an American-influenced pop culture of soul music, cowboy movies, sports cars, instant celebrities, and new forms of mind-altering drugs – the most popular of which was marijuana, a mainstay of the former beat/hipster life-style (Bromberg, 1989; Hebdige, 1979). And in February of 1966, *Time* magazine christened "Swinging London" the center of the international counterculture youth movement.

These were the days when the Beatles, according to John Lennon, "were more popular than Jesus." They were the days when "flower power" dominated the scenes in Coventry Garden, Hyde Park, Carnaby Street, Kings Road, and Piccadilly Circus. They were the days of Jimi Hendrix at the Marquee; of R. D. Laing lecturing on LSD at Cambridge; of Bob Dylan and the Band at Royal Albert Hall; and of *Blow-Up,* Michelangelo Antonioni's documentary film about the Swinging London era.

They were the days when the Beatles, a scruffy group of retooled beatniks from Liverpool, were received and honored by British royalty. These were the days of hippie boutiques, Owsley's "Orange Sunshine," the Ad Lib and the Indica Gallery, the "Summer of Love," *Sgt. Pepper's Lonely Hearts Club Band,* Cream's *Disraeli Gears,* the Maharishi, Mary Quant's "Chelsea Look," Marianne Faithfull, Timothy Leary, and the ascendancy of the Rolling Stones as "The World's Greatest Rock 'N' Roll Band." They were the days of hot pants, crushed velvet bell-bottoms, snakeskin jackets, love beads, long hair, star-spangled shirts, blue jeans, fringed buckskin boots, and catch phrases like "Sock it to me," "POW," "Tune in, turn on, drop out," and "Make love, not war." In essence, it seemed as if the entire London youth scene had been bounced on its head, exploding in a cacophony of acid rock, brilliant pageantry, and splendid youthful exuberance. But more important, the subculture itself had achieved an unprecedented maturity. And with this maturity, there came respect from the society at large.

These events fundamentally changed the British youth scene forevermore. Most notably, they placed the hippie – not the idealized alienated urban black male, not King Edward VII, nor Elvis Presley – at center stage in the construction of a subcultural style.

Like the beats, the hippies almost sanctified poverty; but like the teddy boys, the hippies were given to wearing flashy Carnaby Street clothes. Unlike any other youth subculture before, the hippies exalted eroticism – particularly Eastern religious themes derived from the use of the psychedelic drug LSD. Marijuana, hashish, amphetamines, and even heroin (another mainstay of the beatnik life-style) were also used to seek an instant humanism wherein hippies could explore more deeply the suffering of others, allowing them the ultimate chance to determine goodness for themselves through the expression of compassion and kindness to fellow human beings in a world they saw as becoming progressively more flawed. Thus, the hippies became—at once—committed to individualism, mysticism, and withdrawal wherein they used contemplation and "inner work" to achieve their own sense of self-actualization, and to the glorification of sexuality, country living, and togetherness. Because of this, the semiotics of the hippie style included concepts such as "love," "here and now," "do your own thing," "higher consciousness," "inner life," and "peace."

Homology

This rich blend of values and life-styles—individualism, eroticism, mysticism, and altruism—created the basis for what social anthropologist Claude Levi-Strauss called homology. Levi-Strauss (1969) originally used the term *homology* to refer to the symbolic confluence of values and life-styles of postwar European societies. As applied to the London hippies of the sixties, however, the term *homology* relates primarily to the subjective experiences of individual hippies and the musical forms they used to express or reinforce these focal concerns (Clarke, 1976b; Frith, 1978; Hebdige, 1979). "It was that music," says one observer of the era, "which linked the youth of the world, a universal language they all understood, a musical badge of their brotherhood. It was the music that goaded them into their excesses, their indifference to consequences, their insistence that their lives were to be lived as swiftly as possible" (Hotchner, 1990:39).

Unlike the beats, hipsters, teddy boys, and mods (whose music and subcultures were based on intellectual abstractions and improvisational rituals and customs) the internal structure of the hippie subculture was characterized by an orderliness and a tight fit between an original system of values and style and the musical expression of values and style. In other words, the hippie subculture was *homologous*. Each part of the subculture (music, values, and style) was "organically related to other parts and it [was] through this fit between them that the subcultural member [made] sense of the world" (Hebdige, 1979:113).

The articulation and dissemination of information related to this world was another important product of the hippie subculture. Sometime around the "Summer of Love" (1967), London hippies began to publish a series of underground newsletters and magazines that expressed social and political commentary about their subculture. These included the *New Musical Express, Disc and Music Echo, Oz,* and *BOMP.* Here, hippies could gain information about everything from fashion, new musical releases, and rock tours, to the political activities of groups like Britain's Radical Student Alliance and the Revolutionary Socialist Student Federation, to record reviews, information about backstage passes, and gossip. Essentially, this underground press established a nebulous but authentic source of news about the hippie subculture and symbolized the formation of trends in music, values, and style.

In sum, the homology between an alternative *value system* (expressed by the slogans "Tune in, turn on, drop out" or "Make love, not war"), *style* (Carnaby Street clothing, long hair, drugs, altruism, peace, and eroticism) and *music* (acid rock) congealed into a meaningful and coherent way of life for individual hippies. This life-style was then reinforced, printed, and disseminated to the subculture by a vibrant underground press. In one way or another, the quest for this well-developed homology has been at the heart of every British youth subculture since the heady days of Swinging London.

ROCKERS, HARD MODS, AND THE SECOND COMING OF THE TEDDY BOYS

By decade's end, the unrestrained consumerism enjoyed by British youth began to grind to a painful halt due to Prime Minister Wilson's inability to come to grips with the nation's powerful trade and labor unions. Aggravated by the worldwide energy crisis of the early seventies, Britons became mired in a wave of unmanageable industrial strikes, rising unemployment, housing shortages, hospital closures, power outages, and three-day work weeks (Hebdige, 1979:113; Bromberg, 1989; Clarke et al., 1976; Frith, 1978). Meanwhile, the relentless outpouring of positive energy that characterized popular culture in London during the sixties began to fade as well. Subjected to media pressures, market forces, aging, and the chaotic and self-destructive nature of rock and roll itself, the hippie subculture began to break down into a number of different scenes. One of these belonged to the rockers.

Unlike their subcultural predecessors, the rockers of this period were youth who came of age in a time of economic austerity. The average London rocker was unskilled and earned less money during the early 1970s than did the beats, hipsters, teddy boys, mods, and hippies of the 1950s and 1960s (Hebdige, 1979). Moreover, the rockers were a subculture of poor kids.

Unlike the hippies, however, the rockers did not place themselves at center stage in the construction of their subcultural style—they placed someone else. That is, the rockers adopted a style that was not of their own creation. Rockers dressed in blue denim, long hair, Harley Davidson T-shirts, and black leather jackets. Similar to the teddy boys, the rockers adopted this look from the American 1950s. Specifically, they borrowed it from Marlon Brando in his performance as the archetypical American rebel in the *Wild One* (Hebdige, 1979).

Rocker music was a fast and furious blend of highly amplified, blues-based rock—created by white males—featuring shrill vocals expounding the values of misogyny, mysticism, nihilism, decadence, and drug imagery (Hebdige, 1979; Eddy, 1985). Its roots were in British singles of the mod era such as the Who's "My Generation" and the Kinks' "All Day and All of the Night." Rocker music was meant to appeal to working-class British boys and young men between the ages of fifteen and twenty-four, who liked their rock to be loud, Anglo-Saxon, and violent. Their drugs of choice were amphetamines, barbiturates, cheap wine, and a new soporific called Mandrax (Quaalude in the United States).

The most influential rocker band was Led Zeppelin, and they brought a new dimension to the music scene in Great Britain. While British rock stars were known for their notorious acts of rebellion and self-destruction, they were never particularly known as evil people. Jimmy Page, guitarist extraordinaire, changed all of this. And he did so with extraordinary style and elegance.

Led Zeppelin projected a sense of the occult to their predominantly juvenile audience. Although the Rolling Stones had dabbled with these matters in *Their Satanic Majesties Request* and "Sympathy for the Devil," Led Zeppelin was the first British band to build its entire persona on occult images, thereby establishing a private covenant of youthful mystique. By 1972, Jimmy Page owned the world's largest collection of artifacts (robes, manuscripts, weapons, etc.) once belonging to Aleister Crowley, the intellectual father of modern day Satanism. Included among Page's holdings was the deed to Boleskine House, Crowley's former mansion on the shores of Loch Ness in Scotland. Whereas Crowley described himself as "The Wickedest Man in the World," Page would come to be known by millions of white teenagers around the world as Sosa—the evil sorcerer of the Tarot.

Page portrayed himself as a wizard possessed by a dark magical alchemy. And in his black silk stage costume, spangled with crescent moons, silver stars, and the Mark of the Beast (666), amid his smokebombs and laser lighting, with his double-necked eighteen string electric Gibson, and onstage catastrophes, the frail and afflicted Jimmy Page took "Stairway to Heaven"—Led Zeppelin's universal anthem of teenage redemption—to the top of the international music charts, and it stayed there for nearly five years. This had never been seen before. Even to this day, nearly twenty years after its release, radio programmers in Britain and the United States still consider "Stairway" the number one rock song of all time. As a result, Jimmy Page became one of the wealthiest and most influential personalities in rock and roll.

Led Zeppelin's occult message was based on the proposition that things were better in the past, a million years ago when the forces of nature ruled the everyday activity of men and women who roamed the land as heathens, barbarians, and shamans. This can be read in the text of such Zeppelin classics as "Dazed and Confused," "No Quarter," "The Crunge," "The Battle of Evermore," "Bron-Yr-Aur Stomp," and the crypto-historic saga of death and annihilation called "The Immigration Song." In the words of an enormously gifted music scholar, Led Zeppelin represented

a fascination with Celtic Britain and the tides of English history, especially the four-hundred-year period from the eighth to eleventh centuries when the English fought for their island with generations of Viking invaders from Denmark and Sweden. "The Immigration

Song," with its images of barbarous Norse seamen and pillaged abbeys, was the first of Led Zeppelin's many hammers-of-the-gods threnodies. . . . "The Immigration Song" cast the band in the role of Viking invaders raping, burning, pillaging, and whispering tales of glory. . . . [Led Zeppelin became] a Viking death squad riding the winds of Thor to some awful satanic destiny. (Davis, 1985:117, 119–20, 161)

Led Zeppelin's overwrought Dark Ages fantasies provided the standard psychic background for heavy metal (sometimes referred to as head-banger music because of the tribal tradition of banging one's head against the stage during Led Zeppelin rave ups). This led inevitably to the commercial success of such first wave heavy-metal bands as Black Sabbath, AC/DC, Thin Lizzy, and Blue Oyster Cult. And this led to the success of a second wave of heavy-metal bands including Def Leppard, Great White, Judas Priest, Slaughter, Skid Row, Metallica, and Megadeth. Because heavy metal was based on fantasy, it appealed to a large number of British youth of the early seventies, who were suddenly shoved into a near-lumpen status because of the nation's severe economic problems.

As for the rockers, they staked their claim to working-class dance halls in London's East End where they created the art form of "idiot dancing" (Hebdige, 1979). Idiot dancing was a crazy, uncontrolled, physical gyration that eventuated in aggression against other dancers as a symbolic statement deriding the social forces experienced by the rockers at the time. Idiot dancing also led to indiscriminate acts of violence. Especially unsettling for the rockers were fat old hippies with their Carnaby Street clothing and spaced-out demeanor, and leftover mods with their high-classed, sissyfied sportcoats and motorscooters. This polarity (rockers versus hippies and mods) soon began to take shape among other subcultures as well.

During the early 1970s, those in the forefront of London's fashion industry began to find the few remaining teddy boys of the late 1950s interesting once again. Accordingly, they began to market old Elvis Presley records, Edwardian coats, string ties, brothel creepers, photographs of James Dean and Marilyn Monroe, and slick jackets emblazoned with legends such as "Confederate Rock" and "Gene Vincent Lives" (Hebdige, 1979; Bromberg, 1989). This business enterprise, combined with the economic austerity of the times, caused a resurgence of the teddy boy subculture.

Meanwhile, community anxieties began to form about the effects of new Pakistani immigration on employment, housing, welfare, and the quality of life in London's working-class neighborhoods. At the same time, Britons underwent a profound patriotic transformation in which a wartime spirit ensued in their search for an enemy to blame for the faltering economy. Based less on concrete suffering than on blocked expectations, panic set in; so did the urge to seek revenge. Onto this social stage stepped two actors: the resurrected teddy boy and the highly visible Pakistani immigrant. When these actors met, racial violence once again became a style among the white youth gangs of postwar Britain.

Moreover, the resurrected teddy boy style was based on an "obstinate fidelity to the traditional 'bad guy' stereotype" (Hebdige, 1979:83) and "hidebound political conservatism, sexism, and racism" (Bromberg, 1989:38). Like the rockers, this second generation of teddy boys would also carry on the tradition of intergroup polarity. For the resurrected teds, their target became a recycled version of the mods called the hard mods.

As the revitalized teddy boys started to commit random acts of violence against Pakistani immigrants (Paki bashing), a group of leftover working-class mods began to polarize themselves against hippies and other youth who gave off a sixties look. In reaction to the commercial elitism of acid rock, long hair, and androgynous Carnaby Street finery, the hard mods adopted a tough, clean look that favored heavy boots, work shirts, blue jeans, and short hair (Coplon, 1989; Hebdige, 1979). Their music, unlike any British youth subculture before, was based on the tribal rhythms of Jamaican reggae and ska—a music of the oppressed set to simple but brilliant staccato impulses. Although they were threatened by the new teddy boys, the hard mods proved tough enough, and mean enough, to defend their subculture at any cost. Out of this space walked the world's first original skinhead.

SKINHEADS: THE FIRST GENERATION

To understand the skinhead subculture, it is necessary to define the genesis of its music, values, and style. In effect, we must examine the skinhead quest for homology.

More than anything else, the early skinheads represented both a suppression of and rebellion against the bourgeois influences of British culture in the 1950s and 1960s (Cohen, 1972). Whereas the teddy boys, mods, and hippies sought to explore and exploit the upwardly mobile options produced by the economic affluence of an earlier era, the skinheads—much like the rockers—sought to explore and exploit the spiraling downward options presented to them during a period of economic austerity.

The skinhead value system began by mixing two seemingly incompatible sources, the culture of the black Jamaican immigrant and the white working-class worker (Hebdige, 1979). In the beginning, the skinheads became fascinated by the style of a flashy, tough, Jamaican street gang called the rude boys whose criminal exploits were immortalized in a string of early reggae recordings such as the Wailers' "Rude Boy," Desmond Decker's "Shanty Town," the Slickers' "Johnny Too Bad," and Prince Buster's "Battle on Orange Street" (Hebdige, 1979).

The hero of this music was seen by the early skins as a "lone delinquent pitched hopelessly against an implacable authority" (Hebdige, 1979:37). The rude boy style included short cropped hair, a porkpie hat, and shiny suits made from the raw materials of the Caribbean. Rude boys spoke an exotic, opaque-sounding Jamaican dialect known as patois, a language developed by West Indian slaves. Early skinheads found this style highly attractive. More than any subculture around, it seemed to offer them a solution to the problems they were experiencing *rude boy style*

in their own working-class neighborhoods. Therefore, the rude boy style was viewed by certain working-class white youth as a functional and coherent answer to difficulties associated with growing up under harsh economic conditions.

Superimposed onto this system of values and style, the early skinheads placed a mythical image of the traditional British working-class community. (Much of which had been eroded by a shrinking economy that mocked traditional values.) This included a pride in neighborhood territory; a rough machismo demeanor; obsessions with football (soccer) and beer drinking; and a stripped-down, regres- *general* sive approach to consumer capital.

At center stage of the early skinhead subculture, therefore, stood a heroic Jamaican criminal overlaid with an idealized image of a traditional British patriot. The style emerging from these two very different value systems produced a subculture that was proletarian, puritanical, chauvinistic, clean-cut, and aggressive (Hebdige, 1979; Clarke, 1976a; Frith, 1978). But the skinheads were not ostensibly xenophobic or homophobic. Nor did they believe in Nazism. All of that would come later.

Phil Cohen (1972:55) has described the early skinheads as a "kind of caricature of the model worker" and Dick Hebdige refers to them as a "hard stereotype of the white lumpen male" (1979:56). The early skins (also referred to as suede heads or boneheads) cut their hair in a short rude boy crop, wore work jeans or stay-pressed trousers, plain button-down Ben Sherman or Fred Perry shirts, black felt "donkey jackets," "Blue-beat" hats, and highly polished dockworker boots called Doctor Martens (Hebdige, 1979; Frith, 1978). From the rude boys, the early skins adopted an argot of street vulgarity and an affinity for reggae, ska, and rock steady (Hebdige, 1976). In the words of John Clarke, "the Skinhead style . . . attempted to symbolically recreate . . . the traditional working-class community" (1976a:99). The skinheads took to the streets, the all white football terraces, the youth clubs, and dance halls of London's East End during the early 1970s. And when they did, several additional features were grafted onto their style.

Intergroup Polarization

First, like their parent culture, the hard mods, skinheads began to polarize themselves against hippies. This polarization centered mainly over the issue of hair. The long hair worn by the hippies represented an expression of the kindness and gentleness that was necessary for love and eroticism; the sui generis of life. For the hippies, hair was to be celebrated: it should be long and flowing, beaded, braided, twisted, headbanded, ponytailed, and windblown; but never cut off. Long hair was sacred. It was ultimately expressive of the hippie quest for homology.

The close-shaved hair of the skinheads, by contrast, represented a direct flaunting of antihippie sensibilities. Short hair was a rejection of elitist acid rock; Carnaby Street fashion; and exotic drugs such as marijuana, hashish, and LSD.

Short hair required no combing, braiding, or care. In fact, short hair sent a strong symbolic message to the hippies: "Fuck you! I'll do as I please." Yet there was a more pragmatic reason for the skinhead fascination with a shaved head. Short hair could not be grabbed in a street fight, and the early skinheads increasingly preferred fighting over anything else (Coplon, 1989; Frith, 1978).

Hippie Bashing

The second feature added to the skinhead style came from the rockers, and this was the art of idiot dancing (later referred to as slam dancing). This led to numerous dance hall fights between the skins and hippies, and then to police calls; and soon, skinheads were fighting with the police (Coplon, 1989). These fights also began to spill over from the dance halls to the soccer games and the streets, leading to still more police action against the now-famous skinheads of London.

Paki Bashing

The third feature incorporated into the skinhead style came from the teddy boys, and this was the style of Paki bashing. "Pakistanis," writes Hebdige, "were sharply differentiated not only by racial characteristics but by religious rituals, food taboos and a value system which encouraged deference, frugality and the profit motive, [therefore] the Pakistanis were singled out for the brutal attentions of the skinheads" (1979:102).

Queer Bashing

Last, the skinheads started to scapegoat other alien groups and they also fell victim to the skinhead style of violence. Specifically, the skins went after middle- and upper-class students at the London School of Economics and Cambridge. Among their new targets were homosexuals (Hebdige, 1979; Knight, 1982). "Queer-bashing," suggests Clarke, "may be read as a reaction against the erosion of traditionally available stereotypes of masculinity [caused] by the hippies. The Skinhead operational definition of 'queer' seems to have extended to all those males who by their standards looked odd" (1976a:102).

By the early 1970s, London skinheads therefore constituted a youth subculture which had achieved a unique identity. Its values included proletarianism, puritanism, chauvinism, and aggression. These values were supported by a specific style (short hair, hiked-up jeans, Ben Sherman work shirts, Doc Marten boots, hippie bashing, Paki bashing, queer bashing) and music (rude boy reggae). Through their pursuit of subcultural homology, the early skinheads avoided internal conflict and achieved a sort of magical recovery of their working-class communities (Clarke, 1976a; Hebdige, 1979). However, two historical trajectories would quickly undermine the organizational apparatus of this first generation of skinheads, temporarily relegating them to the boneyard with the beats, mods, and hippies.

Rasta Man Vibrations

The first important change occurred when Jamaican reggae—like so many forms of British pop music before and since—underwent a dramatic transformation. This change was brought about by the religion of Jamaican Rastafarianism (Rasta). Once again, the superb insights of Hebdige:

reggae became darker and more African. . . . The lyrics became more self-consciously Jamaican, more dimly enunciated and overgrown until they disappeared altogether. The "dread," the ganga, the Messianic feel of this "heavy" reggae, its blood and fire rhetoric, its troubled rhythms can all be attributed to the Rasta influence. (1979:36)

In effect, the Rasta influence turned Jamaican reggae bands, such as Bob Marley and the Wailers (who lived in London at the time), into underground sensations and removed the rude boys from center stage of skinhead style. Around 1972, young Jamaicans in London began to cultivate a more natural African image and, hence, a more political image. Suddenly gone were the stovepipe hats; short, rude boy crops; and slick gangster suits. In their place came red, green, and black caps woven with home-grown Jamaican materials, combat jackets, and muddy "natty" dreadlocks. As a result, the entire British reggae scene became mired in a heavy cloud of ganga smoke, biblical revelations about Babylon, and romantic tributes to an imagined Africa. Essentially, "the rude boys had come of age and the skinheads were sentenced to perpetual adolescence" (Hebdige, 1976:150).

London Crackdown

The last thing to catch up with the early London skinheads was their racial violence. In August of 1972, Scotland Yard waged an unprecedented law enforcement campaign against the skinheads. A youth subculture was one thing, but victimizing innocent people was quite another. The crackdown effectively edged the skinheads into decline and nothing more was heard from them for about four years (Coplon, 1989; Laing, 1985). Thus, by the mid-70s the London skinheads were a subculture without a coherent system of values, style, and music. Furthermore, they were wanted by the law. But similar to the racist teddy boys who came before them, in time a new wave of British popular culture would transform a second generation of London skins into a street-fighting gang of historical proportions.

PUNKS AND THE IDEOLOGY OF FUCKYOUISM

While the skinheads took to the sidelines during the mid-70s, other British youth were desperately trying to stake a claim to a meaningful subcultural identity. These were the days when the British economy plummeted to its lowest point since World War II, bringing the nation a host of new social ills. With massive unemployment now affecting nearly every London working-class neighborhood,

the ominous specter of racial violence became an all-too-frequent feature of British society. Race riots, once again, erupted in Notting Hill, Grunwick, Lewis-
ham, and Ladywood (Dancis, 1978; Hebdige, 1979). Amid these gloomy,
apocalyptic events, Tory leader Margaret Thatcher began to gain unprecedented
popular support for sharp monetary revolution and promises of "a return to the
Victorian values of hard work, thriftiness, and the virtues of meritocracy"
(quoted in Bromberg, 1989:281).

Within this historical context, a highly unique and remarkably profane youth
subculture arose. This radically new subculture was highly complex because it
both combined and denied various elements of all the major postwar subcultures
that came before. It was the celebrated phenomenon known as punk.

Much like their subcultural predecessors, punk values and style had their roots
in music. Put another way, "punk began as music and punks themselves began as
music fans and performers" (Laing, 1985:xi). Yet punk "immediately discredited
the music that preceded it. . . . [By] [d]estroying one tradition, punk revealed a
new one" (Marcus, 1989:39).

Punk music started with the values of narcissism, nihilism, gender confusion,
and sadomasochism inherent in what was known then as glam rock (or glitter
rock). Glam rock was a cross between the full-tilt rhythm and blues of the Rolling
Stones and the Who, the highly amplified sound of acid rock (à la Jimi Hendrix),
and the "doo-wop" of American female soul groups such as the Supremes and the
Ronnettes. Glitter rock was David Bowie ("Ziggy Stardust and the Spiders from
Mars"), Lou Reed ("Take a Walk on the Wild Side"), Iggy Pop ("D.O.A."), Mott
the Hoople ("All the Young Dudes"), and the New York Dolls ("Pills").

Onto this penchant for glam rock the punks added the exotic new Rasta-influ-
enced reggae with its call for an African revolution. Punk then crossed glam rock
and reggae with the early music of the mods that had produced what was called
"Northern Soul" (an indigenous form of 1960s British pop) bringing the tradition
of secrecy and hysteria (fast, jerky rhythms and, of course, amphetamine use) to
the complex punk style (Hebdige, 1979). Punk was rounded out by a then-emerg-
ing form of American juvenile rock put out by the Ramones ("Teenage Lobot-
omy"), the Crime ("I Stupid"), and Patti Smith who had scored a top ten hit with
her punk version of Van Morrison's "Gloria" (Hebdige, 1979).

This esoteric blend of musical forms created the values and style for the punks
of London during 1976 and 1977. This subculture is most clearly exemplified in
the short-lived musical phenomenon known as the Sex Pistols. The Sex Pistols
were led by Johnny Rotten, self-described as a "rhesus monkey in a wind tunnel,"
and Sid Vicious, the tragic character portrayed in the Hollywood cult saga of
heroin addiction and murder, *Sid & Nancy.*

Talent? Well, it's not a question of talent: it's a question of style. Call it the Style of Fuckyouism: *Fuck you, fuck off, "don't waste my time"* (Rotten's favorite expression). Not some
precious, aesthetic response to the world, but something they have to feel: *Fuck you, fuck
off, "don't waste my time."* Without it these Sex Pistols would merely be one more musical
fad. (Bromberg, 1989:xiv–xv, emphasis in original)

On this basis, the punks defined their subcultural space through symbols of nihilism, sexism, anarchy, and violence (Dancis, 1978; Hebdige, 1979; Laing, 1985; Marsh, 1977). Yet unlike the skinheads, punk violence was more abstractly expressed. While skinheads were most likely to attack specific targets (hippies, Pakistanis, Asians, and homosexuals), punks were likely to attack anyone—including each other and themselves.

This provided something new in postwar popular culture: Punk offered "a voice that denied all social facts, and in that denial affirmed that everything was possible" (Marcus, 1989:2). For starters, punk clothing took the form of confrontational dressing in which the most sordid mixture of contexts were used to say—like the skinheads before them—Fuck You! London punks began mutilating their faces with common household objects (safety pins, plastic clothespins, television parts, and razor blades). Punk hair was dyed either hay yellow, jet black, pink, or bright orange with tufts of green or white often carved out in question marks (?) on the side of the youth's skull. This hairstyle was often set off in a spike or Mohawk held together with Vaseline.

Put simply, punk was deliberately meant to shock and offend everyone. "We're into chaos," said Johnny Rotten, "not music." This anarchy was expressed in the names of the original punk bands (Generation X, the Unwanted, Rejects, Damned, Dogs, Sex Pistols, Slits, Clash, Exploited, Worst, and Richard Hell and the Void Oids) and in titles of their songs: "If You Don't Want to Fuck Me, Fuck Off," "I Wanna Be Sick on You," "Anarchy in U.K.," "Kill Me Today," "Blank Generation," "No Fun," "Submission," and "No Feelings."

Part of this profane system of values, style, and music would soon come to moderately influence the next generation of London skinheads. Yet two specific punk creations would have a major impact on the second coming of the London skins.

The Empty Effect of Nazism

First, in 1976 David Bowie, Lou Reed, and Iggy Pop entered what they called their Berlin phase. Through their fascination with these glam rockers, punks developed an interest in the decadence and evil of Nazi Germany. Yet this Germany was less a place than an ideological construct. It was a construct, like Britain, that had no future. Therefore, in the tradition of fuckyouism, the odious sign of the swastika was adopted as a new punk symbol. However, like the abstract way in which they expressed their violence, the punks themselves did not adopt the ideology of Nazism denoted by this symbol (Dancis, 1978; Laing, 1985). Hebdige argues that

The signifier (swastika) had been willfully detached from the concept (Nazism) . . . and although it had been re-positioned (as "Berlin") within an alternative subcultural context, its primary value and appeal derived precisely from its lack of meaning: from its potential for deceit. [The swastika] was exploited as an empty effect. (1979:117)

Using symbols of Nazism only for their shock value was consistent with the ideology of fuckyouism. Therefore, London punks began to wear T-shirts and jewelry emblazoned with symbols of the Iron Cross, the SS insignia, and the swastika. This influenced the music scene as punk rockers Johnny Rotten, Sid Vicious, and Mick Jones of the Clash (who had briefly fronted a punk band called the London SS) began to perform their music wearing swastikas and other Nazi regalia. Even heavy-metal artists got into the act, as the famous Jimmy Page, on at least one occasion, performed in concert wearing the uniform of a Nazi stormtrooper (Davis, 1985). At the Rainbow Theater in May 1977, the Clash played their song "White Riot" and chairs were ripped out of the floor and thrown on stage in a symbolic act of approval for this new style (Dancis, 1978; Marsh, 1977). Offending all sensibilities about the Nazi Holocaust, in 1976 the Sex Pistols released a single called "Belsen Was a Gas." In 1978, a punk band called the Cortinas had a minor hit with their song "Fascist Dictator," and in 1979, the Exploited released a single appropriately entitled "Hitler's in the Charts Again." These were the days when a band emerged calling itself Elvis Hitler.

Fanzines

The second important punk creation that would be passed along to the next generation of London skinheads was to be appropriated from the hippies. To provide an alternative space within the subculture to counteract the increasingly hostile media coverage of the punks, a series of underground fanzines was established sometime around 1978. These included *Sniffen Glue, Ripped and Torn,* and *Jolt.* These fanzines were written and published by punks themselves and consisted of record reviews, editorials, and interviews with punk celebrities. They were produced cheaply, stapled together, and distributed through record shops and punk boutiques.

NEO-NAZI SKINHEADS: THE SECOND GENERATION

By 1982, the Thatcher administration had implemented a series of reforms to ameliorate the troubled British economy. In essence, economic growth was supposed to come from the leisure goods industries. Therefore, thousands of new low-skilled and low-paying jobs were created in which the nonaffluent working class was to provide goods and services to the affluent upper class. Moreover, the new working class would be built on other people's leisure (Frith, 1985). This economic principle was similar to the trickle-down effect of Reaganomics that was being implemented across the Atlantic.

At the same time, the British government began to adopt a conservative approach to immigration. On the eve of her election to office, Mrs. Thatcher commented that she "understood the feelings of those who fear that the British culture may be swamped by an alien one" (quoted in Bowling, 1990:2n). This rhetoric of nationalism led a number of analysts to conclude that Thatcherism had facilitated the incorporation of a commonsense form of racist logic into mainstream political thought.

Out of this historical context came two new youth subcultures. The first was the "casuals." The casuals were akin to an eighties version of the original mods, without the secrecy and without the widespread use of amphetamines. Still remaining, however, was the penchant for American soul music. Reacting to the extraordinary profanity of the punks, the style of the casuals was decidedly provincial, but largely gay. The casual style is exemplified in the leisure rock music of Boy George and the Culture Club ("Karma Chameleon"), Duran Duran ("Bang a Gong"), Bow Wow Wow ("Homosexual Apache"), and Frankie Goes to Hollywood ("Relax"). This style was meant to portray an idyllic image of the beach in summertime, far from the streets of London. And far from the din of heavy metal and Elvis Hitler.

The second youth subculture was the resurgence of a relatively small, but influential and violent band of London skinheads who came about partially in response to this brazen new subculture of homosexuals called the casuals with their leisure rock. A more critical reason why the London skinheads came along again has to do with a deliberate, well-organized recruitment and indoctrination campaign to bring thousands of European youth into the ranks of right-wing extremism.

The Skinhead Nation

The emergence of the skinheads as an international youth subculture is largely attributable to the musical talents, political action, business acumen, and good fortune of one Ian Stuart Donaldson. Unlike the working-class urban skins of the early seventies, Donaldson came from a middle-class suburban background. Ian Stuart Donaldson was born in 1958 in Blackpool, England—Britain's most successful seaside holiday resort located on the North Coast. His father was a successful businessman and his mother was a housewife (Center for Democratic Renewal, n.d.).

Blackpool was also the site of one of the first full-scale rock and roll riots in history. In early 1964, the Rolling Stones embarked on their second tour of British cities and villages. One venue brought them to Blackpool's Empress Ballroom where some 5,000 teenagers went berserk after guitarist Keith Richards aimed a kick at a young fan who had run onstage and tried to attack him. The audience overran the stage, smashing amplifiers, drums, and guitars. Stones piano player Ian Stewart had his baby grand piano hurled off the stage; it was shattered into pieces by an angry mob of boys. More than 30 fans were later treated for injuries at Blackpool's Victoria Hospital (Hotchner, 1990). Gaining international media attention, the event marked indelibly into the minds of Blackpool youth the sort of power and mass lunacy that rock and roll music could generate, and catapulted the Rolling Stones into the status of an underground icon for an entire generation to come.

Ian Donaldson was only fourteen years old when the Rolling Stones released their most critically acclaimed record album of all time: *Exile on Main Street*. One song on this record was entitled "Tumbling Dice," written and performed by the legendary Keith Richards, Mick Jagger, and the pianist Ian Stewart — who would also play on Led Zeppelin's historic hymn of spiritual evocation, "Stairway to Heaven" (Davis, 1985). "Tumbling Dice" was a wailing, full-tilt blues saga of paranoia, romance, gambling, and violence. It captured the attention of young Donaldson like nothing before, and he began to obsess about its underlying meaning.

In 1975, seventeen-year-old Donaldson started a British grammar school band called the Tumbling Dice (Center for Democratic Renewal, n.d.). To further align himself with the dark and rebellious world of post-sixties rock and roll, he dropped his surname and became known as Ian Stuart. In young Stuart's mind, the Tumbling Dice followed the street logic of Keith Richards: Everyone has to watch out for their own against the crapshoot of life. Thus, in a classic teenage portrayal of prepunk alienation, Ian came to believe that his existence was being threatened by low-down gamblers and other sinister things far beyond what he could see in his own middle-class social world in the seaside resort town of Blackpool.

In 1976, the Tumbling Dice began playing the South and East End dance halls of London. And Stuart started to mix with teddy boys, hard mods, rockers, and a crazy new bunch of youth called the punks. He also met a handful of leftover skinheads. Of these subcultures, Stuart saw the tough, no-nonsense style of the skinheads as coming closest to espousing the views in "Tumbling Dice." After all, the underground skinheads, at this point, were the real exiles on Main Street.

In 1977, Stuart renamed his band Skrewdriver (not the conventional spelling, screwdriver — but *Skrewdriver*), thereby putting a distinct punk-spin on its image (Center for Democratic Renewal, n.d.). By this time, Stuart had also developed into a gritty, soulful performer in the tradition of Howlin' Wolf via Mick Jagger (Coplon, 1989). And so, Skrewdriver started to share billings with popular punk and reggae artists working in the dance halls of London. But Stuart soon came to view punk and reggae as being too left wing and thus ineffective when it came to protection against the crapshoot of life. Something more was needed.

Accordingly, Stuart moved his beliefs beyond the art form of rock and roll. He built up a small following of youth sympathetic to his vision of survival in post-sixties England, and in early 1979 Stuart rented a loft in London's East End, where he established a political action group called White Noise. The goal of Stuart's organization was to promote Skrewdriver's unique philosophy of survival and rebellion. This combination of music and politics soon captured the attention of more powerful forces on the far right, and soon White Noise had forged an alliance with the neo-fascist organization known as the British National Front (NF) (Coplon, 1989). In Skrewdriver, the National Front — whose musical awareness at the time started and ended with Wagner and SS marching songs — saw an opportunity to attract a following of young whites into the ranks of the NF by offering them rock concerts that would be heavily racist and anti-Jewish, but not too political. Yet 1979 was also a bad year for Skrewdriver. It was then that Chiswick Records released the band's first album, *Anti-Social*. Nobody bought it. These were the days when the Clash dominated the British pop charts with songs that would eventually end up on their historic 1980 album, *London Calling*. (According to *Rolling Stone* magazine, *London Calling* was the most important record album released during the decade of the 1980s.) Meanwhile, Skrewdriver and White Noise slipped quietly into financial doldrums. If they were to survive, something was needed to challenge and provoke the new wave musical creations of the Clash.

Stuart closed down the White Noise office and retreated to Blackpool where he took a job in a textile factory (Coplon, 1989). After work, however, Stuart continued his relationship with NF members through frequent letter writing and telephone calls. He also became a frequent contributor to an emerging underground punk press. Somewhere around the time that the swastika became a widely used symbol of the punk movement, the young factory worker and his friends came to embrace a full-throttled neo-Nazi ideology. In order of importance, they were anti-immigrant (anti-black), anti-communist, anti-Semitic, anti-gay, and anti-IRA (Coplon, 1989).

With savings from his job at the textile plant, Stuart soon moved back to London. And in the spring of 1981, Skrewdriver was re-formed and the political arm of the band was renamed the Blood and Honour Club. By this time, the nationalistic and anti-immigration rhetoric of the Thatcher administration was at fever pitch. These events, combined with the political action of the National Front, led to a resurgence of the London skinhead subculture and an increase in racial violence. In February 1981, the Home Office released a report on racial violence in Britain, indicating that

In most places, it was said that the problem had deteriorated significantly within the space of the last year, and that the main perpetrators were of the skinhead fraternity. Assaults, jostling in the street, abusive remarks, broken windows, slogans daubed on walls—these were among the less serious kinds of racial harassment which many members of the ethnic minorities (particularly Asians) experience, sometimes on repeated occasions. The fact that they are interleaved with far more serious racially motivated offenses (murders, serious assaults, systematic attacks by gangs on people's homes at night) increases the feeling of fear experienced by ethnic minorities. . . . In many places . . . Asian families were too frightened to leave their homes at night or to visit the main shopping center in town on weekends when gangs of young skinheads regularly congregate. (Joint Committee Against Racialism, 1981:11)

In the foreword to the report, Conservative Home Secretary William Whitelaw declared that the actions of the skinheads were "wicked crimes which can do our society great harm" (Joint Committee Against Racialism, 1981:iii). The foundation was being laid for an international skinhead youth movement.

Yet during the early eighties, forces within the popular culture of Britain were also beginning to coalesce against racism. By 1982, the Clash, the Police, the Jam, the Boomtown Rats, the Pretenders, Elvis Costello, Graham Parker, and Bob Marley and the Wailers had transformed the London pop music scene into a progressive and outright leftist art form—a kind of Marxist, postpunk, brand of rock and roll. Naturally, then, London's pop music establishment began to criticize the activities of the racist National Front. Johnny Rotten, for example, had this to say about the NF: "I despise them. No one should have the right to tell anyone they can't live here because of the color of their skin or their religion or whatever" (quoted in Dancis, 1978:78).

Because of this subcultural transformation, British punk (as it existed after the fall of the Sex Pistols) became stripped of its nihilism, sexism, and violence. In its place came a new wave, hard-edged, hippielike value system of altruism, pluralism, and peace. But in true British fashion, another group of youths soon came along to polarize themselves against the visionary music of the Clash and the other new romantics of the era.

Around 1982, several punk bands began to adopt the devolved, back-to-the-basics sound of British Oi music. Oi is an old gypsy term used by cockney workers years ago meaning, "Hey!" ("Oi, you!"). The punked-up version of this stupid Oi music was created by a group of now defunct bands of middling renown: Cocksparrer, Oi Polloi, Last Resort, Criminal Class, Cockney Rejects, and 4-Skins. To set themselves apart from the Clash legacy, these bands based their music on the tradition of British pub sing-alongs and male surge-chanting about the "glory of the British state" (Dancis, 1978; Jewell, n.d.; Laing, 1985).

Skrewdriver copied this drunken, patriotic style of British pub sing-alongs. There was a reason for this. Skrewdriver's Oi effectively attacked the values of all other British pop music at the time: new wave, reggae, and the casual rockers like Boy George. On top of this counterrevolutionary form of punk music, Ian Stuart laid his own brand of heavy metal, with its themes of escape through fantasy. When combined with the banality and patriotism of Oi, Stuart's din-of-battle heavy metal produced a sort of mystical and occult-oriented bully-boy appeal for a clean white Britain in which the Viking—that mythical and noble European warrior of Led Zeppelin folklore—once again emerges to rule the British Isles. Essentially, "Skrewdriver turned the clock back hundreds of years and glorified the age where life was a day to day battle for survival, disease was rife, war ever present, and the mass of people lived as virtual slaves" (*Cable Street Beat review*, n.d.:4).

In 1982, White Noise Records of London (owned and operated by the NF) released the second Skrewdriver long-playing record entitled *Hail the New Dawn* (Center for Democratic Renewal, n.d.). The album cover displayed a group of Vikings standing on a beach in front of a glorious sunrise. *Hail the New Dawn* contained Stuart's anthems to human survival in modern-day Britain, including "White Power," "Nigger, Nigger," "Race and Nation," and "Rudolf Hess (Prisoner of Peace)."

Largely through the political action of the National Front, Skrewdriver then emerged as the premier white power rock band in England (Center for Democratic Renewal, n.d.; ADL, 1988c; Coplon, 1989). This was due mainly to the fact that a number of hard-core London punks were still flirting with the vacant but violent and reactionary images of Nazism (Laing, 1985). Suddenly, Ian Stuart was in the right place at the right time. Breathing intendment to the otherwise meaningless punk symbols of Nazism, Stuart and his skinhead associates created a subculture that was homologous.

There was, once again, a tight fit between subcultural values (Nazism), style (Paki bashing, hippie bashing, queer bashing, Nigger bashing, shaved heads, white power T-shirts, Doc Martens, and Viking and Nazi regalia) and music (white power rock). At this point, "armies of skinheads tattooed their faces with swastikas and taunted onlookers with *Seig Heil* salutes, and many joined Britain's right-wing resurgence" (Coplon, 1989:86). The Skinhead Nation was born.

By 1984, Skrewdriver's popularity had won them a contract with a West German recording company known as Rock-O-Rama Records. Recognizing the marketing potential of violent and racist lyrics, Rock-O-Rama would soon emerge as the major distributor of white power rock throughout Europe, Canada, and the United States. Accordingly, between 1983 and 1985, a number of white supremacist Oi bands adopted the heavy-metal sound of Skrewdriver; setting up thriving venues in working-class clubs throughout England, East and West Germany, Holland, Belgium, Sweden, France, Canada, Brazil, and Australia (Coplon, 1989; ADL, 1988c, 1989a; Came, 1989). Today, these bands are living legends among second generation neo-Nazi skinheads. They include Brutal Attack, No Remorse, Vengeance, Condemned 84, Close Shave, Skullhead, White Noise, and Doc Marten.

As the youth of London were being introduced to this new white power rock, Stuart and his companions—now closely aligned with the National Front as a result of *Hail the New Dawn*'s success—formed the NF's Instant Reponse Unit to provide security at NF meetings and Skrewdriver concerts. A standard uniform for the security force was simple: black trousers, black Skrewdriver T-shirts emblazoned with the SS insignia, black bomber jackets with swastikas, and Doc Martens. Every member of the Instant Response Unit was tattooed from shoulder to wrist, often on the bald head (and probably elsewhere) with symbols of Vikings and Nazis. They were, alas, the most menacing force ever seen in the London underground.

In early 1985, Stuart and a skinhead companion were arrested and received six-month prison terms for brutally stomping a Pakistani man during an Instant Response Unit patrol of London's East End (Center for Democratic Renewal, n.d.). When Stuart came out of prison, the twenty-seven-year-old rock star found himself a celebrity for the cause of white supremacism throughout Britain and Europe. Because of this, Stuart was now able to establish a vibrant white power political action group in London.

In his rented quarters at the Ferndale Hotel in Kings Cross, Stuart began to entertain a number of leaders from the European extreme far right, including

French presidential candidate Jean-Marie Le Pen and West Germany's leading neo-Nazi/terrorist, Manfred Roeder (Center for Democratic Renewal, n.d.). In the months following these international visits, the NF established a boutique called the Cutdown in an old launderette near London's Oxford Street. The Cutdown featured a wide range of swastika armbands, SS rings and badges, white power T-shirts, Doc Martens, Viking posters, and records by Skrewdriver, Vengeance, Brutal Attack, No Remorse, and others from the growing stable of Rock-O-Rama artists.

Meanwhile, skinheads throughout Europe started to amass an unprecedented record of vandalism, racial assaults, and murder (ADL, 1988c; Came, 1989). In Britain alone, the number of racial attacks reportedly increased to 70,000 a year, including 74 murders of Afro-Caribbean, Asian, and Pakistani men (Brown, 1984; Gordon, 1990; Hiro, 1991). During this period, one study found that one in every four black residents had been the victim of some form of racial harassment in the previous twelve months, and more than two-thirds of these victims had been victimized more than once (London Borough of Newham, 1986). This wave of violence crested in May of 1985 when skinheads from four European nations instigated the historic Brussels soccer riot leaving 38 dead and 200 wounded (Cooper, 1989). Amid these events, Stuart composed a special song to commemorate the birth of the Skinhead Nation. It was a horrific, two-chord heavy-metal number entitled "Dead Paki in a Gutter" (Owens, n.d.).

Simultaneously, Stuart and his associates began publication of a Nazilike bulletin called *Blood and Honour.* This fanzine reported on the activities of various racist bands, like Skrewdriver, whose music Stuart called "a celebration of being white" (quoted in Bishop, 1988:17). In their inaugural issue, the editors of *Blood and Honour* proclaimed: "We will follow the example of the one uncorruptible ideal: —National Socialism, and its great martyr Adolf Hitler" (quoted in *Cable Street Beat* review, n.d.:1). About the future of Great Britain, the *Blood and Honour* manifesto ran as follows: "For a start there wouldn't be any black people here, lesbians and gays would crawl back into the sordid holes they crawled out of, and the sensible socialists would see the wisdom of Nationalism" (*Cable Street Beat* review, n.d.:1).

At length, *Blood and Honour* was disseminated in the United States to members of the Ku Klux Klan and the American Nazi Party. One of these readers was a middle-aged television repairman from Fallbrook, California, named Tom Metzger.

3

From Haight-Ashbury to Plymouth Rock: The Rise of the American Neo-Nazi Skinheads

No collective category, no class, no group of any kind in and of itself wields power or can use it. Another factor must be present: that of organization.
— John Kenneth Galbraith
The Anatomy of Power

We get new members each time one of those idiot TV guys gives us air time. Get it?
— Alden Ernst
Fictional neo-Nazi organizer in the made-for-
television movie *Hail the New Dawn*

The American punk scene took root on the heels of the 1977 Sex Pistols tour of North America. Although the Sex Pistols offered American youth a dramatic introduction to the punk phenomenon, the U.S. version of punk never evolved into the sophisticated social force that eventually came about in Great Britain. As we have seen, British punk rock was based on themes derived from youthful unemployment and blocked opportunity for a better life. American punk rock had little of this sharply defined class-based dimension. Because of this, the American punk scene was restricted in its ability to develop strong, Clash-like messages of social protest. Essentially, American punk turned out to be little more than an angry and meaningless form of social posturing (Dancis, 1978; Marcus, 1989).

Nevertheless, by the early 1980s the insipid American punk movement had spawned a number of homegrown bands in major urban areas across the nation. These defunct acts included the Dead Boys from Cleveland, the Avengers from San Francisco, and New York's Blondie, Television, the Nuns, and the Dead Kennedys. Here, American youth assembled piecemeal some of the essential elements of the British punk style: confrontational dressing, colored Mohawk hairstyles, and the language of anarchy. This borrowed style was supported by a borrowed musical form, and neither was sustained by a coherent value system. In other words, American punk generally became an overnight failure because this subculture never came close to setting up the elements essential for achieving tribal homology.

It was in much the same way that the American skinhead subculture initially experienced its transatlantic bypass. In the early years, the racist American skinheads were an utter failure inasmuch as they were never able to galvanize a large number of youth around a clearly defined system of values, style, and musical expression. Complicating their plight, the original American skinheads were organized by young men who suffered severe mental and emotional disabilities.

THE RISE AND FALL OF ROMANTIC VIOLENCE

In 1979, a nineteen-year-old high school dropout named Clark Martell received a four-year sentence in an Illinois prison for the crime of arson committed against an Hispanic family in Chicago (*Social Education,* April/May 1988). While in prison, Martell was diagnosed as having a serious mental problem. Yet it was also here, in the sanctity of his cell, that this mentally infirmed high school dropout read every page of Adolf Hitler's *Mein Kampf* (Leo, 1988). He also began to draw elaborate and meticulous pictures showing the glories of Nazism (field notes).

Upon his release from prison in 1983, twenty-three-year-old Martell returned to his home in Blue Island, Illinois, and immediately joined the Chicago-based American Nazi Party. Because of his artistic abilities, the leadership of the Chicago Nazis put young Clark to work drawing cartoons for the party's newsletter, *Public Voice* (ADL, 1988a).

In the summer of 1984, Martell began his own cartoon business by producing a line of T-shirts portraying a human skull emblazoned with a "Death's Head Muscle" logo in honor of the notorious Nazi SS Death's Head Battalions. Few kids on the streets of Chicago knew what this meant, and Martell's cartoon business quickly went as dead as the picture on his ill-fated T-shirt.

In September of '84, Martell was arrested for painting swastikas on public property in the Chicago suburb of Oak Park. Despite his status as an Illinois parolee, Martell was soon released from custody. Without a job, Clark then rented a post office box in Blue Island, and began a more focused business campaign by advertising his Death's Head Muscle T-shirt in *Public Voice* and the underground teen press (ADL, 1988a).

During this period, record stores in the Chicago area began to stock the new white power Oi music from Britain. Suddenly, there were records by Brutal Attack, No Remorse, Skullhead, and of course, Skrewdriver. From contacts made through the sales of his Death's Head Muscle T-shirt, Martell organized a small group of youths who began to meet in Martell's Blue Island apartment where they would listen to this new white power rock and drink copious amounts of beer. Here, Martell and his companions would carry on serious discussions about Skrewdriver songs such as "Nigger, Nigger," "Rudolf Hess (Prisoner of Peace)," "Race and Nation," and "White Power" (field notes).

Out of Martell's Blue Island apartment came America's first neo-Nazi skinhead street gang. They took the name Romantic Violence and began to pattern themselves after the skinheads of Europe (field notes). One of their first activities was to print and disseminate a leaflet based on Martell's awkward paraphrasing of a passage from *Mein Kampf:*

Our heads are shaved for battle. Skinheads of America, like the dynamic skinheads in Europe, are working-class Aryan youth. We oppose the capitalist and communist scum that are destroying our Aryan race. The parasitic Jewish race is at the heart of our problem. (quoted in *Social Education,* April/May 1988:290)

In early 1985, Martell and his associates began a campaign to bring Skrewdriver to Chicago for a white power rock concert. Through arrangements made with a local record store, Romantic Violence started to sell Skrewdriver records and cassettes on a consignment basis through Martell's Blue Island post office box (field notes). Advertisements for this service were contained in a Nazi-like leaflet, "Skrewdriver News," distributed by Martell and his gang. Here is an excerpt from "Skrewdriver News":

For nearly nine years SKREWDRIVER have been offering White Youths a glimmer of hope for the future and the chance to momentarily escape from our nightmare world of multi-racialism, unemployment and degradation. SKREWDRIVER have become an institution, a stance of courage, determination, loyalty, honor and a will to win.

During the spring of 1985, members of Romantic Violence formed their own white power band called the Final Solution. At the very few Final Solution gigs that took place in and around Chicago during 1985, Martell could be seen passing out copies of "Skrewdriver News" portraying his gang as "a new breed of heroes [who] have sprung from the midwestern soil, brave skinhead patriots ready to fight for race and nation" (quoted in ADL, 1987b:3). By the summer of '85, Romantic Violence had captured the interests of more powerful elements on the extreme right.

In June, the American Nazi Party organized a Chicago march to protest the city's annual Gay and Lesbian Pride Day. Leading this march was Clark Martell and his new gang of shaven-headed neo-Nazis (ADL 1987b:3). Martell subsequently made two visits to the seventy-acre farm of Robert Miles in rural Cochoctah, Michigan, to meet with hate group activists from around the country. (Miles is the former Michigan Grand Dragon and national Chaplain [Imperial Klud] of the United Klans of America. At the time of his meetings with Martell, Miles was under indictment on charges of plotting to overthrow the U.S. government [ADL, 1988a; Toy, 1989].)

Following the Cochoctah meetings, Romantic Violence committed a spree of serious hate crimes in the Chicago area. On three occasions during 1987, Martell committed aggravated assault against six different Hispanic women (ADL, 1988c). On the evening of November 9, 1987 — the forty-ninth anniversary of

Nazi Germany's *Kristallnacht*—Romantic Violence smashed the glass doors to the entrances of three Chicago-area synagogues and left behind red swastikas on the synagogue walls. They proceeded to devastate two kosher markets, a Jewish bookstore, and several other Jewish-owned businesses (*Social Education,* April/ May 1988). This crime spree reached its pinnacle of hate in December of '87 when Martell broke into his girlfriend's apartment, beat her until she bled from the mouth, maced her, and then drew a swastika on the wall with her own blood because she was seen talking to black people on the street.

Martell was arrested and jailed for this crime spree in January of 1988. This effectively neutralized the skinheads of Chicago, as some members of Romantic Violence splintered into a group known as CASH (Chicago Area Skinheads) and others migrated to Milwaukee (ADL, 1988c; Tomaso, 1990). Today there are few racist skinheads in Chicago, and Martell is once again confined to an Illinois prison cell where he has begun to envision the American skinhead movement as the living embodiment of God. Says the now seriously infirmed Martell:

How we cried out for help, *for vengeance,* for life. And yet our plea went unanswered for years, until it came—the plan of salvation, the hope of redemption; we became warrior Skinheads. We now have hope for life where once only black despair filled our thoughts. We have hope today, because today we have Skins and the movement thereof. Today we have met the father God, and he is us. Skinhead!!! (Martell, n.d.:14, emphasis added)

THE IDIOTS OF HAIGHT-ASHBURY

The second original U.S. skinhead gang emerged during 1985 in (of all places) the Haight-Ashbury district of San Francisco, where twenty years earlier hippies had forged the international subcultural paradigm of peace and love. Like their counterparts in Chicago, the San Francisco skinheads were organized by a single, highly disturbed young man.

During the summer of 1984, Robert Heick, an eighteen-year-old high school dropout with a lengthy juvenile arrest record, traveled from his native San Francisco to London where he became exposed to the British skinhead style and the new white power rock (field notes). On his return to San Francisco, Heick shaved his head, changed his name to Bob Blitz, and began wearing a bomber jacket, a Fred Perry shirt, Levis, red suspenders, and steel-toed Doc Martens (Coplon, 1989). In late '84, Heick and a friend broke into and vandalized a Haight Street anarchist bookstore, leaving behind this message. "Punks, Communists, Anarchists, Hippys [sic], and homosexuals. . . . We the SKINHEADS will not tolerate your spreading of unwanted diseases both mental and physical. . . . YOUR DAYS ARE NUMBERED" (quoted in Gatewood, 1989:14).

By 1985, twenty-year-old Heick had organized a handful of San Francisco teenagers into a skinhead gang called the American Front (ADL, 1988c). Together, these youths moved into an apartment on Judah Street in the Buena Vista Park area near Haight-Ashbury and claimed the section as Skinhead Hill (Coplon, 1989). At this point, Heick marked his body with sixteen tattoos of swastikas, eagles, and Vikings. On the inside of his lower lip, Heick tattooed the word SKINS (ADL, 1988c). During the summer of '85, the American Front spray-painted swastikas on the sidewalks around Skinhead Hill and began attacking longhairs and interracial couples on Haight Street. In the words of Bob Blitz:

That was a bitchin' summer. We'd get in fights with bunches of hippies and blacks and punks and anarchists. Kids were coming in from the suburbs . . . and everyone was hanging on Haight Street — it was like a big party. And any time anyone gave us any lip, we just bashed 'em, because this was *our* street. (quoted in Coplon, 1989:87)

By 1986, Skrewdriver records were available in selected San Francisco record stores, and another dozen-or-so teenagers joined Heick's American Front; as Heick himself began a homegrown Oi band called the Stormtrooper Five. But his popularity as a musician was limited, and soon Heick let his hair grow out and took a job as a mail-room worker in a department store (Coplon, 1989:87).

Heick then transformed his Bob Blitz image from traditional skinhead style to a look that has rarely, if ever, been seen again in the skinhead underground. Gone were the Fred Perry shirt, red suspenders, bomber jacket, and Levis. Also gone now was his shaved hair. In their place came a Nazi-like uniform set off by a respectable crop of well-combed hair. Still remaining, however, were the sinister-looking Doc Martens (Coplon, 1989:87).

Because of his newfound respectability as a mail-room worker, the heavily tattooed high school dropout became fascinated with the U.S. Postal Service. In late 1986 Heick purchased a copying machine and began to print and mail a series of leaflets reading: "The Future Belongs to the Few of Us Still Willing To Get Our Hands Dirty: Political Terror, Its the Only Thing They Understand" and "Get Out Jew While You Can." Both flyers were emblazoned with the swastika and a gun and were mailed to hundreds of California youths who had listed their addresses in an emerging underground punk press (ADL, 1988c).

During this period, Heick and his companions allegedly ran their automobile over a gay man in the Castro Street area of San Francisco, crippling him for life. They also reportedly kidnapped and tortured a prostitute in Oakland, and made another assault on the Haight Street anarchist bookstore (ADL, 1988a; Gatewood, 1989). Then, suddenly, Heick's reign of terror was over.

By 1987, the Haight-Ashbury Merchant's Association had persuaded the San Francisco Police to crack down on the local skinheads. And after this, Heick and the American Front rarely ventured out en masse and stopped spraying swastikas on the sidewalks of Buena Vista Park (Coplon, 1989). For Bob Blitz, the bitchin' summer of '85 was over. Although the American Front would survive and go on to organize yearly White Workers Day parades down Haight Street, Heick's gang eventually dwindled to less than ten members and their hate crimes became limited to minor scuffles and occasional spray-painting of racist graffiti (ADL, 1989b). Instead of a serious threat to San Francisco's population of "Punks, Communists, Anarchists, Hippies, and Homosexuals," Heick's group turned out to be little more than "a floating community of transients [rather] than a well-established gang" (ADL, 1989b:16).

The fact that Heick's gang turned out to be such a failure should not be surprising to any observer of contemporary youth subcultures. After all, the American Front was a product of San Francisco and there has always been a dark side to the youth subcultures of that city since Jack Kerouac first wrote about North Beach beatniks back in the mid-fifties. Indeed, no less a foreboding figure than the convicted mass murderer Charles Manson has passed through the San Francisco subcultural scene and stories abound about ritualistic murders and Satanic cults (Kahaner, 1988), including cabals who feast on human afterbirth (Grogan, 1972) and those who deliberately plan the birth of a child who will one day become the "Idiot Bastard" of the human race (Doyle, 1970). Because they were so damnably esoteric, these youth cults were never able to achieve a coherent political identity in San Francisco, nor anywhere else in California.

The oddball skinheads, though, were different. Instead of drifting off into obscurity, hundreds of other Bay Area skins were soon organized into a statewide hate group. Tim Yohannan, editor of the Berkeley-based *Maximum Rock 'N Roll* fanzine, has aptly described this subcultural development: "There were always idiots [in California]. Now there's idiots with ideology" (quoted in Coplon, 1989:87).

But it would take a much more portentous force to accomplish the spread of youthful hate across California than the small handful of idiots from Haight-Ashbury.

TOM METZGER

The central hypothesis of the present research is this: Were it not for Tom Metzger—the Fallbrook, California, TV repairman who subscribed to Ian Stuart's newsletter *Blood and Honour* back in the winter of 1985—the American neo-Nazi skinheads would never have become more than scattered, short-lived groups led by disturbed individuals. Because of his importance in the American skinhead story, Metzger's life history deserves a careful explanation and analysis.

Tom Metzger was born in Warsaw, Indiana, in 1939. He grew up in this small Indiana town, and throughout his youth he remained virtually unexposed to blacks, Jews, and homosexuals (ADL, 1988b). After graduating from high school, Metzger was drafted into the U.S. Army and achieved the rank of corporal before his twenty-first birthday (ADL, 1988b). This intense drive to assert himself in a unique fashion would become a recurring pattern throughout his life. It was also here, during the early years of the Cold War, that Metzger claims to have developed a "segregationist ideology" (Brown, 1989).

In 1961, twenty-two-year-old Metzger ended his tour of duty in the army and moved to Los Angeles where he found employment as an electronics technician in a military plant (ADL, 1988b). Sometime around 1963, Metzger began experimenting with far right radicalism. First, he joined the ultraconservative John

Birch Society. For Metzger, the John Birch Society held revolutionary ideas that offered a compelling response to the dangers of Cold War America. Metzger quickly embraced the organization's concept of a communist infiltration into American government and news media. At length, Metzger began to theorize that Jews were at the heart of this conspiracy (Langer, 1990).

However, Metzger soon withdrew his membership from the Birchers when he was prohibited by the leadership from using the organization's name in behalf of his public defilements of Jewish bankers and businessmen (ADL, 1988b). In essence, Metzger's beliefs had become too radical for the Birchers of Los Angeles. Searching for the correct organizational form to express his extreme views, Metzger then joined the Los Angeles-based Minutemen; but he soon found the Minutemen to be old, stodgy, and mindlessly patriotic. And so, Metzger gave up his membership in this organization as well (ADL, 1988b; Brown, 1989).

By 1964, Metzger had become an ardent supporter of conservative presidential candidate Barry Goldwater. Following Goldwater's defeat in the '64 elections, Metzger fell out of sight in conventional California politics (although he would reappear briefly as a George Wallace campaign worker in 1968 [Brown, 1989; Langer, 1990]). With the Summer of Love, the Watts riot, and the anti-Vietnam War movement just around the corner, it seemed that few Californians were interested in Metzger's ultraconservative theories about communist infiltrators and racial segregation.

In what would become a common theme running throughout his career over the next two decades, Metzger then avoided the more moderate position of radical libertarianism and became a secretive and highly skilled organizer of extreme right-wing factions dedicated to clandestine forms of militarized racial and ethnic violence. By 1970, Metzger—who had recently fathered the first of his six children, a son named John—came to believe that Jews, especially Secretary of State Henry Kissinger, had forced the United States into an Asian war that was not in the best interests of American whites. Furthermore, he started to blame deteriorating urban conditions on black criminals, welfare cheats, and Mexican immigrants. In response, Metzger formed an organization called the White Brotherhood to carry out his new vision of creating a mass racist movement with a selective cadre of well-trained young white men dedicated to armed terrorism against Jews and minorities throughout California (Brown, 1989; Langer, 1990).

Nineteen seventy-four was the year that the United States Congress voted to impeach President Richard Nixon because of his involvement in Watergate. Disco and cocaine were quickly becoming the rage among American youth subcultures, and Tom Metzger joined the Ku Klux Klan. Following this, Metzger merged his White Brotherhood with the national Knights of the Ku Klux Klan which was led by a twenty-four-year-old former CIA counterinsurgency employee and American Nazi Party activist named David Ernest Duke (Brown, 1989; Langer, 1990.) At the time, Duke was the rising young star of an emerging "New Klan" devoted to transforming the image of the KKK through the skillful use of the print and broadcast media. In their new image, the Klan were to be perceived as the champions of white rights in the modern age of affirmative action (Brown, 1989).

By 1978, however, Metzger had become disenchanted with David Duke and his New Klan. Metzger then initiated a California-based Klan election that ultimately gave him the title of Grand Dragon of the Knights of the Ku Klux Klan (Brown, 1989; ADL, 1988b). This was a matter of significant importance within the KKK. Until the 1979 California enclave, the state's Klan elections were always coordinated by the national Klan office in New Orleans, Louisiana. Therefore, the establishment of an independent and autonomous California "Realm" – with its own leader, Grand Dragon Metzger – became a matter of serious concern in New Orleans. This was especially so for the newly elected Imperial Wizard of the national Knights of the Ku Klux Klan – the ever-vibrant David Duke. (David Duke – the first Imperial Wizard of the Klan to hold public office in history – is currently a member of the Louisiana State Legislature and was briefly a Republican candidate for president of the United States. He is the former president of the National Association for the Advancement of White People, and one of the most detested political figures among minorities throughout the world [Zatarain, 1990].)

In reaction to Duke's anger over the unorthodox California Klan elections of 1978, Metzger withdrew his membership from the national KKK and formed a breakaway group called the California Knights of the Ku Klux Klan (ADL, 1988b; Langer, 1990). Once again, Metzger had become too radical for the racist underground. "To Metzger," writes David Duke's biographer, "Duke was not a true white racist because he was 'too soft' on racist issues. Duke generally limited his anti-Semitic attacks to Zionists, while Metzger . . . focused on the 'individual Jew' " (Zatarain, 1990:229).

Following his break with Duke and the New Klan, Metzger took an even more outlandish position to gain attention for his radical beliefs. In late 1979, he turned to the pulpit and became an ordained minister in the New Christian Crusade Church. This was an Identity Church based on an obscure, century-old anti-Semitic doctrine known as British-Israelism that contends God's "chosen people" are not Jews, but rather descendants of the Lost Tribes of Ancient Israel who ultimately became the Anglo-Saxon-Teuton Whites of the British Isles (Hexham, 1984). According to the Identity Church, Jews are thought to carry the "seeds of Satan" and blacks are considered monkeys or "mud people" who are descendants of the "Forces of Darkness" led by Lucifer (Sapp, 1991). Moreover, Metzger's New Christian Crusade Church sought to justify racism and bigotry through a perversion of biblical scripture.

Sustained by his religious transformation, the forty-year-old Metzger then took one of the boldest steps down the road of right-wing radicalism since the American civil rights movement. During the spring of 1979, Metzger organized a small band of armed Klansmen from the Marine Corps base at Camp Pendleton into a group known as the Border Watch. Their purpose was to look for illegal aliens along the U.S.–Mexican border near Tijuana (ADL, 1988b; Brown, 1989). Eventually, the Border Watch extended from the Pacific Ocean to Brownsville, Texas, as hundreds of Klansmen were recruited into the patrol (Zatarian, 1990).

The Border Watch, however, was eventually found to be repulsive by sheriffs, lawmakers, and immigration officers on both sides of the U.S.–Mexican line. And in early 1980, INS officials in San Diego arrested Reverend Metzger for his border patrol activities. Said INS regional commissioner L. J. Castillo at the time: "We do not condone and will not allow the Ku Klux Klan to make border arrests in California" (quoted in ADL, 1988b:5). The arrest made Metzger aware that the road before him had become a difficult one. In the immediate future, he would have to be more careful.

Therefore, in an attempt to transcend the traditional stereotype of the racist as a redneck bigot, Metzger went in search of a deeper and more refined system of political action that could produce real solutions to the problems he foresaw in America's future. And in early 1980, Tom Metzger became a candidate for election to the United States House of Representatives. Shortly after announcing his candidacy, Metzger addressed a journalism class at San Diego State University. "You don't make changes having fiery crosses out in cow pastures" said Metzger. "You make change by invading the halls of Congress and the Statehouse" (quoted in Langer, 1990:88).

Accordingly, Metzger disbanded the New Christian Crusade Church and opened a combination TV Repair Service and multipurpose political action center in a modest house located in the Latino section of Fallbrook, California, north of San Diego (Langer, 1990:88). It was at this point that Metzger also became a connoisseur of conservative business suits, stick-pin ties, freshly laundered white shirts, and polished penny loafers (Coplon, 1989). His was the corporate look that became so popular during the American eighties. Essentially, Metzger had packaged his beliefs in a new and modern format that allowed him to reach out to thousands of people who would have never been attracted to his brand of extremism before.

By this time, former California governor Ronald Reagan had gathered unprecedented national support for a new wave of right-wing American populism. Although Metzger appropriated this populism as part of his own campaign rhetoric, he also took positions no sensible Democrat or Republican would ever support. This trait had followed him from his past and would guide him into the future. Like the "racist messiah" David Duke, Metzger's political biography reveals that he has consistently found strength in maintaining loyalty to his own beliefs, rather than in gaining approval from others (Langer, 1990;. Zatarain, 1990).

For example, Metzger may have been the first American political candidate to ever promote a public policy calling for elementary school children to be taught rifle marksmanship. He may also have been the first candidate to make opposition to affirmative action programs and the need to seal off the borders against foreign immigration the cornerstones of a serious political campaign. To demonstrate the importance of these issues, Metzger delivered his campaign speeches wearing a bulletproof vest (ADL, 1988b; Brown, 1989; Linker, 1989).

In October of 1980 (on the eve of Ronald Reagan's presidential election), Metzger received 33,000 votes and became the surprise winner of the California Democratic Congressional Primary in the state's forty-third district (ADL, 1988b; Langer, 1990). Metzger had successfully translated his extreme views into victory at the ballot box because he had effectively cast extremism into a language appropriate for American populism. In essence, Metzger promised to look out for the little white guy by opposing taxes and fighting urban crime and drug use.

Although Metzger had been victorious in the primaries, he was defeated in the general elections by Republican incumbent Clair Burgener, who beat Metzger by more than 250,000 votes (Langer, 1990). Adding insult to injury, in late 1980 the California Democratic Central Committee voted to strip Metzger of his party credentials because of his affiliation with the Klan (Langer, 1990; Wallace, 1985). In response, Metzger changed the name of his California Knights of the Ku Klux Klan to the White American Political Association (WAPA). Whereas the stated goal of WAPA was to promote pro-white candidates for public office, lying beneath the organization's outer appearance of respectability was something dark and dangerous.

During this period, Metzger created a second uniformed security force; this time called the Klan Bureau of Investigation to act as guards for WAPA officials. As before, most members of the security force were recruited from the Marine base at Camp Pendleton. Metzger's followers soon became involved in violent clashes with police and anti-Klan demonstrators across California. One such clash took place in March of 1980, when Metzger led thirty armed members of his security force into a confrontation with anti-Klan demonstrators in Oceanside, leaving seven people injured (ADL, 1988b).

Simultaneously, Metzger's WAPA began to promote future far right paramilitary activities by distributing instructional handbooks on terrorism and guerrilla warfare. These included works such as *The Anarchist's Cookbook, The White Man's Bible, White Power,* and a science fiction novel entitled *The Turner Diaries,* which is considered by many to be the contemporary Bible of hard-core racists in the United States (Flynn and Gerhardt, 1989; Langer, 1990; Sapp, 1991; Singular, 1987; Wallace, 1985).

Metzger's true genius did not lie solely in his pursuit of this radical agenda; rather, it came from his newfound ability to look both ways. Even though he was politically trounced and repudiated in 1980, by 1982 Metzger had made peace with the state's Democratic party. He then ran in the California Democratic Primary for the United States Senate. Metzger placed fourth in the race, receiving 73,987 votes—or 1.5 percent of the vote necessary for election (ADL 1988b). Defeated, yet somehow elated by his growing popularity, Metzger retreated to his television repair shop to concentrate on what he knew best.

THE CULTURAL CONSTRUCTION OF
DOMESTIC TERRORISM

By the mid-1980s, the mainstream culture of the United States had become anchored in conservatism, Republicanism, patriotism, and traditional family values that were at the heart of a growing religious revival waged by the Fundamentalist Christian Right. By the time of Ronald Reagan's 1984 victory over Walter Mondale, the Reverend Jerry Falwell of the Thomas Road Baptist Church in Lynchburg, Virginia, headed a 6.5-million-member political action group known as the Moral Majority, which was waging a strong campaign for the acceptance of Christian education in public schools and legal sanctions against abortion, pornography, homosexuality, and other forms of "immorality" (Singular, 1987).

In 1985, 1,000 of America's 9,642 radio stations and more than 200 local television stations were affiliated with evangelical or fundamentalist Christianity (Singular, 1987). Of the 80 million television sets studied by the Nielsen rating service during this year, nearly 68 million were tuned at least once a month to evangelical or fundamentalist programs such as Pat Robertson's *The 700 Club*, *The Jimmy Swaggart Ministry*, *The Oral Roberts Ministry*, and Jim and Tammy Faye Bakker's *PTL Club* (Singular, 1987).

The Christian right also turned their religious beliefs into a strong political force as the Reverend Pat Robertson became a viable candidate in the 1988 presidential campaign. Meanwhile, Jerry Falwell and Jim Bakker became frequent guests at the White House; and President Reagan himself—now one of the most popular politicians in American history—showed up as a guest celebrity at *PTL* and *The 700 Club* and became a beloved speaker before the National Association of Evangelicals (Shepard, 1989; Sternberg and Harrison, 1989).

The symbolic incorporation of fundamentalist religion into federal government was not the only significant change brought about by Ronald Reagan. From the beginning, the highest priority for the Reagan administration was to reduce the size of the federal government and its budget relative to the economy. This was to be accomplished through severe cuts in federal spending for civil programs and lower taxes—especially for those Americans who earned more than $50,000 a year (Dalleck, 1984).

This system was known as supply-side economics, Reaganomics, or—as George Bush described it in 1980—voodoo economics. It is premised on a microeconomic theory predicting that low taxes for the wealthiest members of society should fuel major economic expansion. In turn, this expansion should reduce unemployment and, therefore, actually provide increased tax revenues because more people are put to work. It was, moreover, the same economic principle employed by Margaret Thatcher's government during the early days of the British neo-Nazi skinhead movement.

For wealthy Americans, the benefits of Reaganomics were simply outstanding. By lowering taxes for the rich, Reagan administrators drew support from some of the most prosperous business enterprises in the nation. In return, the Reagan administration awarded these free-enterprise groups with special benefits including tax write-offs for accelerated depreciation of assets, travel, entertainment, legal fees, and the near elimination of real estate taxes (Polenberg, 1988; Sternberg and Harrison, 1989).

For the first Reagan administration, the benefits of this partnership were equally outstanding. With the projected tax revenues generated by Reaganomics, the federal government set forth a two-pronged strategy to ensure Ronald Reagan's reelection in 1984. The first strategy was to lower the federal deficit. When Reagan took office in January of 1981, the national debt was $800 billion and growing (Polenberg, 1988). At the time, it was thought that his 1984 reelection would turn on his administration's ability to solve this problem (Dalleck, 1984).

The second strategy was to increase military spending. Between 1981 and 1984, the U.S. military budget rose from 5.5 to 8 percent of the gross national product (GNP) (Tobin, 1988). In total, the first Reagan administration spent approximately $1.8 trillion on military programs, representing the largest military buildup in American history (Dalleck, 1984; Smith, 1986).

By the time Ronald Reagan faced off against Walter Mondale in the '84 election, Reaganism was being heralded as the most successful counterrevolutionary tactic ever waged by the United States government (Kymlicka and Matthews, 1988). Reaganism had produced an overall 25 percent reduction in taxes, steady economic growth, declining inflation rates, a drop in oil prices, a stabilization of unemployment rates, and a strong military (Dalleck, 1984; Polenberg, 1988; Tobin, 1988). Journalist Paul Duke described the mood of America at the time:

the Reagan [administration] had its nostalgic side, a yearning for easier, less complicated times and a return to a period when America reigned supreme. But fundamentally it symbolized the country's willingness to strike out in new problems—even if some of them sounded dangerously simplistic. Implicit was the message that the heyday of the welfare state was finally over. (1986:13)

The Reagan administration did, in fact, take major strides toward eliminating the heyday of the welfare state. Billions of dollars were cut from welfare, health care, and educational enhancement programs for the poor during President Reagan's first term in office (Dalleck, 1984). During this period, federal expenditures for human resources fell from 11.75 percent of the GNP to 11.4 percent; cash assistance payments dropped from .26 percent of the GNP to .22 percent; and compensatory education grants were slashed in half, from .6 percent to .3 percent of the GNP (Falk, 1987). And as the number of welfare recipients declined approximately 3 percent between 1980 and 1984, the U.S. poverty rate increased by almost as much (Gottschalk, 1988; Weaver, 1988).

Simply put, by 1984 Reaganism had made conditions worse for the dispossessed and disenfranchised, and exceedingly better for the wealthy. Because of this, the United States had become a nation where the formulation of public policy was largely dependent on the physical capital brought forth by private business groups—many of whom were funded by the U.S. military (Sternberg and Harrison, 1989). As such, big money had replaced participatory politics as the critical element of American democracy. These policies had two widesweeping impacts on American culture.

First, the formulation of physical capital by private business groups led to a boom in the construction of shopping malls, luxury hotels, and gambling casinos (Tobin, 1988). This led to increased incentives for personal consumption, severe economic dislocation, and an accelerated weakening of the social fabric in American neighborhoods begun by the economic policies of the 1970s (McNiven, 1988). Second, Reaganism produced the most sophisticated brand of weaponry ever seen in human history. Between 1983 and 1987, Reagan administrators introduced the world to the MX and Tomahawk intercontinental ballistic missiles, the B–1 and F–15 bombers, the neutron bomb, enlarged naval and army fleets, and plans for the elaborate Strategic Defense Initiative known as Star Wars (Dalleck, 1984; Stevens, 1988).

These events strongly influenced the youth subcultural scene in America. In many ways, white youth under Ronald Reagan—like white youth of early postwar Britain—never had it so good. In April of 1985, the U.S. unemployment rate among white youth sixteen to nineteen years old reached its lowest point in twenty years. At the same time, the percentage of white youth attending and graduating from high school reached its highest point in 112 years of American public school education (Lane, 1986).

These were the days when the Coca Cola Company brought back its original formula, as MTV saturated the cable television market playing videos twenty-four hours a day. Often dressed in flashy paramilitary jump suits, Michael Jackson, Prince, and Madonna rode the charts with their sexy, syncopated dance tracks like "Beat It," "Kiss," and "Like a Virgin." According to the *World Almanac Poll* of American high school students, the raucous comedian Eddie Murphy was the top hero in 1985. Not surprisingly, next to Eddie Murphy the American high school populace selected Ronald Reagan as the top hero. Sylvester Stallone ("Rambo") followed the president in order of importance (Lane, 1986). Fashion and entertainment industries responded to the symbolism of these times by flooding U.S. shopping malls with camouflage suits, bomber jackets, combat boots, martial arts costumes, Rambo dolls, and computerized war games.

Yet as the country's mainstream conservative forces were becoming more powerful and institutionalized, those who belonged to the American far right were drifting into decline. By mid-decade the membership in the Ku Klux Klan had fallen from a high of 11,500 in 1981 to about 5,000 in 1985, and membership in the American Nazi Party dwindled from 1,200 to about 400 during the same period (ADL, 1988a; Reed, 1989). Large Klan rallies began tapering off; Klan and neo-Nazi leaders started fighting with each other, and eventually more than thirty different national Klan and neo-Nazi organizations emerged to compete with each other for attention. During the Reagan era, not a single Klan leader was elected to public office in the United States (David Duke would be elected during the Bush administration). And a series of new hate crime laws, together with numerous civil and criminal lawsuits, caused hundreds of Klansmen and neo-Nazis to drift away from the far right (ADL, 1988a; Dees, 1991; Singular, 1987).

While their numbers were dropping rapidly during the mid-eighties, those who remained loyal to the beliefs of the Ku Klux Klan and the American Nazi Party drifted toward an extreme form of activism. Whereas previous generations of or-ganized white racists were predominantly rural-based and middle-aged, the neo-Nazis of the American eighties sought to build a grand coalition of young Aryan terrorists whose primary objective was to rid America of what they called a Zion-ist-Occupied Government—ZOG (Langer, 1990).

Moreover, the American neo-Nazis began their politics with an aggressive re-jection of the symbols of eighties conservatism (e.g., the Reagan White House, voodoo economics, corporate America, and Star Wars). "Instead of welcoming the conservative shift in the country," observed Stephen Singular in 1987, "[ex-tremists] tended to loathe it, for it drew members from their ranks toward more conventional center-right politics. It left them isolated on the fringe, without a liberal in the White House to rail against" (1987:85).

Yet, the extremists remained deeply committed to the core values of main-stream conservatism at the height of the Reagan era. Essentially, the neo-Nazis adopted a synthetic ideology combining their vitriolic anti-Semitism and tradi-tional hatred of African-Americans, gays, and liberals with extreme militarism, love of family, and fundamentalist Christianity.

As such, cross-burning Klansmen in bed sheets and goose-stepping neo-Nazis were not only passé but also an embarrassment to the far right (King, 1989). In their place came a secret collective of paramilitary survivalists, tax protesters, bankrupt farmers, bikers, prisoners, Odinists, and devotees of the Identity Church who were linked together by an elaborate network of computer bulletin boards, cable access television, desktop publications, and telephone hotlines (ADL, 1988a; Langer, 1990).

Out of this space came one of the most dangerous and criminally competent terrorist organizations ever seen in the United States. In the spring of 1984, forty-three white men from the remote mountains of Metaline Falls, Washington—most all family members and devotees of the Identity Church—began a secret army known alternatively as the Silent Brotherhood (or *Bruders Schweigen*), the Or-der, and the White American Bastion. Although the Order existed for less than eighteen months, they committed an unprecedented spree of terrorist acts in an attempt to act out a sophisticated fantasy portrayed by William Pierce (aka Wil-liam McDonald) in his science fiction novel, *The Turner Diaries*.

The Turner Diaries can be considered a blueprint for right-wing revolution in the United States. It depicts an underground extremist army that wages a 1990s race war against a Jewish-controlled American government. In the book, the Co-hen Act has outlawed gun ownership and has invested human relations councils with police powers to force integration and miscegenation on the public. In response, a white guerrilla force led by the book's protagonist, Earl Turner, has been formed and its secret elite set of commanders are known as The Order. Turner and his guerrilla band wage warfare against the Jewish-controlled government through the successful truck-bombing of FBI headquarters and a mortar attack on the U.S. Capitol Building. Along the way, The Order also stages a series of small-scale strikes, counterfeiting operations, armored car robberies, and assassinations of Cohen Act supporters. In the end, 1999, the white revolutionaries win their war against the government after gaining territory in Southern California, killing thousands of Jews and minorities, and commandeering the nuclear missiles at Vandenberg Air Force Base to annihilate the nation of Israel.

THE EMERGENCE OF THE AMERICAN NEO-NAZI SKINHEADS

In late 1984, the FBI launched its hardest-fought battle against the extreme right in history. And by April of '85, the FBI issued a federal RICO indictment against twenty-three members of the Order charging them with:

- the machine gun execution of Alan Berg, an outspoken Jewish radio personality from Denver
- the bombing of a Boise, Idaho, synagogue
- the murder of an informant
- counterfeiting, racketeering, conspiracy, transporting stolen money, and sedition
- the stockpiling of large amounts of automatic weapons and explosives
- a series of commando robberies that netted the Order more than $4 million in cash (Flynn and Gerhardt, 1989)

It was within this context that the ever-radical Tom Metzger jumped back into the fray. Specifically, Metzger implemented seven initiatives designed to interject the Skinhead Nation into American culture. Although these initiatives covered a wide range of recruitment strategies, they all had one thing in common: Each sought to appropriate British skinhead values, style, and music to bring thousands of American youths into the revolutionary movement initiated by the Order.

W.A.R.

Metzger's first initiative was to create an organizational structure that would appeal to working-class American youth of the Reagan era. Following his retirement from electoral politics, Metzger changed the name of his California-based WAPA to the White Aryan Resistance (W.A.R.). Jeff Coplon has aptly described the objectives of this organization.

Where the Old Right was aging, isolated, rural-based and mindlessly patriotic, Metzger's New Right (W.A.R.) would be dynamic, hip, urban, and the champion of a white working class against a treasonous white ruling elite. It would be a place where alienated skinheads could feel right at home. (1989:82)

To attract the few alienated skinheads who existed in California at mid-decade, Metzger began to intensify his relationship with Ian Stuart and Skrewdriver. Coplon's 1988 interview with Metzger leaves no doubt about the recruiting potential he saw in British white power rock. Explained Metzger,

I became friends with the British skins about three years ago. The more I worked with them, the more I saw their potential to drag the racialist movement out of the conservative right-wing mold and into a newer era. I figured the music of these people could do that. I'm 50 years old, and I grew up with early rock 'n' roll—Elvis Presley, Jerry Lee Lewis, Fats Domino. I don't always catch all the words (in skinhead music), but I'm impressed with the power of it. I feel this anger coming from these white street kids—I get taken up in it. (Coplon, 1989:82–83)

W.A.R. was highly unique because it was the first American hate group to build its organization on the emotional appeal of rock and roll music. But W.A.R. was unique in more ways than this. Consistent with previous clandestine hate groups organized by Metzger (The White Brotherhood, The Klan Bureau of Investigation, and The Border Watch), W.A.R. was hardly an organization at all. Traditional hate groups, like the Knights of the Ku Klux Klan and the American Nazi Party, require elaborate induction ceremonies, rituals, and costumes. Most Klansmen and American Nazis, for example, carry membership cards. None of this was necessary in W.A.R. That is, the White Aryan Resistance was not a membership organization (Langer, 1990). Metzger explained this in a 1988 telephone hotline message:

W.A.R. wears no uniform, carries no card, and takes no secret oaths; [it] doesn't require you to dress up and march around on a muddy field; [it] works the modern way, with thousands of friends doing their part on the job, behind the scenes, serving their race. (Langer, 1990:89)

The War Zine

Metzger's second initiative was to publish and disseminate a slick youth magazine entitled *WAR*. Instilling hatred of Jews and minorities into those receptive to his beliefs has long been a key to Metzger's recruiting success. In this regard, *WAR* is Metzger's quintessential message of hate.

This monthly publication devotes pages to glorifying perpetrators of racial violence and vilifying minorities (called niggers, black assed coons, spooks, congoids, monkeys, black baboons, spics, mud people, kikes, pathetic queers, Jewish lesbians, and brown rot) through highly sophisticated (R. Crumb-like) comic strip presentations. Recent issues have called for an "all-out race war" against Jewish bankers and media representatives. *WAR* has called Pope John Paul II a white race traitor, described the now-imprisoned members of the Order as our highest living heroes, and saluted the revolutionary efforts of the Howard Beach mob for killing a young black male. *WAR* has featured long, detailed revisionistic accounts of the lives of Adolf Hitler and Rudolf Hess (referred to as a shining symbol and savior for mankind), and it carried a full-page photograph of a Tampa, Florida, skinhead killer named Dean McKee over the caption: "Winner of a Fight with Negro."

As a special feature, each issue of *WAR* contains addresses of avowed skinheads, and extensive lists of incarcerated white extremists called POWs. Included are mailing addresses for ten imprisoned members of the Order and other well-known racists such as Germany's Manfred Roeder, and Americans Clark Martell and James Earl Ray.

The cornerstone of *WAR* is a regular section devoted to the music of Skrewdriver. Since its inception in 1985, nearly all issues of *WAR* have carried a picture of Ian Stuart howling his white man's Oi from a black and white portrait usually situated in the center of the zine. Each issue also tells readers how they can order Skrewdriver and other white power music through the W.A.R. network. In addition, *WAR* offers readers the opportunity to purchase hard-to-find racist books, racist videos, cassettes, stickers, Nazi jewelry, white power T-shirts, and Viking posters (listed under the banner, Aryan Entertainment).

The purpose of all this, according to Metzger, "is to inject some ideology into the skinheads" (quoted in Coplon, 1989:85). This ideology is centered around what Metzger calls the Third Position. In its Third Position manifestos, *WAR* speaks of an "international pan-Aryan movement" that it describes as "an emerging global struggle of whites against Jews and mongrels." Moreover, the Third Position emphasizes race, ecology, and violence to the near exclusion of economics, religion, and public policy. In its U.S. manifestation, Metzger envisions the Third Position as the "Alamo of the white race" that is aligned with the "Mother Continent of Europe" (quoted in Langer, 1990:90).

To Metzger, skinheads are the vanguard of the Third Position. In his words, "If you're going to do anything, you need to have somebody with you who's going to stand their ground, and most conservatives won't. The skinheads have already got the main thing, and that's guts" (quoted in Gatewood, 1989:14).

"Race and Reason"

Metzger's third initiative began early in 1986 when he created a videotaped series for public access television entitled "Race and Reason." Metzger took this name from a book written by Carlton Putnum; *Race and Reason—A Yankee View* offers a variety of reasons why racial integration should fail and ultimately generate conditions favorable to poverty and crime. Wearing his corporate look, the naturally active Metzger—who had spent the last half-decade cooped up in his repair shop inspecting the circuitry of red and black TV wires—became something of a television star himself.

"Race and Reason" was videotaped in Metzger's repair shop and it seemed to be an exciting time in his life (Brown, 1989; Wallace, 1985). Throughout these videotapings, Metzger would elevate the traditional message of hate espoused in secret Klan rallies into the white heat of electronic public performance. A typical broadcast occurred in early 1987 when WAR Skin David Mazzella elaborated on the finer points of skinhead politics. Said Mazzella: "We can start gassing all the niggers and get rid of them because there's no need to keep paying taxes on their worthless lives" (quoted in ADL, 1987c:1).

The fact that Metzger had the audacity to broadcast such flammatory statements made him a folk hero to many on the far right. To be sure, in this age of remarkable developments in public access television (e.g., the rise and fall of Jim Bakker, Jimmy Swaggart, and Morton Downey, Jr.), Tom Metzger ultimately overcame the regionalism that had plagued the ultra right during the mid-eighties, and "catapulted himself into the American living room" (Langer, 1990:89). By 1987, "Race and Reason" had been introduced to new and vibrant audiences in San Francisco, Los Angeles, Phoenix, Las Vegas, Atlanta, and Memphis (ADL, 1988b; Brown, 1989).

Oprah and Geraldo

Metzger's fourth initiative began quite fortuitously. In December of 1988, he was invited to Chicago to appear on the most popular television program in America: "The Oprah Winfrey Show." Accompanied by Bay Area Reich Skins Brad Robage and Marty Cox, this forum gave Metzger a chance to be heard and seen by millions of people throughout North America (Klanwatch, 1989). In the audience were members of the Chicago Area Skinheads (CASH).

When Oprah asked Brad Robage to explain the philosophy of the American skinheads, he replied: "What makes a skinhead? Attitude. White power. Cause Niggers suck. Niggers and Jews. They're half monkeys. They should all be killed" (Klanwatch, 1989:54).

Following this, the skinheads in the audience shouted "Yea!" "Fuckin' right on!" and "Go for it!" Oprah cut to a commercial. Off the air, Tony Cox—then on federal parole for assault—called Oprah a monkey and a skinhead from CASH called her a "nigger whore" (Klanwatch, 1989, field notes).

When the cameras returned, the skinheads marched off the set with their arms clenched in a Nazi salute (Gatewood, 1989). Metzger then presented a calm and reasoned explanation for skinhead attitudes about race. A few curious questions to Metzger followed from the audience, but Oprah was strangely silent; sensing that something was terribly wrong with this whole production. After the show, Oprah told a Chicago reporter: "I have never seen such hatred in all my life" (quoted in ADL, 1988c:4).

"The Oprah Winfrey Show" did more than increase public recognition of Tom

Metzger and the American skinheads. In time, skinheads began to appear on other nationally syndicated TV programs, and *Rolling Stone, Time, Newsweek,* and the *New York Times* featured exclusive interviews with a number of American skinheads. In one of these interviews, talk show host Geraldo Rivera suffered a much publicized broken nose from a 220-pound New York City skinhead named Wyatt Kaldenberg. Metzger's *WAR* would later report that "Thousands of inquiries and millions of viewers now recognize a White Separatist Movement. . . . 40 million people tuned in to see this dirty Kike [Geraldo] get his beak broken, making it the most watched talk-show ever in history" (*WAR,* n.d., 7, no. 6:2–3). (*The Geraldo brawl was broadcast on the afternoon of November 11, 1988. The following evening, Mulugeta Seraw would die at the hands of skinheads in Portland.*) Yet there was another war dividend to be gained from this extraordinary media coverage.

Because Metzger had contributed so much to Oprah's television ratings, she invited the former Klansman back for a second visit in September of 1989. But this time Metzger said little about the skinheads. Instead, he defended the Ku Klux Klan's right to broadcast on cable TV. Unlike before, Oprah had nothing to tell the press after this show. But two months later, Morton Downey, Jr. – the pit bull of TV talk shows during the eighties – told CNN reporters that he had been attacked by Reich Skins in a restroom at the San Francisco International Airport. The hangdog, chain-smoking Downey was filmed before a worldwide audience with his hair crudely botched-off and a swastika drawn across his forehead.

Moreover, Tom Metzger had gained an audience far beyond the idiots of Haight-Ashbury. In a period when most American neo-Nazis were turning away from public appearances, Metzger and his mean-spirited band of skinheads had, in fact, become racist celebrities of national stature.

The W.A.R. Board

Metzger's fifth initiative was to develop computer links between skinheads and other hate groups operating in the United States. Beginning in his Fallbrook repair shop during 1985, Metzger created an electronic bulletin board known as the "W.A.R. Board." He did this by rigging a Commodore 64 personal computer, which lumbered along at less than 300 bytes per minute, with a single telephone modem so that callers could download his various messages of hate (Stills, 1989). When he did this, Metzger's single telephone line immediately became overloaded. With this, Metzger discovered that there was a high demand for computer online white-extremist materials, and that his callers knew the technology necessary to access such information.

Through the W.A.R. Board, Klansmen and neo-Nazis (and members of splinter groups such as the Aryan Nations and the Posse Comitatus) could communicate freely with skinheads (or potential skinheads) all across the country (ADL, 1987a). But Metzger's simple Commodore 64 created what is known in computer management systems as the problem of multiple memberships. This problem involves having individuals affiliated with several different organizations and not being able to determine to which organization they actually belong.

In the case of Metzger, this meant that his electronic bulletin board effectively mixed known skinheads' names with those other extremists. Consequently, this led to a breaking down of the distinguishable features of these groups. In essence, Metzger had unintentionally created a large computer-driven management information system that made it impossible to tell a skinhead from a Klansman, a Klansman from a member of the Aryan Nations or the Posse Comitatus, or a member of the American Nazi Party from a skinhead, and so forth.

The messages transmitted over the W.A.R. Board ranged from innocuous statements about wolves and romance to prescriptions for murder. Here is a communique sent by an anonymous user:

Title: Killing
From: User #1
To: Kinsmen
Date: May-24-1986
Time: 17:15:11.7
Lets get serious now folks. The fact is that the only way to be free of what threatens you is to kill it. So learn to kill. Quickly. Quietly. Without witness.

A very neat trick is to loosen the fittings to a car's master cylinder so there is a gradual loss of brake fluid as the brakes are used. Finally resulting in no brakes and a lot of unchecked inertia.

The old standby is to drill a small hole in [the enemy's] lightbulb and fill it with gunpowder. When the light goes on, he goes out. GFTT [meaning "Go for the throat."]. (quoted in Ridgeway, 1990:173)

The W.A.R. Hotline

Metzger's sixth initiative was directed toward those youths who didn't have the skill or technology to access the W.A.R. Board, and for those who didn't like to read or wanted more than what was published in the *WAR* zine. For them, Metzger created a series of telephone hate lines known as the W.A.R. Hotline. Relying on no more than the presence of a single follower willing to house the phone, Metzger started to tape telephone bulletins that offered what he termed the "Latest Movement Information" (Langer, 1990). These call-in messages were replete with Third Position manifestos, news about skinhead activities, and declarations of solidarity with the Order. For example, one of Metzger's long-standing methods of drawing attention to his philosophies is to accuse Jews of being the true fascists. Here is an early W.A.R. Hotline message concerning abortion:

ALMOST all abortion doctors are Jews.

ABORTION makes money for Jews.

Almost all abortion nurses are LESBIANS.

JEWS will do anything for money; including the rape of innocent children followed by the ripping and tearing of the living child from the young mother's womb while still squirming.

JEWS must be punished for the HOLOCAUST and MURDER of WHITE BABIES along with their perverted LESBIAN nurses who enjoy their jobs too much.

Other messages have detailed the release of Ian Stuart from a London jail (for a second assault against a Pakistani man in the East End), and the conditions of imprisonment afforded Clark Martell in the Cook County Jail (ADL, 1988c). Still other messages have exposed the work of antiracist organizations. Metzger had invited call-in listeners to write him for a list "of where these slime ADL hide out in your area" (ADL, 1988a:7) and to "call W.A.R. and tell us everything you know about the John Brown Anti-Klan Committee, where they live, where they eat, where they sleep" (Gatewood, 1989:4).

Finally, through the W.A.R. Hotline Metzger began to reward American skinheads for their racial violence. This was played out dramatically in the Portland case. Mulugeta Seraw was buried by his Ethiopian parents in Portland on the afternoon of November 16, 1988. Later that evening, Metzger sent out the following Hotline message.

Dateline: Portland, Oregon

And now the oppressed await the decision in the skinhead/Ethiopian case. We may believe that many of these Negroes had long arrest records. Many of the beautiful Negroes were also high on crack. SOUNDS LIKE THE SKINHEADS DID A CIVIC DUTY.

The Aryan Youth Movement

The final critical initiative employed by Metzger to create a national neo-Nazi skinhead confederation began in May of 1987. Its short-term objective, like the unintentional consequence of the W.A.R. Board, was to further cloud the distinctions between the various hate groups operating in America today. This outreach involved Metzger's takeover of a small California organization called the Aryan Youth Movement (A.Y.M.).

A.Y.M. was founded in a Sacramento pizza parlor during 1979 by one Greg Withrow, a seventeen-year-old art student from American River College. In May of 1987, Withrow fell in love with a woman who convinced him to renounce his affiliation with A.Y.M. (Ridgeway, 1990). Two things happened as a result of this:

First, Withrow was severely beaten by his former A.Y.M. companions. Sacramento police found Withrow near death on August 9, 1987. His hands had been nailed to a six-foot wooden plank and his neck had been slit with a razor blade. Second, Metzger's nineteen-year-old son, John, then emerged as the new president of this racist youth group (ADL, 1988c; Hackett, 1987).

After this, the major goal of A.Y.M. was to transform California high schools and college campuses into forums for Tom Metzger's views and recruiting grounds for skinheads. The Metzgers began by publishing a crude monthly bulletin called *The White Student* that they distributed to high school and college campuses throughout California, and eventually to other parts of the nation. The first issue of *The White Student* called for cooperation with "White Aryan Resistance, White Patriots Party, Creativity, Aryan Nations, Odinists, Christian Patriots, Nazis, Identity, Atheists, Ku Klux Klan, Bruder Schweigen, the Order, Dualists and many, many more. Our enemies understand only one message: That of the knife, the gun, and the club."

On balance, the marriage between W.A.R. and A.Y.M. freed Tom Metzger to develop more sophisticated recruitment strategies because it allowed him to let his own flesh and blood, John, take the reins of his growing empire of magazines, television productions, and computer/telephone communications. But perhaps more importantly, this strategy allowed Tom Metzger to recast the American skinhead movement into a more moderate appearing political force. Metzger reflected on this fundamental shift in a recent interview with journalist James Ridgeway. Said Metzger:

I've been trying to convince the skinheads to let their hair grow out and work into regular situations, melt into the public scene. A lot of them resisted that *because they felt they had [to make] their fashion statement.* Now the government is pushing them so hard they are being forced to do that. (1990:172, emphasis added)

Such is the case of John Metzger. John does not shave his head, wear Doc Martens, red suspenders, bomber jackets, or white power T-shirts. He does not wear swastikas or SS badges, nor does he *Seig Heil* people on the street. From what he has ever said or written about the American skinheads, it is doubtful that John has even listened to Skrewdriver, let alone Brutal Attack, No Remorse, Condemned '84, or Doc Marten.

In essence, John Metzger—like Tom—is not a skinhead. In fact, they are both gross aberrations within the traditional skinhead subculture. John is instead a product of the military-industrial complex of Southern California and a radical neo-Nazi father whom he idolizes. John Metzger dresses in light blue and white business shirts, khaki trousers, and penny loafers. His sandy brown hair is about three inches long and neatly trimmed. Like David Duke, John has superb photogenic qualities. Even though handsome young Metzger is divorced from the American skinhead subculture, by the late 1980s he was considered by some FBI agents to be one of the most dangerous out-of-jail racists in America (field notes).

CONCLUSIONS

On March 6, 1990, U.S. Attorney General Dick Thornburgh addressed the first National Leadership Conference of the Simon Wiesenthal Center in Chicago. "The White Aryan Resistance," said Thornburgh,

is a depravity that confronts goodness itself. [It has] introduced a parasitic plague of anti-Semitic graffiti and an assault upon decency and community sanctity from a pit of racism which represents our worst nightmares. The full force of law is our first priority. [The Attorney General added a word of caution, however.]

We face a sizable threat [in the control of hate crime] because of the malleable young skinhead gangs. [They are] marauding groups of shaven headed youth armed with spray-paints and baseball bats [who] commit copy-cat hate crimes based on credos that have no acceptance in the minds of the overwhelming number of people.

Two weeks later (March 18, 1990) the FBI reported a "remarkable growth [in the number] of skinheads in the United States" (Tafoya, 1990). The following day, an ADL representative reported that more than 3,000 youths in thirty-one states — from Plymouth Rock to the Haight-Ashbury — had now become neo-Nazi skinheads (Sandberg, 1990). Today, American neo-Nazi skinheads have infiltrated the ranks of the United States Army (ADL, 1989b), have instigated rioting and the increase of Nazi regalia seen on college campuses across the nation, and have become law enforcement officers in various police departments in the United States (Tafoya, 1990).

This evidence suggests that the American neo-Nazi skinheads are a highly unique criminal subculture. Indeed, never before in history have Americans been faced with "marauding groups of shaven headed youth armed with . . . baseball bats [who] commit copycat hate crimes." And never before have such vicious crimes been based on such esoteric credos "that have no acceptance in the minds of the overwhelming number of people."

4 _____

The Internal Structure of a Terrorist Youth Subculture

We don't know why gangs are forming today in some cities and not in others. We don't know how the gangs in smaller cities are similar or different from gangs in the metropolis. There isn't much data to go on.

—John M. Hagedorn
People and Folks

The Skinheads are [simply] white mean machines who deliver honest casualty reports.

—Tom Metzger

To thoroughly understand the American neo-Nazi skinheads, it is necessary to properly define them. This exercise serves an important purpose far beyond the concerns of academic theorizing. Moreover, a concise definition of the skinheads can play a crucial role in formulating public policies to control their proclivity for violence.

The traditional starting point for understanding criminal youth subcultures was neatly summarized by criminologist Gerald D. Suttles more than twenty years ago: "Street corner groups can be understood in large part by examining their place in the local community, rather than the society at large" (1968:4). Based on this intellectual model, public policies have been implemented to control street gangs through the strengthening of community organizations—schools and tutoring and recreational programs (Spergel, 1984), increased and specialized local law enforcement (Maxon and Klein, 1983; Zatz, 1987), and negotiation with gang leaders (Hagedorn, 1988; Horowitz, 1987; Stokes and Hewitt, 1976). Other jurisdictions have simply denied the existence of their gang problems altogether (Huff, 1989).

Each of these approaches to the control of American street gangs has met with varying degrees of success. As models for public policy to control the skinheads, however, these strategies have little relevance. Why? Because the neo-Nazi skinheads, for all intents and purposes, do not conform to the classic definition of a street gang.

THE DIFFERENCES BETWEEN STREET GANGS AND NEO-NAZI SKINHEADS

The skinheads constitute a unique criminal subculture for several important reasons. To begin with, scholars have found that gangs are a largely immigrant, adolescent, underclass phenomenon, but they have not found racism to be an organizing principle for gang membership. In those instances where racism has been discovered by gang researchers, it has usually been cited as an excuse for juvenile delinquency. That is, gang delinquency is a function of youthful rebellion against oppressive conditions caused by racism in the larger society (Cloward and Ohlin, 1960; Erlanger, 1979; Hagedorn, 1988; Spergel, 1964; Vigil, 1990).

This is not the case, though, for the neo-Nazi skinheads of North America. For them, we consistently discover that skinhead membership is an explicit function of their own strident racism.

Many scholars have also pointed out that violence, like racism, plays only a small role in gang behavior (Hagedorn, 1988; Klein, 1971; Merry, 1981; Miller, 1958; Morash, 1983; Moore, 1978; Suttles, 1968). In fact, some researchers have shown that gangs often have a positive relationship with their local communities and even serve as auxiliary police forces (Horowitz, 1987; Sanchez-Jankowski, 1991). Others have found that when gang violence does occur, it is often related to the use and/or distribution of highly addictive drugs such as heroin and crack cocaine (Fagan, 1989; Huff, 1989; Taylor, 1990), disputes over turf (Erlanger, 1979; Horowitz and Schwartz, 1974; Thrasher, 1927), ethnic and cultural differences between neighborhoods (Moore, 1978; Suttles, 1968), poverty and social disorganization (Curry and Spergel, 1988), or general economic interests (Spergel, 1984).

Once again, the evidence on the neo-Nazi skinheads stands in instructive contrast to this body of criminology. For the skinheads, violence is their signature trademark because *violence is part of subcultural style*. Instead of turf disputes, socioeconomic disadvantage, social disorganization, drugs, or economic interests, the skinheads seem to use violence for the explicit purpose of promoting political change by instilling fear in innocent people.

This was evident in Clark Martell's Romantic Violence, Robert Heick's American Front, David Mazzella's WAR Skins, and John Metzger's Aryan Youth Movement. It was ultimately the case in the killing of Mulugeta Seraw. There are virtually hundreds of other cases where American neo-Nazi skinheads have used violence for the specific purpose of instilling fear in innocent people.

Among these cases are the following:

- On December 4, 1987, a skinhead in Tampa, Florida, (Dean McKee), used an eight-inch hunting knife to kill a homeless black man sleeping in his bedroll outside a local art museum (ADL, 1988c).

- On September 15, 1987, a skinhead in Van Nuys, California, used a switchblade knife to slit the throat of a Hispanic woman because she refused to turn off a cassette recording by the Miami Sound Machine (Klanwatch, 1989; field notes).

- On February 9, 1988, a skinkhead in Las Vegas, Nevada, used a .38-caliber snub-nosed revolver to kill a young black female clerk at a 7-Eleven store. He then turned on an elderly black female customer in the 7-Eleven, and fired two shots into her spine. No money was taken from the cash register nor were the victims sexually molested (Klanwatch, 1989; field notes).

- On April 2, 1988, four members of the Detroit Area Skinheads (DASH) used knives to murder a twenty-year-old black woman. About the murder, the leader of DASH told police, "All I could do was feel confused and happy" (Dees, 1990).

- On March 4, 1988, four skinheads from La Verne, California, assaulted an Iranian couple, their two-week-old son, and a black man who tried to intervene. On arrest, the skinheads confessed that they thought the couple was Jewish (Dees, 1990).

- On December 10, 1988, a skinhead in Reno, Nevada, used a .45-caliber Smith & Wesson revolver to kill an unidentified black male (Klanwatch, 1989; field notes).

- On February 7, 1988, eight skinheads attacked a group of homeless advocates in Santa Barbara, California, stomping them with Doc Martens and beating them with baseball bats (Klanwatch, 1989).

- On January 7, 1988, seven members of San Diego's WAR Skins assaulted a group of Vietnamese immigrants outside a restaurant near Ocean Beach (ADL, 1988c).

- On January 1, 1988, seven skinheads in Washington, D.C.'s Dupont Circle attacked a party of homosexuals and beat them with baseball bats and steel batons. One of the victims, Rodney Johnson, received a fractured skull, broken ribs, and a broken shoulder as his skinhead attackers shouted, "Die, faggot, die!" On arrest, one of the skinheads told a *Washington Post* reporter that if Johnson had died, "I don't think I would have felt any remorse about it" (ADL, 1988c; Shapiro, 1990:6).

- On March 15, 1988, two skinheads approached two lesbian women outside a Philadelphia bar and beat them with beer bottles (ADL, 1988c).

- On April 21, 1988, three skinheads from Halifax, North Carolina, abducted an eighteen-year-old black male and tortured him with a boa constrictor. Then the skinheads slit the young man's throat with a hunting knife, killing him (Klanwatch, 1989; field notes).

- On December 3, 1988, five skinheads in Minneapolis, Minnesota, attacked a group of black kids playing basketball. One fourteen-year-old victim was seriously beaten with a wooden club wrapped in barbed wire (Dees, 1990).

- In July 1989, eight affluent teenagers belonging to a group known as BRASH (Buffalo Rochester Aryan Skinheads) were arrested and charged with beating a thirty-year-old man. Later, members of BRASH became suspects in more than two dozen attacks against gays in the Rochester, New York, area. One skinhead suspect told police during his interrogation: "Gay bashing is when we lure a gay guy into our path and jump him. Sometimes his wallet gets stolen, but mostly we just beat him up bad" (John Brown Anti-Klan Committee, 1990b:2).

- On March 15, 1988, two members of the Los Angeles Reich Skins plead guilty to assault with a deadly weapon for pointing a gun at a Hispanic teenager after breaking into his home (ADL, 1988c).

- On June 6, 1988, a fourteen-year-old skinhead stabbed a black junior high school student three times in the back on a playground in Ventura, California (ADL, 1988c).
- On February 4, 1989, a thirteen-year-old skinhead pulled a loaded .357 Smith and Wesson revolver and threatened to shoot a Glendale, California, teacher who refused to let the skinhead wear a white power T-shirt for his school yearbook picture (ADL, 1989b; field notes).
- On May 4, 1989, four skinhead members of Tampa's American Front were stopped in Taveras, Florida, after two of the skinheads had pulled automatic assault rifles on an elderly black couple (ADL, 1989b).
- On March 18, 1989, David Timoner was shot to death with a 9-mm automatic weapon wielded by a skinhead in Denver. The skinheads then set Timoner's car afire. During a police chase the following day, one of the skinheads took a hostage while brandishing a .22-caliber handgun, proclaiming to a police negotiator that he wanted "to go out in a blaze of glory" (ADL, 1989b).
- On February 3, 1990, five members of the Confederate Hammer Skins were found guilty of putting poison gas into a Dallas synagogue's air-conditioning system, and of other racially motivated hate crimes against Hispanics at a Dallas park during the summer of 1989 (Clarke, 1991; the *New York Times,* February 4, 1990). Since then, the Confederate Hammer Skins have been linked to more than forty hate crimes in the Dallas area, including attacks on blacks and gays, and anti-Semitic and anti-Moslem vandalism (John Brown Anti-Klan Committee, 1990c; Thornburgh, 1990).

Neo-Nazi skinheads have clubbed and knifed the punk music scene into submission in Detroit, San Diego, and Los Angeles (Coplon, 1989). And following the murder of Mulugeta Seraw, Portland skinheads were implicated in forty-six hate crimes including assaults with deadly weapons (ADL, 1988c; Shapiro, 1990). During 1989 alone, the Southern Poverty Law Center discovered more than 200 skinhead arrests and prosecutions throughout the United States for murder and assaults on blacks and minorities (Dees, 1990).

Finally, academic gang theorists have traditionally based their sociological models on the following proposition:

The violent gang is a natural, lower-class interstitial institution, resulting mainly from the weaknesses of secondary institutions, such as schools, local communities and ethnic organizations, and to some extent from the weakness of primary institutions such as the family, to provide adequate mechanisms of opportunity and social control, particularly in the transition of males from youth to adulthood. (Spergel, 1984:201–2)

This means that violent gangs are a natural outgrowth of urban, underclass cultures where schools are lousy, parents don't control their children, and there is no community or ethnic organization to join when life becomes just too much for young men to endure. This is the classic sociological definition of alienation. When this happens, contemporary criminology predicts that certain young men will meet each other in the neighborhood and start a violent street gang because it is a natural product of their environment.

Yet this pre-paradigmatic construct is based on research that focuses exclusively on poor, urban, African-American, Hispanic, or Asian youth. Rarely has a study focused exclusively on a white street gang (although Short and Strodtbeck, [1965] and Yablonsky [1962] offer partial exceptions). And never has a study examined a white gang that is international, rather than interstitial, in nature.

There is good reason for this. White international criminal youth subcultures are a very recent phenomenon in America. Indeed, it was not until 1986 that the word *skinhead* was even introduced into the mainstream vernacular in the United States (Coplon, 1989). As a result, social science has yet to catch up with this unique development. For example, a recent analysis entitled *Gangs in America* (Huff, 1990) includes fourteen original criminological studies of U.S. street gangs written by foremost scholars in the field of gang research. Within this 345-page volume, the word *skinhead* is not mentioned once. Nevertheless, today thousands and thousands of violent neo-Nazi skinheads are scattered throughout the United States, Great Britain, Germany, France, Spain, Holland, Belgium, Portugal, Denmark, Canada, Australia, Brazil, and Egypt (ADL, 1989b; Jackson, 1991; Mücke, 1991; Seidelpielen, 1991; Ward, 1991; field notes).

These skinhead groups have emerged under various social, economic, and political conditions. Hence, they do not share a common street corner or neighborhood culture. But they do share a common ideology. According to every published account filed to date, this ideology is *neo-Nazism* supported and sustained by a specific *style* (shaved heads, Nazi regalia, Doc Martens, and racial/ethnic violence) and *music* (white power rock).

For these important reasons, then, the skinheads do not conform to the classic criminological definition of a street gang. In fact, the skinheads seem to violate this definition in a classical way. The skinheads represent something else; something with a wider agenda that is potentially more dangerous to society, and certainly more elusive to academic gang scholars. Hence, instead of viewing the skinheads as a street gang, we must define them for what they truly are. Because of their overt racism, political violence, and links to a homologous international subculture of neo-Nazism, the skinheads constitute what can best be described as a *terrorist youth subculture.*

INSIDE THE WHITE ALAMO

As we have seen, this terrorist youth subculture was unleashed on the American public between 1985 and 1990. Simultaneously, the ex-Klansman Tom Metzger created a complex organization to snare young whites into a national skinhead confederation — the Alamo of the White Race, as he informally refers to it (Langer, 1990). This organization goes by the names of the White Aryan Resistance and the Aryan Youth Movement. It publishes two suave and persuasive youth magazines, *WAR* and *The White Student;* sponsors a widely televised public access program called "Race and Reason"; and maintains computer and telephone bulletin boards for skinhead communications. Metzger's organization recruits skinheads from high schools, junior high schools, and college campuses. It promotes images of neo-Nazism on nationally televised programs such as "The Oprah Winfrey Show."

As such, Metzger has supplied an identifiable leadership for the American neo-Nazi skinheads. Yet Metzger, himself, is not a skinhead. He does not "understand . . . the words in skinhead music" (Coplon, 1989:88) and discourages "skinheads making their fashion statement" through the expression of subcultural style (Ridgeway, 1990:75). Nevertheless, this peculiar organizational arrangement at the headquarters of the White Alamo has supplied the major inspirational stimulus for the U.S. Attorney General to declare a "shocking reemergence of hate group violence" in America.

The Subculture Army

Further insights into the organizational structure of the White Alamo can be gained through interviews with neo-Nazi skinheads who have worked in Metzger's inner circle. According to a recent FBI report, one skinhead with ties to Metzger described his group as "a subculture army. . . . Instead of verbally assaulting people, we physically assault them. . . . We've all had our part in bashing people. We'll assault anybody" (quoted in Clarke, 1991:16).

Other skinheads close to Metzger have talked about a paramilitary structure in which lieutenant was the highest rank one could achieve. According to these informants, by 1986 there were W.A.R. lieutenants in San Diego, Oklahoma City, Tulsa, Tampa, and Dallas. The pinnacle of honor among these skinheads was to appear on *WAR*'s list of POW's—alongside the hallowed names of James Earl Ray, Manfred Roeder, Ian Stuart, Dean McKee, Clark Martell, and a dozen members of the Order (field notes). For example, W.A.R. Lt. David Mazzella recalls that Metzger issued "report cards. When my recruits bashed somebody . . . my position in the organization was moving up" (quoted in ABC's "20/20," December 15, 1990).

But this level of violence came at a high cost. By the end of the 1980s, most of the original W.A.R. lieutenants were either in prison (where they often turned state's evidence), or they had left W.A.R. altogether. Such was the case of Lt. Mazzella. In 1990, he would take the stand in a Portland courtroom and provide further insights into the subculture army by testifying that

It was a whole different world when I entered Metzger's world. I'd walk down the street and see black people and they all looked like monkeys and Asians, they all looked disgusting. They all looked like bugs you could step on. People, ya' know, they didn't look like real people in this world. (quoted in ABC's "20/20," December 15, 1990)

In summary, Tom Metzger appears to be the primary catalyst for creating and sustaining the unique terrorist youth subculture known as the American neo-Nazi skinheads. But I am not so sure that Metzger's elaborate organization has been supported solely by his television repair business. In fact, there is evidence to suggest that Metzger has been propped up by an extraordinary means of right-wing revolution.

DOMESTIC TERRORISM AND THE WHITE ALAMO

On July 19, 1984, thirteen members of the Order—dressed in blue jeans, running shoes, and white T-shirts, and with blue bandannas tied across their faces—used one Ingram MAC-10 automatic assault pistol to rob a Brinks security truck of $3.8 million in cash near rural Ukiah, California. At the time, this was the largest open road robbery in American history (Flynn and Gerhardt, 1989). It is estimated that more than $3 million of this money was never recovered by the FBI (ADL, 1988c; John Brown Anti-Klan Committee, 1990c; field notes). Based on the following circumstantial evidence, we may surmise that a large portion of this robbery money went into the hands of Tom Metzger for his use in creating the White Alamo:

• On December 3, 1983, Tom Metzger and thirteen other neo-Nazis were arrested in Kagel Canyon, located in Los Angeles' San Fernando Valley, after lighting three large crosses at a Klan rally. Among the others arrested were Richard Butler (founder and leader of the Aryan Nations), Frank Silva (Exalted Cyclops of the New Order of the Ku Klux Klan), and his two companions, David Tate and Randy Evans (John Brown Anti-Klan Committee, Summer, 1986; Flynn and Gerhardt, 1989; Wallace, 1985).

• On June 17, 1984, one month before the Brinks robbery, Randy Evans was arrested in Madras, Oregon, for committing assault and battery against a local transvestite. Evans had been sharing a motel room with Frank Silva. Together, they were on their way to Metaline Falls for a meeting of the Order. When the Madras police searched Evans, they found a handwritten phone number for Tom Metzger. The next day, Evans was bailed out of jail by Silva (Flynn and Gerhardt, 1989).

• After the historic July 19 holdup, Frank Silva became a fugitive wanted by the FBI. Shortly thereafter, Silva was interviewed by Metzger on "Race and Reason." Although Silva said little about the Order, he lauded the role of the Ku Klux Klan as a "guerrilla organization fighting for white people" (quoted in John Brown Anti-Klan Committee, Summer 1986:7).

• On August 15, 1985—three years before the Portland murder of Mulugeta Seraw—Silva, Evans, and Tate were sentenced in a Seattle Federal Court to forty years each for their part in the Brinks holdup (ADL, 1988a; Flynn and Gerhardt, 1989). After their verdicts were handed down, Tom Metzger stood on the courthouse steps and told reporters: "They gave us [three] martyrs. A new day is dawning for white people in this country" (quoted in ADL, 1988a:38).

• On December 30, 1985, the lead defendant in the government's case against the Order, Bruce Carroll Pierce, was sentenced to 100 years in prison for his part in the Brinks holdup. And on November 17, 1987, Pierce was convicted of murdering Denver radio talk show host Alan Berg with the same Ingram MAC-10 automatic machine pistol used in the Brink's truck crime. For this, Pierce received another 150-year sentence.

  Facing absolute life imprisonment, Pierce told the FBI (though he later recanted because he claimed to have been drugged) that Metzger received approximately $250,000 of the Brinks robbery money from Order leader Robert Jay Mathews before Mathews died in a fiery shootout with FBI agents on Wibney Island, Washington, in December of 1984 (ADL, 1988a; ADL, 1988c; Flynn and Gerhardt, 1989). Notably, other investigators claim that Metzger may have received more than $1 million in stolen money from the Order (John Brown Anti-Klan Committee, Summer 1986; field notes).

- In October of 1985, while the Order trial was taking place in Seattle, a summit meeting of more than 200 Klan and neo-Nazi leaders from seventeen states and Canada was held at Robert Miles' Mountain Church in rural Cochoctah, Michigan. Honored guests at this event were the widow of Robert Mathews and the wife and children of Bruce Carroll Pierce. Among the other notables present were Richard Butler, Clark Martell, and Tom Metzger (ADL, 1988a; John Brown Anti-Klan Committee, Summer 1986; Toy, 1989).

- On September 14, 1984, (three months before his death) Robert Mathews traveled to Columbus, Ohio, where he met with a white racist history professor who agreed to underwrite the cost of a white power rock band that would appeal to the soon-to-be-emerging skinheads of Southern California (Flynn and Gerhardt, 1989). This activity would be implemented by Tom Metzger three years later.

- And on November 14, 1984, less than two weeks before his death, Robert Mathews set forth his vision of life in America after the White Revolution was delivered by the Order. In his final manifesto (and in accordance with the revolutionary fantasy set forth in *The Turner Diaries*), the thirty-four-year-old Mathews gave Tom Metzger the code name Bear, thus designating Metzger as the official torchbearer of the Order's fantasized struggle against ZOG (Flynn and Gerhardt, 1989; John Brown Anti-Klan Committee, June 1985).

THE NEW ORDER

In addition to establishing the seven recruitment initiatives discussed in Chapter 3, I suspect that Metzger's share of the Brinks holdup money has been used to support even more sophisticated recruitment projects undertaken by W.A.R. between 1986 and 1989. This conclusion is based on the following circumstantial evidence:

- In June 1987, Metzger launched a national recruitment of skinhead bands for an "international punk white power record album" (Center for Democratic Renewal, n.d.:5). Suddenly, a number of moronic racist bands were flown to San Diego to record an album called *The Spirit of Oi* (released in 1988 on White Noise Records of London, owned and operated by the British National Front) (ADL, 1988c; Center for Democratic Renewal, n.d.). These bands included Philadelphia's Arresting Officers, Uprise, New Glory, and Fight for Freedom; Chicago's Johnny Vomit and Out of Order; San Diego's Destructive Youth Patrol; and Tulsa's Midtown Bootboys. (*Maximum Rock 'N' Roll,* September 1989)

- Although Metzger himself cannot be directly linked to this development, between 1986 and 1989 a number of white power zines emerged throughout the nation. These included desktop publications such as Hollister, California's *Skinhead; Final War* and

Hail Victory from Detroit and Southfield, Michigan; *Pit Bull Boy* from Grand Rapids, Michigan; *The National White Resistance* from New Orleans; *Truth and Justice* from Manassas, Virginia; *Pure Impact Skins* from Newton, Pennsylvania; *Skinheads RULE-OK!* from Dallas, Texas; and *Boiling Point* from Oakland, California. Between 1986 and 1989, thousands of these racist zines were disseminated around high schools, junior high schools, and college campuses. In fact, copies of *Boiling Point* and *WAR* were distributed to tourists at California's Disneyland (ADL, 1988a). During this period, Metzger announced on "Race and Reason" that "racialism should be fun!"

- Between 1987 and 1989, Metzger produced and disseminated a series of stickers for skinhead organizations across the nation. Advertising for the parent organization, W.A.R., was done through a sticker depicting the image of a rifle marksman taking aim at what is supposed to be a caricature of a Jewish man over the logo "Get out! Jew Pig!" Four other sticker lines were produced and distributed to various skinhead groups, including Mazzella's WAR Skins. One of these stickers includes a swastika and the phrase "Trash Em! Smash Em! Make Em Die!" and another shows a pistol with a silencer over the caption "Make Em Scared! White Revolution is the Only Solution!" (ADL, 1988c).

- Between 1987 and 1989, Metzger made numerous trips on behalf of W.A.R. to recruit skinheads. He went to Los Angeles, Chicago, San Jose, San Francisco, Seattle, Dallas, Portland, and Oklahoma City. Metzger was often accompanied by Reich Skin Brad Robage (of Oprah Winfrey fame), David Mazzella, John Metzger, and members of the Midtown Boot Boys (ADL, 1988c; *Monitor,* September 1987).

- By 1988, "Race and Reason" had expanded from seven to more than thirty U.S. cities, and Metzger's publications were being printed by the thousands (ADL, 1988b; Klanwatch, 1991; Langer, 1990).

- By 1989, *WAR* had taken on a more sophisticated look. Gone were the small, blurry black and white photographs. In their place came highly defined eleven-by-seventeen-inch colored blowups of skinheads injured in the "line of battle"; white school children *Seig Heiling* alongside Mickey Mouse at Disneyland; and full length features on the sexual exploits of Martin Luther King, Jr. (referred to as "Dr. Martin Luther Coon"); the bank robbing career of the Indiana "Aryan Hero" John Dillinger; and rave reviews for the racist and homophobic Indiana-bred rock band Guns N' Roses.

- During this period, the Aryan Entertainment section of *WAR* expanded from one to two pages. By 1989, no fewer than thirty racist VHS videos, including a "History of W.A.R.: 1975 to the Present," were offered to readers. Also, 393 videotapes of "Race and Reason" became available as well as "Assorted Radio Interviews with Tom Metzger."

- By 1989, the W.A.R. Hotline had expanded to nearly fifty lines in thirteen major U.S. cities including Tulsa, Dallas, Seattle, Phoenix, Portland, San Diego, Los Angeles, San Francisco, New York City, Washington, D.C., Detroit, and Miami (Metzger, 1990).

- By 1989, Metzger had transformed the W.A.R. Board technology from the simple Commodore 64 personal computer, to a multiuser 286-based AT clone with a 40-megabyte hard disk running state-of-the-art FidoNet software. This sophisticated new system also maintained several elaborate layers of password security. Simultaneously, Metzger would claim to have 2,000 bulletin board system users, many of whom were skinheads (Stills, 1989).

- By 1989, most of these skinheads ran their computer network to W.A.R. with cheap IBM clones customized to interact with the FidoNet software. Since then, Metzger's

W.A.R. Board has come to offer users the choice of transfer protocols to even more sophisticated softwares such as Kermit, Zmodem, and sliding-window protocols such as W/Xmodum. In addition to the "Latest Movement Information," the W.A.R. Board began to hawk racist stickers and videotapes, concert tickets, Nazi jewelry, white power T-shirts, Viking posters, Skrewdriver news, and computer diskettes containing the formulas for making homemade bombs (Stills, 1989; field notes).

- Although Metzger cannot be directly related, between 1987 and 1989 hundreds of skinheads from around the country appeared at various Klan rallies to act as security guards (ADL, 1988c; Bishop, 1988; Center for Democratic Renewal, n.d.; Klanwatch, 1989). For example, skinheads from across the Southeastern United States provided security at the September 2, 1989, national Ku Klux Klan retreat on Stone Mountain, Georgia—an event which took place on the same day that seventeen-year-old Yusef Hawkins (a black kid who had been shot in the chest and murdered by seven white assailants on the streets of Bensonhurst, New York) was buried by the Reverend Jesse Jackson before a nationally televised audience (John Brown Anti-Klan Committee, 1990a). This event, in turn, set off "the days of outrage," as the three days of bloody rioting between New York police and citizens came to be known.

- On March 6, 1989, Metzger organized an event meant to replicate the historic celebration of love and peace held in Woodstock, New York, during the rainy August of 1969. More than 100 skinheads from around the country showed up on a vacant lot in Napa, California, for a concert billed as the Aryan Woodstock. Skrewdriver had been denied entry into the United States because of Ian Stuart's lengthy criminal record, but the concert featured some of the leftover *Spirit of Oi* players including the Arresting Officers, New Glory, and the ever-popular Midtown Boot Boys (Gatewood, 1989; McNulty, 1989; *Maximum Rock 'N' Roll,* September 1989). As previously noted, the skinhead security force for this event was armed with automatic assault rifles and sawed-off shotguns.

- Although Metzger cannot be directly related, on April 23, 1989—less than two months after the Aryan Woodstock—more than 100 skinheads attended a party honoring the 100th birthday of Adolf Hitler, sponsored by Aryan Nation's founder Richard Butler. This event was held on Butler's compound near Coeur D'Alene, Idaho, where skinheads from around the country took part in paramilitary training for terrorist activities (Gatewood, 1989; *Terre Haute Tribune-Star,* April 23, 1989).

- Finally, on Memorial Day 1989, more than 250 skinheads gathered together in an empty cornfield near Tomahawk, Oklahoma, to celebrate Tom Metzger's first annual Reich 'N' Roll festival. Music was provided by two new bands: Haken Kreuz from Detroit and Bully Boy from Dallas, and two familiar acts: the Midtown Boot Boys and Bound for Glory. In addition to this "Great Aryan music," John Metzger set up group activities billed as "Great Aryan Fun." These included tug-of-war games, tattooing, swastika lightings, pistol practice, head shaving, and lessons in spray painting (*WAR,* n.d., 8, no. 2).

Amid these proceedings, Tom Metzger walked onto the stage and proclaimed:

This is the New Order. You've heard about the New Order. You saw it around you this weekend. Recognize it. It's here. You are the New Order. Skinheads are in the forefront. You know why? Do you know why the Jews are worried about the Skinheads? Cause the

Skinheads kick ass. They don't walk down the street with their shoulder over like this, hoping no one will pick on them. They don't go down to a rock concert and say gee, hope we can sneak in here and there will be no trouble. The Jews are panic stricken. That's all we hear from the Jews . . . the Skinheads! I had a guy who is an agent, working for us, he met with a Jew leader of the ADL. He was trying to talk about all these different things with the leader of the ADL and all this Jew wanted to talk about were these Skinheads. They're panic stricken! (*WAR*, n.d., 8, no. 2)

CONCLUSIONS

Three general conclusions can be drawn at this point in the analysis. The first conclusion is that much of the research and theory on traditional juvenile gangs has little relevance for understanding the American neo-Nazi skinheads. Because of their overt racism, political violence, and international links to a broader hate movement, the skinheads are properly defined as a *terrorist youth subculture.*

The second conclusion is that Tom Metzger appears to have single-handedly defined the organizational characteristics of this terrorist youth subculture. This conclusion, however, can be buttressed by parts of the gang literature that pertain to why individuals are attracted to criminal subcultures in the first place. For example, through his recruitment initiatives, Metzger seems to have taken what gang scholar Lewis Yablonsky (1962) referred to as a near-group with sociopathic leadership (the early skinhead groups like San Francisco's American Front) and transformed it into an inceptive association of peers with specific roles, codes of conduct, and collective goals (see Horowitz, 1990). Likewise, it further appears that these skinheads became, in Walter Miller's words, "bonded through mutual interests" in British skinhead style and music (1980:121). And like the "street elites" and "bad asses" examined by Jack Katz (1988) in his celebrated *Seductions of Crime,* the neo-Nazi skinheads appear to represent "a dramatic style of presentation of self" (cited in Horowitz, 1990:46).

Therefore, in certain ways the skinheads are highly unique and in other ways they are unremarkable. Similar to other teenage subcultures that have emerged in the U.S. over the course of the past half-century, the skinheads have adopted characteristics that principally serve to render its members distinct from mainstream culture (see Cohen, 1955; Schwendinger and Schwendinger, 1985; Short, 1990). That is, the skinhead subculture appears to reject traditional American role models of success, and in their place, offers a social space for status attainment and enhancement in which certain white youths are capable of functioning.

Also, like the Mexican-American gangs studied by Moore (1978), the African-American gangs examined by Hagedorn (1988), and the Chinese-American gangs investigated by Chin (1986), the neo-Nazi skinhead subculture ostensibly appears to draw its members from among the most marginalized of American youth (e.g., Clark Martell, Robert Heick, Kenneth Mieske, and David Mazzella). In other words, like every other youth subculture to emerge in the American experience, the skinheads are seeking a sense of belonging.

Yet, they have joined a terrorist youth subculture organized by an adult neo-Nazi who has constructed a veritable empire of television programs, fanzine publications, stickers, hotlines, computer bulletin boards, and white power rock distribution outlets. This dramatically sets the neo-Nazi skinheads apart from any other youth subculture that preceded them. Whether this decision to become a skinhead was a rational choice (as in the gang research of Sanchez-Jankowski, 1991), was determined by social and/or economic circumstances (as in the landmark work of Cloward and Ohlin, 1960), or both (as suggested by Horowitz, 1990), is an empirical question addressed in subsequent sections of this research.

The third conclusion we can draw is that Metzger's success in creating the White Alamo depended on large infusions of money. And I contend that this money came from the terrorist activities of the Order. I am not alone on this issue. In September of 1989, FBI agents in Dallas testified during the grand jury investigation into racist skinhead activity that a portion of the $3 million in unrecovered Brinks money could be linked to the Confederate Hammer Skins of Dallas (John Brown Anti-Klan Committee, 1990c). And in his March 9, 1990, address before the Simon Wiesenthal Center, Attorney General Thornburgh revealed that the Confederate Hammer Skins' plot to inject cyanide into a local synagogue's air-conditioning system was formulated at Metzger's 1989 Reich 'N' Roll Festival.

To the extent that these conclusions reflect an underlying dimension of reality, I am prepared to formulate specific hypotheses that can be used to answer the questions posed at the outset of this analysis. The first question is, "Why did the number of racist skinheads increase so dramatically in America during the late 1980s?" My hypothesis is that thousands of American white youth became neo-Nazi skinheads because Tom Metzger deliberately recruited them into his army subculture.

The second (and more important) question is, "Why are racist skinheads so violent?" I hypothesize that neo-Nazi skinheads are violent because violence is part of their subcultural heritage. However, I further hypothesize that Metzger has exploited this style by encouraging and rewarding American skinheads for their hate crimes. Thus, skinheads who closely associate with Metzger's organization are more dangerous than those skinheads who do not.

The final question is, "What is the most efficacious public response to this type of violence?" And my hypothesis is that the American neo-Nazi skinhead phenomenon would, for all intents and purposes, disappear without Tom Metzger and his son John.

The following section of the analysis presents a theory, methodology, and test of these hypotheses. As such, I endeavor to describe more clearly the range of needs that are fulfilled in the minds of those white youths who join a terrorist subculture.

RESEARCH NOTE

The uniqueness of the neo-Nazi skinheads in the American experience is important and warrants further clarification. It is true that America has had previous youth organizations that engaged in violent, illegal terrorist acts and that were characterized by a shared subcultural value, style, and musical expression of value and style. It is also true that these youth subcultures published their own newsletters containing vitriolic attacks against their perceived enemies. It is further true that these subcultures urged violence against their perceived enemies. And it is even arguable that these underground groups were far more international in character than the skinheads — in the sense of having direct interchanges with similarly oriented groups in other countries. Indeed, the Weathermen and Black Panthers of the late 1960s fit this profile as well as the skinheads of the late 1980s. The skinheads can be distinguished from the Weathermen and Black Panthers, however, by their respective struggles for homology.

The Carnal Morality of Skinhead Terrorism

The values of the Weathermen and Panthers were built on a communist model of a small guerrilla *foco* that could catalyze social upheaval and bring down a capitalist empire. Like the neo-Nazi skinheads, the Weathermen and Panthers insisted that race, not class, was the primary factor in fomenting revolution.

Yet for the Weathermen and Panthers, the idea was to "promote a chaos that would cripple America and ultimately cast it into a receivership that would be administered by the morally superior third world" (Collier and Horowitz, 1989:77). The skinheads, on the other hand, sought to topple a fantasy-inspired Zionist Occupied Government and cast it into a receivership that could be administered by a morally superior Aryan Youth of the First World. Because of this fundamental difference in values (Third World neo-communism versus First World neo-Nazism), the style and music of these terrorist groups were vastly different.

More than anyone else, the revolutionaries of the late sixties were inspired by the poetic talents of Bob Dylan. The Weathermen took their name from Dylan's "Subterranean Homesick Blues" ("ya' don't need a weatherman to know which way the wind blows") and the Panthers adopted Dylan's "Ballad of a Thin Man" as their guiding anthem (Collier and Horowitz, 1989; Cleaver, 1967).

For these revolutionaries, Dylan offered epic-length folk-rock extrapolations on the human condition that he has described at various times as "mercurial," "mathematical," and as a "spirit comin' through me." Others have described Dylan's music as "the voice of a generation" or as simply "golden." These songs were based on surrealistic images of real-life experiences at both the personal and political levels of existence.

At the personal level, Dylan introduced the Weathermen and Panthers to exquisite renderings on the pathos of love and romance ("Queen Jane Approximately," "I Want You," "From a Buick 6," "Tomorrow Is a Long Time," "It's All Over Now, Baby Blue," "Just Like a Woman," and the haunting "Sad Eyed Lady of the Lowlands"). Among the revolutionaries — whose own romantic lives were being torn apart by the unexpected consequences of the sexual revolution — Dylan offered a much-needed emotional grounding (Collier and Horowitz, 1989). At the same time, Dylan's music offered extravagant existential tributes to the utopian values of social and political upheaval ("The Times They Are a Changin'," "It's Alright Ma (I'm Only Bleeding)," "Gates of Eden," "Masters of War," "George Jackson," "Like a Rolling Stone," "Chimes of Freedom," and the transcendental "Mr. Tambourine Man").

In short, Dylan's music was perceived by his radical followers as spiritually and intellectually moral because it represented an organic and artistically unrivaled affirmation of their subculture. This morality, in turn, served to undergird the organizational structures of the Weathermen and Panthers as they went about the life-threatening task of waging an American revolution. In the crass words of a Dylan biographer, "The message [of Dylan's music] was: the whole world's a mess. THEY fucked up, now WE have to live with it" (Spitz, 1989:271).

This morality (based on spiritual and intellectual properties) therefore determined the emotional basis for subcultural style among the revolutionaries of the late sixties. For the Weathermen, their style was based on Third-World chic — black berets, military boots, and guerrilla uniforms made popular by Che Guevara and Fidel Castro. Similarly, the Panther style included black berets and military boots, but was set off by a strident but indigenous African-ghetto look (powder blue banlon shirts, black leather jackets, sunglasses, Afro-frizzes, and machine guns).

Hence, the revolutionaries of the late sixties adopted a subcultural style of terrorism that was straightforward, passionate — and in their minds — morally correct. Their enemy was the establishment and their violence represented a well-planned and concrete expression of revolution against American in-groups. The Weathermen bombed courthouses, police statues, and a restroom of the U.S. Capitol Building; while the Panthers fought bloody gun battles with police in the streets of Oakland, Chicago, and Los Angeles, and engaged in tragic knife fights with prison guards behind the walls of San Quentin, Soledad, and Attica.

The American neo-Nazi skinheads, by contrast, were driven by the fantasy-oriented music of Skrewdriver. Within their discography, there is not one Skrewdriver song dedicated to the pathos of love and romance. Thus, Skrewdriver's philosophy of morality was established exclusively on a level of political imagination. This, in turn, shaped the character and direction of skinhead terrorism.

Instead of well-planned acts of violence against in-groups, the American neo-Nazi skinheads of the late 1980s committed acts of terrorism against out-groups in an attempt to act out the messages rendered in Skrewdriver's "Nigger, Nigger," "Prisoner of Peace (Rudolf Hess)," "Dead Paki in a Gutter," and "White Power." Moreover, the entire skinhead revolution was based on an elaborate and convoluted emotional pipe dream. On one hand, they sought to bring down the fictitious ZOG by destroying what Romantic Violence called "the parasitic Jew race." In reality, however, the skinheads turned their violence away from the state — and instead of bombing government buildings and killing policemen and prison guards — the young neo-Nazis committed an incomprehensible number of killings, stabbings, clubbings, knifings, and stompings of poor black Americans and other disenfranchised people. Through this extraordinary level of terrorism, the skinheads elicited a form of carnal morality reminiscent of the post–Civil War Ku Klux Klan, the Third Reich, and the ancient European Vikings.

Are the neo-Nazi skinheads the first terrorist youth subculture in the American experience? No, they are not. The skinheads were preceded by, and arguably inflected by, the romantic revolutionaries of the late sixties. However, these groups were vastly different in their conceptions of morality. Therefore, youthful terrorism can be viewed in a generic sense (it has been part of the American experience at other points in history). Yet such terrorism may also be conceived as historically dynamic (its values, style, and music have undergone a profound transformation). And this is precisely what sociology hopes to find — general principles, along with situation-specific and history-specific qualifications of deviance.

Part II

Inside the Skinhead Subculture

The revolutionary hopes of the 1960s, which culminated in 1968, are now blocked or abandoned. One day they will break out again, transformed, and will be lived again with different results. I mean only that; I am not prophesying the difference.

—John Berger
"Lost Prophets,"
March 1975

5

Sociological Perspectives on Terrorist Youth Subcultures

In sharp contrast to their British counterparts, the American skinheads have not been the subjects of rigorous social scientific inquiry. Without empirical data on this terrorist youth subculture, researchers and policymakers have difficulties trying to coherently account for why it emerged. However, portions of three existing models offer promising explanations for the subculture's development: functionalism, neo-Marxism, and differential identification-reinforcement.

THE FUNCTIONALIST PERSPECTIVE

It is common knowledge among criminologists that the historical foundations of this sociological perspective are found in the nineteenth-century writings of French sociologist Emile Durkheim (1893, 1894, 1897). Durkheim's work includes four key ideas: First, people are egoistic individuals whose wants always exceed their needs. Second, society's rules and regulations are products of value-consensus. Third, various activities and components of the social structure — such as religion, work, and sports — exist because they are functional. In other words, they help stabilize society. Last, Durkheim viewed society as an organism consisting of various independent parts that all work to maintain the equilibrium of the social system (Ellis, 1987).

While Durkheim made a number of contributions to our understanding of current social problems (see Ellis, 1987; Liska, 1981; Beirne and Messerschmidt, 1990), contemporary U.S. formulations (Cloward and Ohlin, 1960; Cohen, 1955; Merton, 1957) of his (1897) anomie theory are of major importance to our understanding of the American skinheads. Briefly, these functionalist theorists assume the existence of a dominant ideology that stresses the achievement of mainly economic goals. Although members of every socioeconomic class and

Co-authored with Walter S. Dekeseredy

ethnic group are socialized to aspire to these goals, lower-class youths and other disadvantaged people, such as blacks, Hispanics, and other visible minorities, are denied equal access to the legitimate means for becoming materially successful.

For these youths, the disjunction between cultural goals and legitimate means becomes initially apparent in the public school system where their inadequate socialization causes them to fail in their attempts to achieve status among middle-class peers. This failure, in turn, is likely to make underclass youths believe that their chances of academic success are extremely limited. Consequently, they develop various adaptations designed to help them overcome the discrepancy between goals and means. One type of adaptation is, according to Robert Merton (1957), rebellion.

Some analyses of this mode of adaptation found membership in a youth subculture a purely rebellious act that is a natural product of the frustration over restricted opportunities. This frustration leads lower-class youths to reject both the cultural goals and the legitimate means to achieve them. The cultural goals (or dominant ideologies) are then replaced with those that can be more readily achieved (the ideologies of the subculture). As such, the youth subculture provides its members with an environment where status ascriptions can finally be achieved. Furthermore, the development of subcultural group norms and boundaries of behavior serves to legitimate youths' decisions to reject the dominant ideology (see Figure 5.1).

One form of rebellion is terrorism. This involves the use of violence to promote political change by instilling fear in innocent people (Beirne and Messerschmidt, 1990; Conklin, 1989). Here, rebel/terrorists try to create a new social structure that will more effectively allow people to meet what the rebel/terrorists consider to be appropriate goals for society. Hence, these youths attack the ruling class's value system and attempt to replace it with an "ideal universal concept of justice" (Schafer, 1974:30).

Instead of being self-centered or egoistic, rebel/terrorists have an altruistic motivation for violent crime. Consequently, violence is most often directed toward nonpersonal goals. Rather than acquiring material rewards through armed robbery, for example, rebel/terrorists are more concerned with setting an example for their subcultural followers and gaining publicity for their violence. Therefore, vandalism, arson, assault, and murder are all logical acts of rebellion/terrorism. These crimes are viewed by rebel/terrorists as necessary sanctions for those who challenge the status quo of the criminal subculture (Blumberg, 1974; Turk, 1982).

Recent studies reveal the social and psychological profiles of hundreds of domestic and international terrorists. Three major findings obtained in this research support the functionalist perspective on terrorist youth subcultures (see Clarke, 1989; Conklin, 1989; Goleman, 1986).

1. While young, terrorists often developed a profound sense of hopelessness mixed with a burning rage over the fact that nobody, not even their parents, could prevent terrible things from happening to them.

Figure 5.1
Functionalist Perspective on Terrorist Youth Subcultures

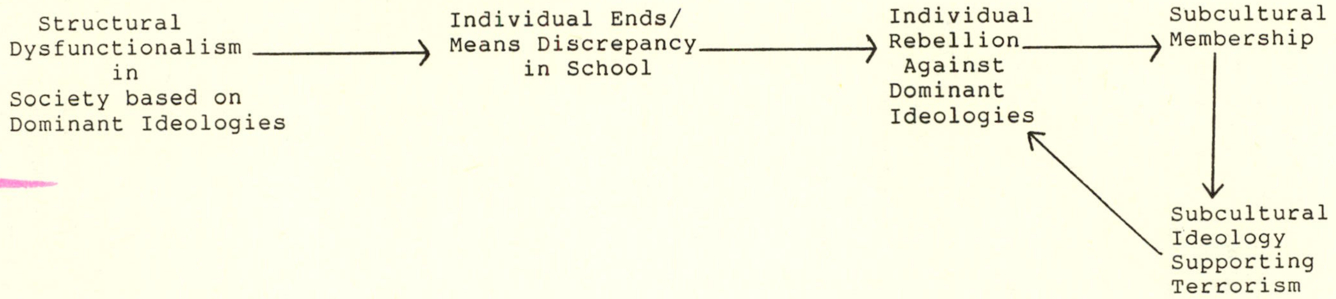

```
Structural              Individual Ends/           Individual              Subcultural
Dysfunctionalism   ───> Means Discrepancy   ───>   Rebellion      ───>     Membership
     in                    in School                Against
Society based on                                    Dominant
Dominant Ideologies                                 Ideologies
                                                                            Subcultural
                                                                            Ideology
                                                                            Supporting
                                                                            Terrorism
```

2. Although young, terrorists often had life-threatening illnesses, which frightened them severely.

3. Later in their lives, this mixture of severe hopelessness and fear led them to deny the risk of death by placing themselves in situations that would threaten their own lives again. This active wager against the forces of death therefore gave the terrorists psychological capacity to commit life-threatening crimes like assassination, hijacking, bombing, and commando raids.

It appears that the functionalist perspective is an adequate explanation of the development of the American skinhead subculture and its behavior. However, this perspective has one major shortcoming. Functionalists cannot explain why some youths who do not reject dominant cultural goals and legitimate means join subcultures (Schwendinger and Schwendinger, 1985; Sykes and Matza, 1957). In other words, by focusing exclusively on poverty and its correlates, functionalists ignore the propensity of middle-class youths to join a subculture (Beirne and Messerschmidt, 1990). In fact, many middle-class youths are the ones who establish American youth subcultures in the first place (see Dylan, 1971; Ginsberg, 1968; Kerouac, 1955; Schwendinger and Schwendinger, 1985).

THE NEO-MARXIST PERSPECTIVE

The second theoretical perspective on terrorist youth subcultures is derived from British neo-Marxist sociology. This school of thought emphasizes the emergence of ideology, culture, and hegemony. From this perspective, culture—not economics—is the linchpin to understanding deviance because culture embodies and defines the true patterns of life within a society (Hebdige, 1979).

British neo-Marxists argue that people are essentially born into many social institutions, not only their immediate families. Their birth within these various institutions causes them to identify their unique space wherever that might be found in society (e.g., the family, school, or street corner). These institutions create specific meanings and relations for youth that are the heart of culture.

According to the neo-Marxist perspective, dominant meanings and relations (culture) always reflect the interests of the most powerful class in society. This dominant class uses its power to create laws so that they may further establish what the culture of society ought to be (Chambliss and Seidman, 1971). At the point where an alliance of powerful groups can exert total authority over all groups in a society, they have established a dominant ideology supported by a specific culture. This is the essence of hegemony.

But hegemony is a wayward child because there will always be those in any society who struggle against it for one reason or another. Those who do so must negotiate a redefinition of cultural meanings and relations. The neo-Marxists view youth subcultures as an example of this negotiation and redefinition process, wherein group members engage in a "struggle over cultural space" (Brake, 1985:4).

British sociologists have found that when youths join a subculture, they inherit a positive reference group which supplies social support and symbolic meaning that allows for the emergence of a counterculture ideology (Brake, 1985:4; Frith, 1978; Hebdige, 1979). This ideology then determines the style of the subculture, which represents the active resistance to hegemony (Dancis, 1978; Frith, 1978). Style is reflected in music, hairstyle, costume, jewelry, and what we might call symbolic terrorism (see Figure 5.2).

Comparing Figure 5.1 with Figure 5.2, we see a great difference between the American functionalist and British neo-Marxist perspectives. Therefore, it demands further explanation. The rebel/terrorist of Figure 5.1 is fundamentally interested in attacking the value system of the ruling class and replacing it with an ideal concept of justice. This person seeks a full-scale revolution—nothing less. On the other hand, Figure 5.2 suggests that subcultural youths engage in acts of terrorism as largely symbolic acts of resistance against the forces responsible for creating hegemony.

The discrepancy between these theoretical models can be explained in the concepts rebellion and resistance. To rebel against the culturally approved goals and means of a society is something quite different than resisting hegemony. Whereas rebellion demands political action that seeks to create a new social order, resistance demands symbolic actions against the dominant law and culture attempting to establish hegemony. Therefore, rebellion is revolutionary, resistance is not.

Because of these fundamental differences, American functionalist research on crime and violence excludes subcultural style; and British scholars, because they treat violence as an incidental feature of the total youth subcultural package, have focused on style to the near exclusion of crime and violence. Whereas American functionalists built their sociological models on observations of criminal activity committed by lower-class, urban street gangs during the 1950s and early 1960s, the British neo-Marxists based most of their conclusions on the emergence of the punk subculture in London during the late 1970s (the historical parent of the neo-Nazi skinheads).

Although British researchers offer very little quantitative data on subcultural development, they provide several important qualitative findings, such as the following (see Brake, 1985; Dancis, 1978; Frith, 1978; Hebdige, 1979; Laing, 1985; Levine and Stumpf, 1983; Marsh, 1977; Muncie, 1981):

1. Punk subcultures are typically dominated by working-class youth and middle-class artists.
2. Punk subcultural ideology is developed by punk music.
3. Punk music, with its intense social content, then raises the political consciousness of those involved in the subculture.
4. Punk style—a function of music—is expressed in hairstyle, costume, jewelry, and theatrical violence, "thus amplifying everything feared in society" (Hebdige, 1979:2).

On balance, British neo-Marxism also appears to provide an excellent opportunity for examining the emergence of the American neo-Nazi skinheads. However, it has two major pitfalls. First, as previously stated, the theory has never

Figure 5.2
Neo-Marxist Perspective on Terrorist Youth Subcultures

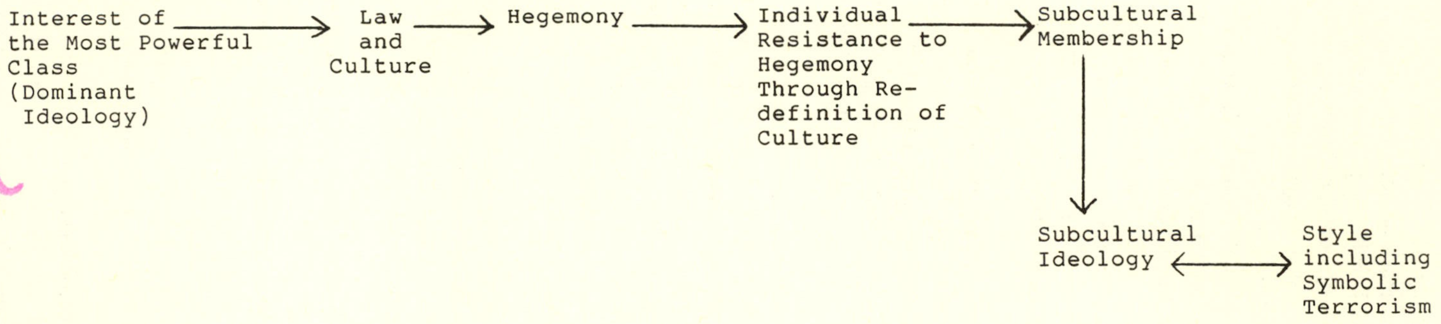

Interest of → Law → Hegemony → Individual → Subcultural
the Most Powerful   and   Resistance to   Membership
Class   Culture   Hegemony
(Dominant   Through Re-
Ideology)   definition of
                                   Culture

Subcultural ⟷ Style
Ideology   including
               Symbolic
               Terrorism

been subjected to even the most rudimentary statistical tests. Hence, we know little about the empirical connection between style and violence. Second, because the theory has never been tested beyond the borders of England and Canada, it may be culturally specific.

British research begins with the premise that punk subcultures consist of working-class youths and middle-class artists who actively resist hegemony. Thus, we should see the punk subculture develop and flourish in societies that produce a great number of young workers and artists, such as Japan. However, there is very little evidence of a punk or skinhead movement in that country. Similarly, no punk or skinhead subculture has emerged in the former Soviet Union, China, or Cuba. As such, the theory fails to explain why the neo-Nazi skinhead movement has emerged and flourished in an advanced totalitarian nation like East Germany (prior to the fall of the Berlin Wall), and at the same time prospered in an advanced capitalist nation such as the United States.

My hypothesis is that neo-Nazi skinheads emerge in a society not because of style, or rebellion. Instead, they emerge through the specific educational and behavioral management efforts orchestrated by adult racists.

THE DIFFERENTIAL IDENTIFICATION-REINFORCEMENT PERSPECTIVE

The third perspective on terrorist youth subcultures is heavily influenced by differential association theory (Sutherland and Cressey, 1970). The starting point for this explanation is that crime occurs because some cultural groups have the power to transmit unconventional norms and values from one generation to the next. That is, the theory focuses on the social psychological processes by which youth are socialized into a deviant subculture.

As articulated by Edwin Sutherland and Donald Cressey, the first principle of this theory is that criminal behavior is learned. Differential association theory therefore predicts that terrorism is neither unique to nor invented by youth. Rather, terrorism is passed on by others. The second principle is that most learning of criminal behavior takes place in face-to-face interaction with others. However, differential association theory was developed before mass ownership of television, before rock and roll and punk music, and long before the days of desktop publishing, telephone hotlines, and computerized bulletin boards.

Therefore, the major changes in the role of the mass media has required a modification of the "face-to-face interaction" principle of differential association theory. This modification has been accomplished through the work of Daniel Glasser (1956), Walter Reckless and Simon Dinitz (1967), and Ian Taylor, Paul Walton, and Jock Young (1973). These scholars refer to this revision as the *theory of differential identification*.

Differential identification theory attempts to explain why people choose models for their behavior. The choice of models does not necessarily involve face-to-face interactions, as required by Sutherland and Cressey. Instead, differential identification theorists argue that "a person pursues criminal behavior to the extent that he identifies himself with real or imaginary persons whose perspective his criminal behavior seems acceptable" (Glaser, 1956:440).

Accordingly, these theorists have emphasized nonface-to-face interaction, and the subjective rather than objective dimensions of social interaction (Liska, 1981). This means that "direct, social and symbolic support for deviance need not necessarily coexist before deviant action is undertaken" (Taylor et al., 1973:129). Under this formulation, the mass media can transmit cultural definitions of deviance that may not otherwise exist in a person's social world. Consequently, individuals become attracted to and identify with deviant people outside of their social world through exposure to television, music, and literature.

Differential association theory has also been revised by Robert Burgess and Ronald Akers (1966). These theorists argue that (1) the process of identifying with deviant cultures refers to mental phenomena that are intrinsically difficult to measure; and (2) the processes of learning deviant behavior are only vaguely described by differential identification theory. Moreover, these scholars argue that researchers should focus on what can be observed—behavior (Akers et al., 1979; Akers, 1985).

Burgess and Akers have, therefore, added a simple theory of operant conditioning to the differential identification model. That is, deviant behavior is a response to rewards and punishments. As rewards increase following deviant behavior, and as punishments decrease, the frequency of deviant behavior will increase. This reformulation holds that deviant behavior is learned and maintained when it is followed by such rewards as money and social prestige.

Combining the Burgess/Akers theory of operant conditioning with the work of Sutherland and Cressey and the differential identification theorists, we are able to specify a *differential identification-reinforcement* perspective on terrorist youth subcultures. Figure 5.3 predicts that youths learn to positively define the act of terrorism through their identification with terrorists who present themselves through the mass media. Once this learning has taken place, the youth joins a terrorist youth subculture. Although the subculture might not necessarily exist in the youth's neighborhood, it does exist in his or her mind. Terrorism is then maintained by a system of rewards. These can include free stickers, zines, airplane tickets to conventions, concert tickets, published notoriety for their violence, the opportunity to meet rock and roll stars, and the chance to appear on TV themselves.

The differential identification-reinforcement perspective on terrorist youth subcultures therefore de-emphasizes the role of subculture, and wholly ignores the influences of class and other socioeconomic factors. The theory does not, however, ignore the impact of style because style is the very essence of mass media presentations. Although the full differential identification-reinforcement model has never been subject to quantitative analysis, certain features of the theory have been tested and the following results were obtained:

1. Watching televised violence is positively related to aggressive behavior by children and teenagers (Goldstein, 1986; National Institute of Mental Health, 1982).

Figure 5.3
Differential Identification-Reinforcement Perspective on Terrorist Youth Subcultures

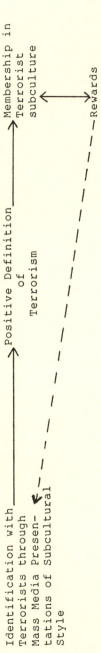

2. The frequency, duration, priority, and intensity of exposure to deviant definitions are
   strongly associated with delinquent behavior (Jensen, 1972; Matthews, 1968; Reiss
   and Rhodes, 1964; Short, 1957; Voss, 1964).

Despite its promise as an explanatory tool, consistent with the functionalist and
neo-Marxist perspectives on terrorist youth subcultures, the differential identification-reinforcement theory has some limitations. The most salient pitfall is that
no empirical data show a direct link between advanced mass media presentations
of terrorist style and positive definitions of terrorism. Thus, four important questions remain unanswered: First, what is the actual relationship between exposure
to racist Oi bands, such as Skrewdriver, and the propensity to commit acts of
terrorism? Second, what is the real effect of racist zines and other publications on
the decision to commit terrorism? Third, what is the impact of racist computer
and telephone linkages on the decision to commit terrorism? Fourth, what are the
true effects of reward on continued terrorism?

The next chapter sets forth a methodology that attempts to apply the analytic
concepts of the functionalist, neo-Marxist and differential identification-reinforcement perspectives to the American neo-Nazi skinheads.

6

Entering the Skinhead Subculture

The majority of criminologists are social scientists only up to a point . . .
and beyond that point they are really social workers.

—Ned Polsky
Hustlers, Beats and Others

This chapter describes the selection of procedures used to enter the American
skinhead subculture, the strengths and weaknesses of these procedures, and the
questions asked once I got there. Parenthetically, I also show that conducting research on the skinheads is somewhat akin to the peculiar subculture itself: In some ways the methods are highly unique, and in other ways, they are
unremarkable.

PROBLEMS OF GAINING ACCESS TO
VIOLENT COLLECTIVES

A number of criminologists have argued that it is unwise, seemingly impossible, and even dangerous to study violent criminals in their natural environments
(Hagan, 1990; Horowitz and Schwartz, 1974; Sutherland and Cressey, 1978). In
this way, there is nothing unique about the present study. Indeed, "gaining access"
to the skinhead subculture presents the same set of problems inherent in gaining
access to other violent collectives. The initial, and most important step involves
the development of a pool of potential subjects. This demands that researchers
overcome two major obstacles.

First, social science research, by its very nature, creates conditions that can
potentially put subcultural members at risk for both arrest by police and retalia-
tion from other members of the subculture. Thus, researchers—whose goal is to
expose the individual and organizational characteristics of such groups—are perceived as threatening to the subculture in general, and to its members in specific.

Because the researcher is an intruder into the collective, members are naturally apt to be paranoid about participating in any study (Becker, 1978; Polsky, 1967).

Second, this paranoia can, in turn, potentially lead to violence against the researcher. For example, Joan Moore's (1978) research team found that observing street-level drug transactions by gang members can put researchers at risk for personal safety. Similarly, in his provocative analysis of Milwaukee street gangs, John Hagedorn (1988) discovered that interviewing gang underlings can cause a "setup" or confrontation between the researcher and gang leaders. And in a study of New York City gangs, a researcher employed by Lewis Yablonsky (1962) was knifed, beaten, and robbed of survey questionnaires by youths in Harlem. Violence was also discovered by investigative reporter Hunter S. Thompson (1967) who documents the story of his own beating at the hands of a gang underling while conducting research for his award-winning *Hell's Angels: The Strange and Terrible Saga of Outlaw Motorcycle Gangs*.

My entry into the skinhead subculture triggered concomitant displays of paranoia and violence. In nearly every case examined, skinheads presented a well-developed skepticism about my intentions. For instance, the leader of the Point Pleasant, New Jersey, Skins explained that, "I can't trust anybody anymore. These days, if I talk to somebody [about our group] I could get shot or meet an agent." This feeling of paranoia was also expressed by the leader of a skinhead collective in Virginia who said:

You're not from the ADL, are you? We won't talk to the ADL. They say things about us that aren't true. They say we're out in the streets bashin' every nigger we see. That's bullshit. The cops read this shit and come down on our ass. The ADL are slime. We're not a bunch of animals out here! We're nothin' like the ADL says.

The implied threat of violence was also encountered in the course of entering the subculture. A skinhead from Milwaukee wrote me a letter saying, "Most likely, your book will be yet another anti-White Kosher Koncoction, however, I took the time to fill out your survey because $10 [payment for filling out the questionnaire] can buy 50 rounds of ammo. I'll be expecting that payment soon." Another Wisconsin skinhead also sent a letter saying, "Try to be honest will you Professor! You will make a lot of people mad. Your own [foregone] conclusions . . . will get you in a lot of trouble."

And like Hunter Thompson's direct form of investigation, my entry into the skinhead subculture also elicited the actual use of violence. Early in the research, I was assaulted by members of the American Front at the corner of Haight and Ashbury in San Francisco. Yet this beating was caused by much different factors than in the Hell's Angels research. Hunter Thompson made the mistake of getting drunk with an Angel who was not part of the gang leadership. As the drinking went on, the biker grew suspicious of the author's intentions. As a result, Thompson was whipped with a motorcycle chain. I made no such technical error. I was assaulted because I was seen by skinheads in the company of an Indonesian woman who was a well-known prostitute in the Haight Street area. For this, I was called a nigger lover and kicked in the shins with a pair of steel-toed Doc Martens.

STRATEGIES FOR ENTERING VIOLENT COLLECTIVES

Criminologists have relied on four primary strategies for entering violent collectives; each attempts to avoid the problems of paranoia and violence. These strategies have generally met with overwhelming success. Indeed, researchers have effectively entered violent collectives as diverse as the Cosa Nostra (see Chambliss, 1988; Talese, 1971), Latin American narcoterrorist cells (Dinges, 1989; Inciardi, 1988; Mills, 1986), and American street gangs from all parts of the nation at different periods throughout the twentieth century. However, these various methods of gathering and recording data have often produced vastly different results concerning the character of violent groups.

That is, as researchers move farther and farther away from their subjects—and therefore farther away from explanations concerning the way subjects view their world—researchers tend to rely more and more on their own value-laden assumptions about human nature and the way society should and does operate. Consequently, this can potentially reinforce prevailing ideologies and the outlook of law enforcement and community agency bureaucrats. If so, researchers confirm official versions of reality that support and sustain the views of social control agents, rather than the empirical realities about the subcultures in which they are interested in the first place.

Therefore, the selection of a research strategy for entering a violent subculture is extremely important. Research methods influence the ideological bias of the investigator which, in turn, affects the criminologist's choice of research questions, theoretical concepts and, inevitably, the recommendation for public policy (Bookin-Weiner and Horowitz, 1983).

Native Field Studies

Historically, scholars' first strategy was to enter violent collectives through the method of participant observation (alternatively referred to as field studies). The field study approach has been preferred among these workers because of its ability to provide the researcher with sensitizing and inductive methods for understanding the individual and organizational characteristics of violent collectives (Hagan, 1990). This method allows researchers to work face-to-face with subjects so they can convince subjects that they have nothing to fear and, thus, remove any cause for personal violence.

Based on this face-to-face interaction and interpersonal trust, criminologists have purposefully attempted to understand phenomena from the standpoint of the violent persons themselves. Why did they join the group? What costs and benefits do they derive from its activities? These were the essential questions dealt with in such American criminology classics as William Chambliss's (1973) "The Saints and the Roughnecks" and Ned Polsky's (1967) study of uncaught career criminals, *Hustlers, Beats and Others.* They were the essential questions posed in more recent sociological exposés on group violence such as Patricia Adler's (1985) analysis of upper-level cocaine smugglers in Northern California and Thomas Mieczkowski's (1986) study of street-level heroin dealers in Detroit. They were also the essential questions raised in the celebrated gang research of Fredric Thrasher (1927), William Foote Whyte (1943), R. Lincoln Keiser (1969), Malcolm Klein (1971), and Walter Miller (1958).

The field study approach was used by University of Birmingham scholars to formulate their seminal theoretical guidelines for understanding British punks and skinheads (Corrigan, 1979; Cohen, 1980; Hebdige, 1979). And this approach has recently been replicated in the first sociological analysis of punks in Canada (Baron, 1989).

In each of these studies, scholars have entered the field as sociological natives. Chambliss, for example, approached the Saints and the Roughnecks outside a Seattle pizza parlor (see Chambliss, 1986). Working independent of criminal justice authorities or community agencies, Chambliss eventually established trust among his subjects; and through his observations, went on to develop important theoretical insights on the relationships between class, subcultural organization, and delinquency. Similarly, Baron independently approached a group of punks gathered on a street corner in Victoria, British Columbia, and simply stated that he was interested in writing about them; and he, too, was accepted with open arms and went on to find important differences between stereotypical and sociological images of the subculture.

Yet both of these archetypical studies can be criticized because they failed to produce large sample sizes. Chambliss' research was based on his longitudinal (two year) study of only fourteen young men (see also Whyte [1943] who based his classic work on interviews with only thirteen subjects, and Shaw [1930], Sutherland [1937], and Chambliss [1975] who drew their often-cited descriptions of *The Jack Roller, The Professional Thief,* and the *Box Man* on only one subject, respectively); and Baron's work is based on observations of thirty-five subjects.

Thus, results produced by the native field study approach can be heralded for their rich and authentic sociological depictions of the organizational and individual characteristics of violent groups. Moreover, these studies produced results indicating that violent subcultures are the product of macro-level social conditions, rather than types of people. Therefore, public policies ought to be forged to ameliorate those structural conditions that lead to organized delinquency and violence. Yet the native field study strategy can be faulted on the grounds that it has produced findings that may not be generalizable to similar subcultures in other geographic regions.

Community Agency Field Studies

Other scholars have used a second strategy: collaborating with current or former members of violent collectives to conduct field studies under the auspices of community agencies. Through this collaborative effort, researchers have generally controlled for paranoia and violence by establishing trust among subcultural members; thereby breaking through what Carl Taylor (1990:43) aptly refers to as the code of silence.

Most notable is the research of Lewis Yablonsky (1962, 1983) who, according to one criminology textbook, "made an important contribution to the understanding of gang behavior" (Siegel and Senna, 1981:255). During the late 1950s, Yablonsky was appointed by a community agency to develop and direct a New York City gang prevention program called Morningside Heights, Inc. on the upper West Side of Manhattan. Yablonsky lived and worked in the area, and gang members would often hang out in his office and occasionally even visit his home (Yablonsky, 1983:xi).

Yablonsky's contribution to gang research was built on gang members' responses to sixteen open-ended questions related to the structure of one Morningside Heights group called the "Balkans." The Balkans were responsible for a string of crimes including robbery, burglary, drug addiction, assault, and homicide. Instead of administering this questionnaire to the Balkans himself, however, Yablonsky used his influence as the director of Morningside Heights, Inc. and offered two Balkan leaders $10 apiece for each completed questionnaire they administered to their gang underlings. This was, moreover, a unique and unprecedented strategy for entering a violent subculture. Gang leaders were now themselves employees of the research project, and their activities were seen as being legitimate (Bookin-Weiner and Horowitz, 1983).

These two gang leaders were named Duke and Pedro, and their method of administering questionnaires was also unprecedented as a social science research strategy. "Their approach," wrote Yablonsky, "seemed to vary between a polite request for information at one extreme and a threatening 'You fill it out 'cause I say so' interview at the other" (1983:103). In essence, Yablonsky recognized Duke and Pedro's coercive authority within the gang, and he began to systematically train them in methods of data collection through intimidation. The following role-playing account is taken from Yablonsky's training session with Duke wherein Yablonsky plays the role of the recalcitrant subject:

YABLONSKY: [referring to the questionnaire] Well, what's that for?

DUKE: A guy I know is writing a book on gangs and I'm doing it for him.

YABLONSKY: No, man. I don't know whether I want to do that, 'cause it's liable to get in the papers or liable to get to the cops or something like that.

DUKE: I'm not giving it to the cops or anybody else; this is just for this guy.

YABLONSKY: How do you know he isn't a cop?

DUKE: Well, you know me—I wouldn't give it to the cops.

YABLONSKY: Yeah, but I can't be sure.

DUKE: Just don't bullshit me; just fill it out (*getting angry*). (Yablonsky, 1983:103–4, emphasis in original)

Yablonsky noted that "Duke's interview technique was 'forceful,' he had a talent for getting information" (Yablonsky, 1983:104). And indeed he did. Within a period of only three weeks, Duke and his Balkan vice-president Pedro conducted a total of 51 interviews for Yablonsky. Yablonsky therefore remained safe from the threats of paranoia and violence by handing these pressures over to Duke and Pedro. Yet they would ultimately pay for this opportunity to participate in academic criminology. As Yablonsky notes:

The gang-boy respondents had mixed reactions to Duke and Pedro as researchers. Some . . . felt they were stoolies working for the cops, and some non-Balkans reacted with overt hostility. On one occasion, Duke arrived at my office, displayed some . . . fresh lacerations on his face, and claimed he had been beaten and robbed of ten filled-out questionnaires by six unidentified Negroes in central Harlem. (Yablonsky, 1983:103)

Despite its ethical ramifications of bringing harm to the subjects of social science research (Babbie, 1989), Yablonsky's strategy has been incorporated into the gang research of many contemporary scholars. Most notable is the often-cited research of Joan Moore (1978) who founded a community-based research project that utilized former East Los Angeles gang members who, in turn, recruited active gang members into her research project. Similarly, Taylor (1990) recruited subjects into his research on Detroit street gangs by hiring former gang members from a rock concert security firm he managed. This method was also used by John Hagedorn (1988) in his analysis of Milwaukee street gangs. Throughout his work, Hagedorn was assisted by a former gang member with strong community ties. Such collaboration was necessary, wrote Hagedorn, because "Gangs don't keep membership rosters" (1990:245).

Like the native approach, the community agency field study method has yielded important findings on the individual and organizational dynamics of violent subcultures including knowledge about the frequency of violence and its relationship to drug use. But perhaps more important, the studies emanating from this tradition have made significant contributions to our knowledge about the origins and subjective meanings of collective violence across various communities (see Hagedorn, 1988; Horowitz, 1987, 1990; Moore, 1985; Vigil, 1988; Zatz, 1985, 1987).

Also like the sociological natives, community agency researchers have built their explanations of violence on information derived from small samples. Hagedorn's research, for example, was based on extensive interviews with forty-seven subjects. Yet unlike his contemporaries, Hagedorn focused his analysis specifically on gang leaders; and this sets Hagedorn's research apart from any other criminological study of violent subcultures ever conducted.

In fact, the community agency field study approach has produced findings that have led those who make policy about criminal justice research to concentrate their attention and resources on community forces that make gang membership

an attractive option for today's youth. Currently, nearly every federal agency concerned with research on gangs assumes the existence of these community forces
and consequently limits research outside this area of interest on the grounds that
such alternative research is less likely to produce results of policy significance.

For example, in its *Research Plan* for 1991, the National Institute of Justice
cites the work of Hagedorn and attributes the nation's gang problem to "family
and other disruptions related to immigration, profound poverty that permeates
communities, and the combination of widespread lack of preventative health care
and the failure of schools to engage and educate a sizable proportion of the youth
population" (U.S. Department of Justice, 1991:28).

Essentially, today's policymakers view violent gang members as normal youths
who have, unfortunately, inherited extremely difficult circumstances in life. In
response, youths have turned to a gang to cope with their profound socioeconomic hardship. Because urban gangs have never been more violent in the American experience than they are today (Spergel, 1990), there is increasing public
effort to control gangs and eliminate their violence. Hence, the research of Hagedorn and others has led to the development of community gang intervention
projects such as the House of Umoja in Philadelphia (U.S. Department of Justice, 1991). The goal of the House of Umoja, seen as a model gang prevention
program by the U.S. government, is to "foster a sense of togetherness and group
unity imparting the values inherent in African culture" (Spergel, 1990:274).

However, such firmly drawn conclusions ignore the different origins and sub-
stantive meanings of collective violence that exist across social contexts of various criminal subcultures. For example, are family problems, "profound poverty,"
and the "widespread neglect of preventative health care and education" also important criminogenic influences on youths who engage in violent forms of organized hate crime? Do these variables explain why a group of middle-class black
youths in New York City recently emerged calling themselves the "wolf pack" to
beat and rape a white Central Park jogger? Do they explain why a group of middle-class Italian youths in Howard Beach, New York, recently organized themselves to commit murder against two black kids who did nothing more than order
a slice of pizza at the wrong pizzeria (Hynes and Drury, 1990)? Do these variables explain why American skinheads have emerged to commit an unprecedented
display of terrorism against urban American blacks, gays, and lesbians during
the late 1980s?

If so, then the dominant research paradigm of American gang scholarship
would hold that neo-Nazi skinheads ought to also be treated in a community-
oriented self-help program—reminiscent of the House of Umoja—which emphasizes "a sense of togetherness and group unity" inherent in the values of Italian,
Irish, French, Polish, Russian, German, and British cultures. That is, skinheads
should be treated with a gang prevention program that promotes the culture of
European Aryans. Such a public policy would be considered racist, however, and
incompatible with the egalitarian principles of a constitutional republic.

Detached Caseworker Studies

A third strategy is a community-oriented technique used by criminologists to formulate explanations of collective violence through survey research conducted by social workers. This technique is exemplified by the research of James F. Short and Fred L. Strodtbeck (1965) — a work which many sociologists consider the high-water mark of empirical analysis on American street gangs (see Hagedorn, 1988; Orcutt, 1983; Spergel, 1990; Regoli and Hewitt, 1991).

In their landmark study, *Group Process and Gang Delinquency,* Short and Strodtbeck examined a total of thirty-eight Chicago street gangs through detached caseworkers employed by the city's YMCA. The detached caseworkers spent most of their time in the field gaining gang members' confidence, steering them away from illegal behavior, and encouraging their participation in more conventional activities, such as playing basketball. Short and Strodtbeck consulted regularly with these detached caseworkers and asked them to fill out an extensive survey questionnaire on each gang member's norms, values, and self-reported delinquency. (Notably, as early as 1960 Short and Strodbeck's detached caseworkers discovered a Chicago-based gang of white youths known as the German Counts who used the swastika as their mark [1965:2].)

Short and Strodtbeck noted two benefits of this approach: First, like Hagedorn would point out a quarter of a century later, they found that the detached caseworkers were necessary because, in their words, "There was, to begin with, no list of gangs from which probability samples could be drawn" (Short and Strodtbeck, 1965:10). Second, the detached caseworker technique provided the researchers with what they called service legitimation. Short and Strodtbeck concluded that "Fruitful observation . . . is possible only when the [researcher] is accepted by the subjects in a role which they perceive as meaningful in relation to their needs" (Short and Strodtbeck, 1965:10).

Using these procedures, Short and Strodtbeck produced a total of 598 completed questionnaires which provided the grist for their legendary theorizing about American street gangs. According to one textbook writer, Short and Strodtbeck's group process theory explains "consistent and revealing patterns of social interaction leading to violence" (Orcutt, 1983:171).

Short and Strodtbeck's theory is comprised of two parts: (1) violent gangs consist of socially unskilled youths who are unable to cope elsewhere in society, and (2) gang leaders are able to dictate levels of organized violence against others. Yet the theory can be criticized on two important counts: First, throughout their two-year study, Short and Strodtbeck failed to identify a single criminal gang in the entire City of Chicago. This happened despite the fact that the Chicago Police Department reported that gangs accounted for 25 percent of all teenage homicides during this era (Spergal, 1990). The authors fully acknowledge this severe limitation by providing the following caveat:

The failure to locate a full-blown criminal group, or more than one drug-using group, despite our highly motivated effort to do so, is a "finding" of some importance, for it casts doubt on the generality of these phenomena, if not on their existence. (Short and Strodt-beck, 1965:13)

In other words, the subjects in Short and Strodtbeck's research were not violent at all. Hence, there can be no "consistent and revealing pattern of social interaction that leads to violence" among youths who have never engaged in violence to begin with. At bottom, Short and Strodtbeck were left with exhaustive survey data on nearly 600 youngsters who were guilty of nothing more than horseplay. "We were led in the end," they write, "to seek groups not primarily oriented around fighting, but with extensive involvement in the pursuit of 'kicks' " (Short and Strodtbeck, 1965:13). Yet there is a second, and more crucial shortcoming of the detached caseworker approach.

During their research, Short and Strodtbeck never actually came in contact with any of the gang members in their study. It is safe to say, in fact, that the most influential gang theorists of the 1950s and 1960s (such as Richard Cloward, Lloyd Ohlin, and Albert Cohen) shared this same characteristic with Short and Strodtbeck: It is likely that none of these criminologists ever met a gang member (see Cullen, 1988; Lotz et al., 1985; Martin et al., 1990; Regoli and Hewitt, 1991). Therefore, they deprived themselves of the sensitizing and inductive strategies implicit in more native approaches to entering violent collectives.

In essence, as the detached caseworker theorists distanced themselves from their subjects, they became more conservative in their social theorizing, more quantitative in their presentation of data, and yet more explicit in their prescriptions for public policy by seeking to "remedy social, physiological, and psychological deficits" of gang members (Short, 1990:237). The more conservative the theory became, the less interest was shown in the violent subculture and its social context. Instead, the criminological focus of gang theorizing began to turn on the personal deficits of gang members themselves.

Thus, theorists working in the detached caseworker tradition have made bold claims about the internal structure of gangs and its relationship to violence. Drawing from the works of Short and Strodtbeck and Yablonsky, esteemed criminologists have recently begun to theorize that

gangs of adolescent males are better characterized as unorganized than as organized. . . . There is, at best, an informal structure of friendship but no hint of formal organization. Gang members do not care much for one another. They do not trust one another. . . . [G]ang members do not come together because they share positive interests or values, but because they share poverty, *unhappy homes,* and social disabilities. (Gottfredson and Hirschi, 1990:207–8, emphasis added)

Under this formulation, gang violence is not a product of group process. Rather, the origins of collective violence are to be found in low individual self-control that is developed in the first six or eight years of life. Hence, these theorists advocate "policies directed toward enhancement of the ability of familial institutions to socialize children [as] the only realistic long-term state policies with potential for substantial crime reduction" (Gottfredson and Hirschi, 1990:272–73). Gottfredson and Hirschi raise a compelling question: Is there empirical justification to assume that such family-oriented policies would control what the U.S. Senate recently called a "rising tide of hate crime nationally" (Koch, 1990:1)?

The Research of Jeffrey Fagan   Recently, the detached caseworker approach has reemerged to assume a position of prominence in the U.S. gang literature. This trend is exemplified by the work of Jeffrey Fagan (1989, 1990a, 1990b; see also Wilson, 1990). Like the YMCA rseearch of Short and Strodtbeck, Fagan recruited his subjects through community center employees (or intermediaries who worked in gang intervention programs, social service agencies, and neighborhood advocacy groups) located in three major cities: Los Angeles, San Diego, and Chicago. These workers persuaded active gang members to come to local neighborhood community centers where they were asked to fill out survey questionnaires by yet another group of proctors also employed by Fagan. On completion of their surveys, Fagan's subjects were rewarded with T-shirts, baseball caps, and music cassettes.

This strategy developed a pool of 151 subjects. Therefore, Fagan's sample provided enough statistical power to establish grounds for quantitative criminology. Through an unprecedented display of complex statistical proofs, Fagan made two important discoveries about the nature of violent collectives in America today. Both contradict the claims made by Gottfredson and Hirschi, Hagedorn, and the U.S. Department of Justice.

1. Organizational structures (and roles of individual members in that organization) reinforce violence.
2. Violence is most often presaged by drug use or drug sales.

In the main, the detached caseworker technique employed by Fagan proved successful because it was entirely safe for both the subject and the researcher. On one hand, gang members were encouraged and rewarded for participating in the research. And on the other, the researcher (Fagan) did not come in contact with his subjects; therefore, he was—like Yablonsky and Short and Strodtbeck—safe from paranoia and violence.

Fagan's research can be criticized on two important counts: First, variances in levels of violence discovered by Fagan may have been an artifact of the detached caseworker technique, rather than a reflection of empirical reality. Fagan did, indeed, discover a uniform prevalence of violence among his subjects. Yet he also found significant differences in the incidence of violence committed by these subjects. As Fagan laments, "Differences were evident. . . . Los Angeles gang members in this study underreported gang involvement in violence. *Their responses may reflect the complex role of the intermediary group with gangs*" (1989:652, emphasis added).

Second, (and as a result) Fagan does not provide a conclusive argument to show that drug use and drug sales equally affect violence across youth subcultures. That is, Fagan's research cannot be generalized to other groups beyond those which he studied using the error-plagued detached caseworker method. Yet he would have us believe as much. In fact, he is unequivocal on this point.

Fagan concludes that "drug use is intrinsic to gang life among more violent gangs" and that gang "delinquency [*does*] *not* occur in the absence of drugs" (Fagan, 1989:654 and 660, emphasis added). Once again, such unequivocal findings ignore the different origins and subjective meanings of collective violence that exist across social contexts of various criminal subcultures. For example, is drug use a necessary precondition for organized hate crime?

Prison Field Studies

The fourth strategy is the long-standing form of surrogate sociology derived from post hoc recollections of organizational and individual characteristics of violent groups rendered by prison inmates (Hagedorn, 1990). In the prison field study approach, the researcher conducts interviews with incarcerated gang members who have been identified by correctional officials. Therefore, the researcher has a steady pool of subjects and the safety of a nearby prison guard trained to eliminate paranoia and violence. This arrangement places the subject in less danger than if he or she were being interviewed in the community while at large for a violent crime (Polsky, 1967).

This strain of criminology is represented by the research of Irwin and Cressey (1964), Irwin (1970, 1980), and Jacobs (1977) who offer exquisite sociological renderings on the dynamics of organized collectives of dangerous men. Like Hagedorn, these scholars have often found that the most elucidating body of knowledge comes from gang leaders.

THE AMERICAN SKINHEADS

The present research relies on a combination and reformulation of the four strategies for entering violent collectives. As such, I try to draw on the strengths while suppressing the shortcomings of each strategy. Through these methods, I explain the American skinheads as a terrorist youth subculture that has arisen from an interaction of individual and social forces. Yet, one unique obstacle presented by this research warrants explanation before the methods are introduced.

Right-Wing Extremism and the Politics of Silence

Right-wing extremist groups present a built-in barrier that transcends the problem of paranoia encountered by generations of gang scholars. Among both gang members and white extremists, there is a well-developed code of silence wherein subjects are naturally prone to conceal information about their criminal behavior. Yet with extremists, like the skinheads, the code of silence assumes a more functional role.

Evidence of a politics of silence among members of the far right is well-documented. In his investigation of the Texas Knights of the Ku Klux Klan, civil rights attorney Morris Dees discovered it is almost impossible to gather even the most elementary information on Klansmen. The following account, taken from Dees' memoirs, delineates the research problem:

> The man . . . a National Socialist and a member of the Klan . . . told me his name was Russell Gregory Thatcher. He refused to give his address. I asked him why. "Hardening the target," he answered. "You minimize the output of information about yourself. . . . [B]ecause I'm a survivalist . . . I minimize my contact with the enemy. . . . It's simple military tactics and procedure." (1991:28)

Thus, withholding information (or silence) becomes a political tool: The less outsiders know about the individual and organizational features of extremist groups, the safer the group becomes from outside threats to control them through public policy (regardless of their criminal exploits). Silence, therefore, serves to "harden the target" of right-wing extremism by providing a paramilitary umbrella over the individual and organizational interests of such groups.

Accordingly, extremist groups have incorporated the values and symbols of silence and secrecy into their racist counterculture ideologies. In other words, silence adds to the mystique of right-wing extremism. Today, the largest hate group operating in the United States is called the Invisible Empire of the Ku Klux Klan (ADL, 1988a; Dees, 1991; Zatarain, 1990). The most dangerous extremist group operating during the decade of the 1980s was, indeed, not even given a name by their leader until nearly a year after they had committed a string of bank robberies, bombings, and assaults. Then, the leader gave the name *Bruders Schweignen* to his group. Translated from German to English, this means the Silent Brotherhood. Over the course of the next year, the leader read the fantasy-oriented underground classic called *The Turner Diaries*. Then, Robert Mathews renamed his group. It was now called simply, the Order (Flynn and Gerhardt, 1989).

Research also shows that extremist workshops and paramilitary training sessions have been offered to members of the far right where they are taught how to: (1) become invisible to investigators; (2) stay out of government files; (3) live nomadically; (4) obtain multiple addresses and multiple birth certificates; (5) use hideouts, deep cover, and money laundering services; and (6) find privacy from tax collectors (Flynn and Gerhardt, 1989; Coates, 1987; Hamm, 1991; Toy, 1989).

Given these conditions, it is of little wonder that American criminology is altogether void of primary research on the subject of organized hate crime (see Gurr, 1989; Spergel, 1990).

Methods

I began to systematically collect data on the American skinheads in the fall of 1989. Drawing from the native field study approach, I started the investigation by visiting various U.S. cities where I tracked down skinheads in their natural habitat (street corners, bars, coffee shops, record stores, survivalist outlets, rock concerts, and motorcycle shops). These subjects were not hard to identify. They all had shaved heads and wore white power and/or Nazi regalia. Two skinheads, for example, were tattooed in the middle of their foreheads with the mark of the swastika. To gain a broader context for the research, I used the same methods to interview skinheads on the streets of Montreal, Vancouver, London, Amsterdam, and Berlin.

Often I would wait hours to see these skinheads in their natural habitat, frequently in heat and humidity, and sometimes at night. I used these native procedures, on and off, between 1989 and 1991.

I simply approached these youths and asked them to participate in a structured interview. No attempt was made to mislead them. I presented myself as an independent sociologist who was not affiliated with law enforcement or any social service agency. To gain their trust, I promised these individuals complete anonymity; I presented the research as an attempt to set the record straight on the skinheads, and at no time were subjects asked to speak into an electronic recording device.

Interviews were conducted on the streets, in face-to-face contact with ten racist American skinheads. (The present analysis does not include interviews with antiracist skinheads, or skinheads from outside the United States.) I interviewed one skinhead in an Indianapolis coffee shop; another skinhead outside a record store in Louisville; two skinheads outside a motorcycle shop in Oakland, California; two Seattle-based skinheads in front of a liquor store in Vancouver; one skinhead on the campus of the University of Illinois in Chicago; and three skinheads at rock concerts in Cincinnati and Indianapolis.

Drawing from the research tradition established by Short and Strodtbeck, these ten interviews were conducted with a forced-choice survey questionnaire designed to capture the responses of more than one subject at a time. Drawing from the techniques used by Yablonsky and Fagan, I offered $10 to any skinhead who agreed to an interview.

Next, I attempted to conduct interviews using the community agency field study approach established so well by Moore, Hagedorn, Horowitz, Vigil, and Zatz. I made written inquiries to various antiracist organizations (the ADL, the John Brown Anti-Klan Committee, the Center for Democratic Renewal, and the Southern Poverty Law Center) concerning skinhead groups operating in different parts of the United States. From these agencies, I attempted to gather the names and addresses of known skinheads for the purpose of collecting more interview data. However, these procedures came to little avail. Therefore, I embarked on an alternative route of data collection which might best be described as a clandestine form of the community agency field study approach.

Unlike street gangs, the American skinheads do keep membership rosters. They often publish their names and addresses in the underground teen press through the nearly 10,000 zines that are currently disseminated across the United

States (see *Fact Sheet Five,* January 1990). In this regard, Tom Metzger's *WAR* provides a short mailing list of American skinhead groups.

Using the *WAR* mailing list, I sent letters to the leadership of twenty-six skinhead groups throughout the United States, inviting them to make long-distance collect telephone calls to me for the purpose of conducting interviews. Again, I made clear my intentions of setting the record straight by promising academic objectivity. I also promised complete confidentiality and a $25 payment for those skinheads who agreed to an interview.

This method yielded nine completed questionnaires on skinhead leaders from Texas, Alabama, New York, California, Wisconsin, Virginia, Michigan, and New Jersey. As such, I spent more than a dozen hours talking to these leaders, and two of them were interviewed more than once. Because of the trust established with these subjects, I gained an unexpected dividend.

Shortly after these telephone interviews, I began to receive unsolicited long-distance calls from other skinhead leaders not listed in Metzger's *WAR.* In essence, I was able to conduct three additional interviews as a result. In each of these bonus interviews, skinhead leaders said that they heard the research was on the level as the leader of the Bronx Area Skinheads (BASH) noted in his apartment in New York City. His interview was particularly instructive inasmuch as there were, at the time, a total of thirty-seven members of BASH, and he was their leader and official spokesman.

For those group leaders who did not respond to the initial invitation for a telephone interview, I sent follow-up letters and five copies of the questionnaire under a simple, innocuous cover. I invited these leaders to fill out the questionnaire and pass the other four along to members of their group. For each completed and returned questionnaire, I promised a $10 payment and complete anonymity. These methods produced a total of eight usable questionnaires from skinheads in Texas, Oregon, Florida, New Jersey, and Wisconsin.

Because of my success in gaining access to the skinheads using Metzger's printed materials, I tried my luck at using his electronic materials. That is, I logged onto the W.A.R. Board, identifying myself as a sociologist with no axe to grind against anybody. I promised to do no harm to W.A.R. or any bulletin board user who came online describing him or herself as a neo-Nazi skinhead. I offered $10 to any taker. I found two skinheads, one from New York and one from Alabama, who were willing to participate in the research through this electronic medium.

Last, I attempted to gain access to the American skinheads using prison field study methods. Working in concert with correctional administrators, correctional educators, and guards, I was able to conduct interviews with incarcerated skinheads in California, South Carolina, Indiana, and Illinois. Two subjects were incarcerated for the attempted murder of racial minorities.

In summary, then, I conducted thirty-six original skinhead interviews using native field study methods, clandestine community agency techniques, and prison field study strategies. I controlled for paranoia by primarily focusing on subcultural leaders—or core members who are likely to display the highest rates and severity of hate crime violence—and by presenting myself as a sociologist operating independent of law enforcement and community service agencies. The early Haight Street assault notwithstanding, I experienced no life-threatening violence by any of the subjects.

MEASURES

As previously discussed, the skinheads are not a street gang. Rather, they are a terrorist youth subculture. There are important differences between youngsters who join a street gang and those who join a terrorist group. These are different forms of deviance and must be approached etiologically for one overarching reason—to facilitate the advancement of public policy on the prevention, control, and treatment of racial, ethnic, and sexual violence.

Toward this end, all thirty-six skinheads were questioned about issues of theoretical and practical concern. Specifically, they were asked questions about class, goals, school, family, politics, style, music, television, literature, computers, religion, drugs, guns, group dynamics, and hate crime. There was a consistent sequence of questions in the interviews, starting with background questions; proceeding to family issues; life-style; drug use; prior criminal record; gun ownership; organizational structure, recruitment, indoctrination, and group status ascriptions; to questions about hate crimes; white power rock; *WAR*, "Race and Reason," and the W.A.R. Board; questions about the W.A.R. reward system; and, finally, questions about alienation, Nazism, and Satanism.

I also explored unanticipated topics that emerged during the interviews, such as the role of skinhead women and their attitudes toward pregnancy. These findings are introduced in the next chapter.

7

Terrorism, Rebellion, and Style

1. We want to sing the love of danger, the habit of energy and rashness.

2. The essential elements of our poetry will be courage, audacity and revolt.

3. [W]e want to exalt movements of aggression, feverish sleeplessness, the forced march, the perilous leap, the slap and the blow with the fist.

9. We want to glorify war—the only cure for the world—and militarism, patriotism, the destructive gesture of the anarchists, the beautiful ideas which kill, and contempt of women.

10. We want to demolish museums and libraries, fight morality, feminism and all opportunist and utilitarian cowardice.

—The Futurists' Manifesto
Rome, circa 1909

The only objective way of diagnosing the sickness of the healthy is by the incongruity between their rational existence and the possible course their lives might be given by reason.

—Theodor Adorno
Minima Moralia

The findings are reported at five different levels of analysis. First, I begin this chapter with a very brief discussion on the background characteristics of the skinheads in this study. Second, I present data that tests for the presence of theoretically relevant variables. This procedure is necessary to determine whether the results are consistent with theoretical expectations on terrorist youth subcultures. Third, I examine the social organization of skinhead groups. Fourth, I parenthetically provide an analysis of the data in light of several commonly held assumptions about the skinheads. And fifth, I examine the data for unexpected operations. This aspect of research design relates to the stimulation of new hypotheses, which if empirically verified, can potentially modify the theoretical discourse on terrorist youth subcultures.

BACKGROUND CHARACTERISTICS OF SAMPLE

The background characteristics of the thirty-six skinheads are summarized in Table 7.1. As the table shows, the sample was comprised of twenty-seven males and nine females, who ranged in age from fourteen to twenty-five years old, with a mean age of 19.6 years. A total of 61 percent of the subjects ($N = 22$) lived away from home and the remainder lived with their parents. Only two subjects had ever been arrested for a felony crime. Length of involvement in the subculture ranged from six months to eight years, with a mean of approximately three years.

As such, these data allow for the construction of a composite picture of the typical skinhead in this study. This person is a nineteen-year-old male who has left home to live by himself or with friends. He has been a skinhead for about three years and has never been arrested for a serious crime. However, as we shall see, he is also likely to be a full-blown terrorist.

TERRORISM

So far, I have presented dozens of cases where skinheads have used violence for the explicit purpose of instilling fear in innocent people. Inspired by the convoluted heavy metal fantasies of white power bands such as Skrewdriver, I contend that the American skinheads have sought to topple a fantasy-inspired Zionist Occupied Government (ZOG) and cast it into a receivership that could be administered by a morally superior Aryan Youth of the First World. They did so primarily by committing a spree of killings, stabbings, clubbings, and beatings of poor black Americans and other disenfranchised people.

This form of violence is, therefore, consistent with the formal definition of American terrorism. Since 1982, the FBI's working definition of a terrorist inci-

Table 7.1
Background Characteristics of Sample ($N = 36$)

```
Sex            .
       Males                                    27
       Females                                   9

Mean Age                                       19.6

Living Arrangement
       Living at home                           14
       Living away from home                    22

Previous Felony Arrest
       Yes                                       2
       No                                       34

Length of Involvement in Subculture
       < 1 year                                  6
       1-2 years                                11
       3-4 years                                 2
       > 4 years                                17
```

dent is a "violent act or an act dangerous to human life in violation of the criminal laws . . . to intimidate or coerce a government, *the civilian population, or any segment thereof,* in the furtherance of political or social objectives" (quoted in Gurr, 1989:203, emphasis added).

Skinhead violence is also consistent with the language expressed in the recent federal Hate Crimes Statistics Act. This law defines a hate crime as an act of prejudicial violence based on race, religion, ethnicity, or sexual preference (Akiyama, 1991). Hence, when skinhead Dean McKee attacked and murdered a homeless black man in Tampa, Florida, for example, he committed both an act of terrorism and a hate crime.

This statement is true only if we can somehow prove that McKee's crime was motivated by (1) an underlying political or social objective and (2) an overt prejudiced against African-Americans. If McKee was motivated by a political or social objective, but was not overtly prejudiced against blacks, he was guilty of terrorism only. If, on the other hand, McKee had only a raw and vitriolic hatred of blacks, but had no broader political or social agenda, he was guilty of a hate crime only.

Therefore, not all acts of terrorism can be considered hate crimes, and hate crimes are not necessarily terrorism unless such prejudicial violence has a political or social underpinning. In McKee's case, there was evidence of both. He was an avowed neo-Nazi covered with swastika tattoos and other white power regalia. And, as we all know, Nazism represents a sustained campaign against certain segments of the civilian population in the pursuit of political and social objectives. There is also proof that McKee's crime was based on prejudice against blacks. Arrested with a Skrewdriver cassette featuring the song "Nigger, Nigger," McKee allegedly called his victim a "fuckin' monkey nigger" moments before he killed him (and McKee did not rob or otherwise molest his victim). Thus, hate crime and terrorism are synonymous in this case.

This venture into the thicket of verbiage on terrorism and hate crime is necessary for establishing my presentation of the data on skinhead violence. I began by asking three questions anchored in the political and social pursuit of violence. First, subjects were asked to respond to the following question: "Why did you join your group?" They were given five response options: "To make money," "To protect myself against other groups or gangs," "To fight for my neighborhood," "To fight for the survival of my race," and "Other."

Second, subjects were asked, "How many fights have you been in during the past two years?" Responses were "None," "One or two," "Three or more," or "Five or more." Third, I asked this question: "How many of these fights were against people of another race?" Response options were "None," "About half of them," or "All of them." Taken together, then, responses to these three questions constitute a reasonable operationalization of both terrorism and hate crime.

The data in Table 7.2 (Prevalence of Terrorism/Hate Crime) show that none of the subjects joined their group to make money, to protect themselves, or to fight for their neighborhood. Instead, a total of 89 percent of these young people became skinheads to fight for their race. For example, the leader of an Alabama

Table 7.2
Prevalence of Terrorism/Hate Crime (N = 36)

	% Responding
Reasons for joining group	
To make money	0
Protection against other groups/gangs	0
To fight for neighborhood	0
To fight for survival of race	89%
Other	11%
Frequency of fights during past two years	
None	19%
One or two	28%
Three or four	19%
Five or more	33%
Frequency of fights against people of another race	
None of them	39%
Half of them	39%
All of them	22%

Note: Percentages may not sum to 100 because of rounding.

skinhead group known as BASH (Birmingham Area Skinheads) said this: "Why'd I become a skinhead? Cause the Jews are takin' over. The Jews, spics, and niggers, and nobody's watchin' out for whitey. But the day will come when ZOG will fall."

Similarly, the leader of a California skinhead group wrote:

The "System" enforces your right to Blow Dope; Turn Queer; Marry a Nigger; Kill the Unborn; and do anything else to destroy America. Some people may be sick enough to accept it . . . but not us. We prefer to SMASH IT! and replace it with a healthy WHITE MAN'S ORDER!

On an equally revolutionary note, the leader of an Illinois group called Death Justice said, "I started the skinheads around here cause it's fuckin' time the white man stood up for his rights. Death Justice, man. Either we get justice, or you fuckers get death!"

Yet Table 7.2 also shows that 11 percent of the subjects cited other reasons for becoming skinheads. In this vein, the founder of the Confederate Hammer Skins said, "I started the group because I wanted to express my views about the white race. My mom's in the Ku Klux Klan and my husband's really into white power."

Two subjects indicated that they became skinheads strictly for cultural reasons. Said the leader of the Point Pleasant Skins: "I became a skinhead because I dug the look. The shaved head, Doc Martens, the music—especially skinhead music from Germany, Portugal, and Spain. I'm a musician myself, and my fiancée's a skinhead from London."

Another subject took a more intellectual road to his subcultural affiliation. The twenty-year-old leader of a Detroit area skinhead group reported that:

I've been a racist since I was fifteen. I started out reading Nietzsche, then I read German history books about the ancient Aryans. I became a National Socialist at about seventeen. I read Hitler's *Mein Kampf* three times in a row. I saw that the racial cohesiveness of the Jews had allowed them to gain power for their own purposes. I started to listen to Wagner and the classic German marching bands. Then I became a skinhead.

Last, a skinhead from Racine, Wisconsin, told the following story:

I joined the skinheads because they're a positive youth culture. I used to be into all kinds of drugs, and really depressed. Now I'm into white power, and I'm gettin' *A*'s in school and I got a girlfriend. But people are really unfair. Like last week, my history teacher came down on me for wearing a black jacket with a swastika on it. You watch, the skinheads are put down everywhere. Did you see "21 Jump Street," last week? They had this story about the skinheads that was really unfair.

Despite these alternative motives, Table 7.2 shows that the vast majority of subjects became skinheads to fight for the survival of their race. The table also shows that, as a group, these skinheads were remarkably violent. The data indicate that more than half of the subjects (52 percent) had been in more than three self-reported fights over the past two years. In total, then, by their own admissions these thirty-six skinheads were involved in approximately 120 acts of violence during the two-year period. But were these fights all acts of terrorism or hate crime? The final presentation of data in Table 7.2 suggests that they were not. The data reveal that roughly 58 percent of these fights were not against people of another race. In other words, of the total number of self-reported acts of violence, less than half (42 percent) can be considered acts of terrorism or hate crime.

In summary, three distinct patterns can be discerned from these data: First, although violence is widespread within the subculture, there are a few skinheads in the sample ($N = 7$) who did not engage in violence. Second, not all acts of violence are directed against minorities. In fact, most fights were, presumably, acts of white-on-white violence. (I more fully explore this finding in chapter 9 and in the Research Note at the end of this chapter.) And finally, therefore, not all skinheads can be defined as terrorists. To be more precise, terrorism varies between subjects.

Research Design

This natural variation between subjects serves as the basis for the study's research design. Because of their own natural differences, I was able to divide the sample into two groups: terrorists and non-terrorists. To be classified as terrorists, subjects had to meet three criteria: (1) they must have indicated that they joined their group to fight for the survival of their race (thereby establishing grounds for the political or social objectives of their violence), (2) they must have engaged in one or two fights in which, (3) at least half were against people of another race (thus satisfying the operational definitions of both terrorism and hate crime). Based on these criteria, I identified twenty-two terrorists and fourteen non-terrorists.

Comparisons of between-subject variations on terrorism lend themselves to the study of theoretical concerns. The diagram in Figure 7.1 (Research Design) accommodates the study of terrorists and non-terrorists (row comparisons) by each set of theoretically relevant variables—functionalist, neo-Marxist, and differential identification-reinforcement (column comparisons). Despite some degree of overlap between these perspectives, this design guides our determination of whether the results are consistent with the following three broad theoretical expectations:

1. Terrorism is a function of rebellion against dominant ideologies (functionalist perspective).
2. Terrorism is a function of subcultural style (neo-Marxist perspective).
3. Terrorism is a function of associations with and rewards provided by Tom Metzger (differential identification-reinforcement perspective).

Figure 7.1
Research Design

Group	Theoretical Perspective		
	Functionalist	Neo-Marxist	Differential Identification-Reinforcement
Terrorists			
Non-terrorists			

TERRORISM AND REBELLION

I began the study of functionalist variables by asking a question about class origin. Following the research path of Stephen Baron (1989), I focused on parental occupation and designed the measure as a simple blue-collar/white-collar/unemployed trichotomy.

By these criteria, Table 7.3 (Class Origin) shows that the majority of terrorists (77 percent) came from blue-collar backgrounds. Conversely, the majority of the non-terrorists came from white-collar backgrounds. Only one terrorist reported that his father was unemployed most of the time (and none of the non-terrorists' fathers were unemployed). The statistic at the bottom of Table 7.3 indicates that these differences are significant.

As such, these data are consistent with functionalist expectations: Terrorists come from predominantly lower-class backgrounds. The average father of a terrorist was either a construction worker, factory worker, truckdriver, carpenter, or common laborer. For example, a New York City terrorist angrily recalled that,

Table 7.3
Class Origin ($N = 36$)

	Background			
	White-Collar	Blue-Collar	Unemployed	Unknown
Terrorists	4	17	1	0
Non-terrorists	10	2	0	2

$X^2 = 16.44$, $df = 3$, $p < .05$

"My father was a cabinet maker. He worked his ass off for fifty years and now he don't have a fuckin' pot to piss in."

In contrast, the fathers of non-terrorists were lawyers, accountants, business-men, teachers, and military officers. A non-terrorist from Texas described her background like this:

My dad was a corporal in the military. In the Marines, I think. He was just real conserva-tive and I grew up thinkin' real conservative too. It just seemed, ya' know, like the thing ta' do! Be a skinhead. Plus, I liked the look. Ya' know, the Fred Perry's 'n' Doc Martens – all that. I just liked the way they looked.

Goals

The mainspring of the functionalist perspective is that underclass youth who experience frustration when the means to attain goals are blocked dismiss domi-nant goals and replace them with goals that can be met through subcultural par-ticipation. In this regard, the experience of youth in the school is cited by functionalist theorists as a major factor in the formation of deviant subcultures because while in school youths recognize that the means to attain future employ-ment opportunities are blocked. Simply put, functionalist theorists predict that terrorism is an outgrowth of rejecting dominant goals associated with education and employment. To test for these expectations, the skinheads were questioned about their future aspirations concerning school and work.

The first set of findings are displayed in Table 7.4 (Educational Goals). The majority of terrorists (55 percent) said they planned to attend college in the fu-ture. Thirty-one percent of the terrorists planned on earning a trade school di-ploma, and the remainder were still in high school and their goal was to graduate. None of the terrorists indicated that they had "no goals" for their future educa-tion. Thus, contrary to theoretical predictions, these terrorists had not abandoned their educational goals on entry into the skinhead subculture. Instead, school was seen as a valuable use of their time because it promised to provide them with marketable skills.

By comparison, less than half of the non-terrorists embraced the goal of attend-ing college, none of them were planning to attend trade school, and one was

Table 7.4
Educational Goals ($N = 36$)

	Attend College	High School Diploma	Trade School Diploma	None
		Goal		
Terrorists	12	3	7	0
Non-terrorists	6	1	0	7

$X^2 = 16.01$, $df = 3$, $p < .05$

planning to graduate from high school. However, fully one-half of the non-terrorists reported that they had no goals for their future education. Therefore, the achievement ideology had not been internalized by non-terrorists as well as it had by terrorists. The statistic at the bottom of Table 7.4 shows that these differences are also significant. As such, they are inconsistent with functionalist expectations.

This pattern of inconsistency with functionalist predictions also runs through Table 7.5 (Occupational Goals). The majority of terrorists (68 percent) planned on blue-collar jobs in the future, and the remainder planned on white-collar jobs. As before, none of the terrorists rejected the dominant goal out-of-hand. Also as before, none of the non-terrorists planned on blue-collar work in the future. Instead, the vast majority (93 percent) planned on white-collar jobs. And last, one of the non-terrorists said she had no goals for future employment.

Means

For terrorists, the foregoing discussion implies that their opportunities to achieve the dominant goals of American society are not blocked. Instead, they demonstrate a strong internalization of the dominant ideology described by functionalist theorists. In the language of functionalist sociology, therefore, these terrorists are properly defined as conformists.

Functionalists also predict that attending postsecondary educational institu-

Table 7.5
Occupational Goals

	White-Collar Job	Blue-Collar Job	None
	Goal		
Terrorists	7	15	0
Non-terrorists	13	0	1

$X^2 = 16.85$, $df = 2$, $p < .05$

tions represents the most obvious means for youth to reach their occupational goals in life (see Downes, 1966). Table 7.6 (Educational Status) provides evidence that these postsecondary educational means may be well within reach of the subjects. Of the twenty-two terrorists studied here, 32 percent were currently enrolled in college. In fact, two terrorists were enrolled in law school and one was a graduate student in fine arts. Yet only 21 percent of the non-terrorists were enrolled in college. Nearly equal proportions of terrorists and non-terrorists were recent high school graduates, and an equal number of the younger skinheads were currently attending high school on a regular basis. Only three subjects in the entire sample (all terrorists) were high school dropouts (one was in prison, and the other two were employed as common laborers). In sum, both terrorists and non-terrorists were conformists in their accessibility and commitment to mainstream education (i.e., there was no statistical difference in their current educational status).

Table 7.6
Educational Status ($N = 36$)

	Current Status			
	Enrolled in College	High School Graduate	Enrolled in High School	High School Dropout
Terrorists	7	10	2	3
Non-terrorists	3	9	2	0

$X^2 = 3.02$, $df = 3$, p = n.s.

This pattern of conformist behavior among terrorists is confirmed again in Table 7.7 (Occupational Status). The majority of terrorists (81 percent) were currently employed at blue-collar jobs. These included occupations such as a stonemason, factory worker, carpenter, construction worker, pipe fitter, fisherman, electrician, railroader, department store clerk, secretary, janitor, short-order cook, and dishwasher (incarcerated subjects were asked to list their most recent

Table 7.7
Occupational Status ($N = 35$)

	Current Status		
	White-Collar Job	Blue-Collar Job	No Job
Terrorists	2	17	1
Non-terrorists	7	3	4

$X^2 = 12.33$, $df = 2$, $p < .05$

employment). By contrast, only three (21 percent) of the non-terrorists held blue-collar jobs. Consistent with their respective class origins, 50 percent of the non-terrorists held white-collar jobs, and only two terrorists (10 percent) wore white collars to work (one was the chef at a large restaurant, and the other was an independent businessman). Consistent with previous findings, Table 7.7 shows that only one terrorist was unemployed; whereas more than a quarter of the non-terrorists (29 percent) were unemployed. These differences are also statistically significant.

This means that terrorists overwhelmingly embraced the American work ethic, yet non-terrorists only halfheartedly embraced it. Yet what is even more striking about the conformism of terrorists is that more than a third of them worked and went to school at the same time! A close inspection of the data in Tables 7.6 and 7.7 reveals that 36 percent of the terrorists who went to school, also held down jobs. This cannot be said, however, for the "rebellious" non-terrorists.

In summary, the foregoing analysis shows that the most dangerous skinheads are socially homogeneous. That is, terrorist youth subcultures appear to be largely inhabited by conformists who exhibit almost hyperactive levels of acceptance of the dominant American social order. They are not rebels at all. This is a finding that functionalist sociology fails to predict altogether.

The Family

The functionalists point out that the family is an important conduit for passing on dominant norms to children. The functionalists predict that children may not always be close to the family, however. Thus, dominant norms are downplayed in the family circle, and this leads to rebellion against dominant ideologies (see also Gottfredson and Hirschi, 1990). These issues are crudely summarized in Table 7.8 (Family Experiences) in three categories: nonfriction, friction, and violence. As the data show, there are no significant differences between terrorists and non-terrorists.

The majority of terrorists (72 percent) reported that they got along with their families and fully 100 percent of the non-terrorists reported nonfriction at home. Yet 22 percent of the terrorists did report chronic friction in the family, and one

Table 7.8
Family Experiences ($N = 36$)

	Presence of Friction		
	Nonfriction	Friction	Violence
Terrorists	16	5	1
Non-terrorists	14	0	0

$X^2 = 4.58$, $df = 2$, $p =$ n.s.

terrorist indicated that he was violently abused by his parents. (This subject was in prison at the time of the study.)

In summary, family experiences do not appear to be important predictors of terrorism. Thus, contrary to the theoretical reckonings of Gottfredson and Hirschi (1990) and the research conclusions drawn by the FBI (see Anderson, 1990), family friction does not appear to be a necessary antecedent of organized terrorism.

Early Childhood Experiences

Recent studies on the social and psychological profiles of domestic and international terrorists confirm the functionalist perspective in two ways: First, these studies show that when terrorists were children, they frequently experienced life-threatening illnesses that frightened them severely. And second, terrorists often developed a profound sense of hopelessness during their childhoods. The mixture of severe hopelessness and fear experienced in early childhood then led these persons to deny the risk of death later in life by placing themselves in life-threatening situations. In turn, this wager against the forces of death gave these persons the emotional capacity to commit acts of terrorism.

Tables 7.9 (Childhood Illnesses) and 7.10 (Childhood Feelings of Extreme Hopelessness) test for these expectations among the skinheads in the present study. As we see, these variables carry little freight. Table 7.9 shows that no one reported life-threatening illnesses while young, and Table 7.10 reveals that only a small and equal number of terrorists and non-terrorists alike reported "feelings of extreme hopelessness." Once again, the functionalist perceptive provides little explanatory power regarding terrorist youth subcultures.

TERRORISM AND STYLE

The British neo-Marxists predict that youths engage in acts of terrorism as largely symbolic acts of resistance against the power-elites who are responsible for establishing cultural hegemony. British neo-Marxists have theorized that when youths join a subculture, they inherit a positive reference group that supplies social support facilitating the emergence of a counterculture ideology.

Table 7.9
Childhood Illnesses ($N = 36$)

	Presence of Early Illness	
	Yes	No
Terrorists	0	22
Non-terrorists	0	14

Note: X^2 statistics cannot be computed when the number of nonempty rows or columns is one.

Table 7.10
Childhood Feelings of Extreme Hopelessness ($N = 36$)

	Presence of Extreme Hopelessness	
	Yes	No
Terrorists	1	22
Non-terrorists	2	12

$X^2 = 1.06$, $df = 1$, $p = $ n.s.

According to the neo-Marxists, the counterculture ideology is manifested in subcultural style that represents the active resistance against the forces responsible for creating cultural hegemony.

Skinhead style—like the style of the punks, rockers, hard mods, new wavers, beats, and hippies—is read in the text of contemporary music. This music is then reflected in politics, hairstyle, costume, jewelry, and symbolic terrorism. Moreover, skinhead music is thought to support a political belief system and a subcultural style that allows skinheads to display their resistance to cultural hegemony in visual terms for the general public to see: shaved heads, Nazi regalia, stormtrooper boots, and violence against blacks and other disenfranchised groups. Therefore, I organize the analysis of the neo-Marxist perspective on terrorist youth subcultures around the complex relationships between skinhead music, politics, and counterculture style.

Skinhead Music

Neo-Marxists predict that skinhead ideology is developed and sustained by white power rock. This music, with its intense social content, raises the political consciousness of skinheads. Once this has occurred, terrorism is only a matter of style. Table 7.11 (Musical Preference) represents a quantitative attempt to examine this issue. Each subject was asked to respond to the following item: "Perhaps the most important aspect of youth culture is music. List your favorite bands (beginning with your most favorite)." (When interviews were conducted on a face-to-face basis, subjects were simply asked, "What's your favorite band?")

Table 7.11
Musical Preference ($N = 36$)

	Favorite Band	
	Skrewdriver	Other
Terrorists	20	2
Non-terrorists	3	11

$X^2 = 17.90$, $df = 1$, $p < .05$

Table 7.11 reports the most unequivocal finding of the study thus far. We see that terrorist preference in music is homogeneous. A total of twenty terrorists (91 percent) reported that their favorite band was Skrewdriver. One terrorist listed the classical composer Ludwig van Beethoven as his favorite, and another listed the blues rocker George Thoroughgood and the Destroyers as her favorite band (neither of which have anything to do with the anger of youth or a critique of the social order).

The table shows a wider variety of music preferred by the non-terrorists. Although three (21 percent) non-terrorists listed Skrewdriver as their favorite band, an equal number cited the British band Slade as their favorite. And here, the distinctions between terrorists and non-terrorists become even more intriguing.

Slade preceded Skrewdriver as a London skinhead band by more than a decade. Emerging from the first-generation British skinhead scene around 1971, Slade had its roots in early reggae music. Although Slade espoused beliefs that were no doubt racist, they were not a neo-Nazi band. The pattern of diversity among the non-terrorists also extended to other forms of British rock: two non-terrorists listed the Clash as their favorite band, one listed the new wave band the Jam as a favorite, and four listed the Skrewdriver clone bands, Brutal Attack, No Remorse, and Ra Ho Ah as their favorites.

Further confirmation of the homogeneous nature of terrorist preference in music comes from an inspection of other frequently listened to bands. In this regard, terrorists were more likely than non-terrorists to limit their choice of music to white power rock. Among the frequently listened to bands, terrorists preferred the music of Last Resort, Midtown Boot Boys, Brutal Attack, War Zone, Danzig, No Surrender, White Noise, and Doc Marten. Seven terrorists also reported that they frequently listened to American country western artists such as Merle Haggard, Dwight Yoakum, Conway Twitty, and Hank Williams, Jr. Four terrorists reported that they also listened to the classical music of Beethoven, Vivaldi, Stravinsky, and Mozart; and four terrorists listed the early Who and Beatles as frequently listened to bands. Contrary to popular beliefs about the skinheads, only one terrorist reported listening to a speed metal band (Metallica) and none reported listening to death metal.

In summary, these findings suggest that the musical preferences of skinheads are homologous with terrorism. That is, the channeling of dissent and anger through the white power rock of Skrewdriver appears to raise or reflect a political consciousness that precipitates the long-standing subcultural style of racial violence among skinheads. The following terrorist responses confirm this notion:

- Back in 1985, Skrewdriver *was* the skinhead movement. They provided the ideology for what we did back then.
- I have very diverse musical interests but as you probably guess my favorite bands are Skrewdriver and Brutal Attack. Why? Because they're radical!
- To me Skrewdriver means pride in my race and pride in my womanhood.

• I started out as a punk rocker then got into the skinhead scene. I was a "glam freak" for a while too but now I'm all the way into the European-American thing. I'm racialist, and Skrewdriver's done a job puttin' our beliefs out there.

Political Beliefs

The political element of youth subcultures has been debated in the neo-Marxist literature. On one hand, researchers argue that music serves to raise the political consciousness of subcultural members. Yet on the other hand, researchers suggest that the political element translated through music fails to confront the individual problems of subcultural members (Baron, 1989; Brake, 1985; Frith, 1978; Laing, 1985; Marsh, 1977; Muncie, 1981). Yet missing from this debate among the neo-Marxists is a clear definition of political beliefs and a systematic analysis of the ways in which musical messages manifest themselves in violence. Next, I attempt to grapple with these issues. Such a task, however, demands a brief digression.

As discussed in chapter 2, Skrewdriver's music is based on a complex fantasy that has produced a sort of occult-oriented bully boy appeal for a clean white European social order in which the mythical Viking reemerges as a noble warrior and hero of the Skrewdriver pipe dream. Skrewdriver's music is, therefore, dominated by themes of masculinity, racism, and violence. Skrewdriver's style, in turn, reflects a celebration of the modern day Viking—the German Nazi. It was in this way, after an initial flirtation with punk music, that the swastika, the SS insignia, the Iron Cross and other Third Reich regalia became Skrewdriver symbols, and ultimately, symbols for the entire Skinhead Nation. Hence, an analysis of the moral meaning of these two signifiers—the Viking and the Nazi—should serve as a springboard for understanding of the political values of those skinheads who have become so enamored with Skrewdriver's brand of white power rock.

Vikings History reveals that the Vikings were a barbaric culture that pillaged and plundered the European continent more than a thousand years ago. The earliest Viking attack on England recorded in the *Anglo-Saxon Chronicle* exemplifies their vicious nature:

In the year 793, the pagans from the North came with a force of ships to Britain like stinging hornets and spread out on all sides like terrible wolves, robbed, tore, and slaughtered not only beasts of burden, but even priests and deacons, and companies of monks and nuns. And they came to the church at Lindesfarne and laid everything to waste. (quoted in Poertner, 1971:152)

A later account of Viking brutality reads:

When the Norse marauders took Nantes by storm in 843, they started a senseless bloodbath slaughtering men and women alike, and in the sheer exuberance tossed infants to each other as [if] they were playing ball, to catch on their spears. (Poertner, 1971:152)

History also indicates that when Vikings were on the warpath they adopted a style known as berserking. To go berserk meant that Vikings were "raging, half-mad, and insensate. They went into battle without armor, like mad dogs or wolves, biting their shields, strong like bears or bulls, mowing down everything in their path" (Poertner, 1971:152). Down through the years, the Vikings have come to represent a mighty nation of powerful men who possessed enormous courage and fighting skill. As one historian comments: "The Vikings did not know the meaning of the word defeat—they never turned their backs on their enemies but slayed or were slain" (Gibson, 1972:15).

Historians write that Viking morality was sustained by a fantasy-oriented pagan religion. The Viking god Odin represented the supreme Nordic man as he was said to be able to turn himself into a bear or a wolf or a bird when necessary (Donovan, 1964). Yet it was the god Thor who became the ultimate Aryan warrior because "he rumbled through the clouds on his chariot, roaring and bawling, looking for a fight and finding it every time" (Poertner, 1971:232).

Nazis At the height of their popularity, Skrewdriver proclaimed that they would "follow the example of the one incorruptible ideal—National Socialism, and its great martyr Adolf Hitler" (quoted in *Cable Street Beat* review, n.d.:4). As envisaged by Hitler, national socialism represented a coherent program of action based on three major concepts: anti-Semitism, the social Darwinian belief that struggle was the basis of all human existence, and a newfound conviction that Germany's destiny lay in conquering the whole of Europe (Carr, 1976). Also known as natural law, the law of history, or biological determinism, social Darwinism was interpreted by the Nazis to mean that a stronger nation possessed a natural right to dominate or even exterminate weaker nations in the general struggle for survival (Von Maltitz, 1973). In essence, the Nazis believed that by annihilating inferior races, they were fulfilling a historical mission.

These natural laws, unlike human laws, were thought to operate necessarily and logically beyond the pale of good and evil, right or wrong. In Nazi Germany's struggle for dominance, therefore, all ethical and legal considerations were suspended. Under such a philosophy, the individual German soldier became "a willing participant in the implementation of supreme laws and if he violated man-made laws, he would be immune from prosecution or moral blame" (Von Maltitz, 1973). As a member of the master race, an individual would be able to free himself of orthodox values and suppress moral scruples, "in a word, he was able to conquer his very moral self" (Wegner, 1982:27). And in this way, the most horrendous acts of oppression and extermination became special proofs of heroic moral virtue and patriotic allegiance to the state.

The supreme form of law enforcement and political control under Nazi rule was the SS Death's Head Battalion administered by Reichsfuhrer Heinrich Himmler. The SS, or *Schutzstaffeln*, was "characterized by both its fighting spirit and combat effectiveness in defeat as well as victory and by its ruthless behavior in the execution of political and military tasks against enemy soldiers and civilians"

(Snydor, 1977:314). According to another historian, the SS "was based on the
. . . combination of primitive instincts and lust for cruelty with a fanatical conviction of the higher legitimacy of such crimes" (Bracher, 1976:223). During
Nazi rule, soldiers of the SS were held up as "the model for National Socialism as
they represented loyalty, unconditional obedience, and readiness for self-sacri-
fice" (Baird, 1990:212). About the SS, Himmler once said that "death holds no
string for us because individuals die while the people live on." He was referring,
of course, to Aryan people only.

Concerned more with the future of the Aryan race than with his own safety, the
SS officer "would bravely and willingly seek death whenever necessary" (Baird,
1990:213). Ever present in the SS campaign—especially at rallies attended by the
Fuhrer—was the theatrical pathos of Richard Wagner's operas, an elaborate system of propaganda activities, and a cult of uniforms that attracted large sectors of
the German populace—especially youth—who inevitably became politically integrated and committed to SS policies and procedures (Arendt, 1963; Bracher,
1976; Mommsen, 1976). These politics of energy—fueled by music, propaganda, and uniforms—influenced not only the ideological goals of Nazism but
also the organization of a mass counterrevolutionary movement displaying overwhelming power and leader worship of Adolf Hitler.

Skrewdriver The primitive instincts and primal emotions of the barbaric Viking were incorporated into skinhead music as a resignification of the Viking
image that promoted Nazism. Skrewdriver viewed the Nazis as something other
than a gangster regime which had destroyed traditional social, cultural, and political structures throughout Europe only to proliferate corruption, administrative
mediocrity, and crimes of historical proportions (see Mommsen, 1976). Instead,
Skrewdriver created a musical text based on historical revisionism: Skrewdriver
portrayed the Nazis as heroic and honorable warriors who gallantly defended the
Aryan culture from outside influences. Subsequently, violence against minorities
and homosexuals became the taproot of Skrewdriver's fantasy because violence
was an explicit, functional, and real way of promoting and defending the inner
values of national socialism—faith, sincerity, loyalty, rigidity, decency, and above
all else, courage (see Bracher, 1976). Through this mystical, romantic, and anti-
intellectual cult of feeling, Skrewdriver's music appears to have offered skinheads
the perverted moral energy necessary to commit acts of paki bashing, queer
bashing, and terrorism.

Fascism The actions of Nazi Germany against Jews in Germany, Poland, Romania, Holland, and France have been the object of countless reports and polemics, and of extensive research and interpretation. These actions have prompted
political scientists, psychologists, and sociologists to study the social and psychological nature of the German people who ultimately became ubiquitously
complicitous in the greatest crime in human history—the Holocaust. As Hannah
Arendt has so eloquently written, "the Holocaust . . . was no ordinary crime,
and the . . . criminal, . . . was no common criminal" (1963:224).

The earliest accounting of the inner logic leading to this crime was recorded by

Erich Fromm (1941) in his tract entitled *Escape from Freedom*. Fromm's work provided a meticulous analysis of the German character structure (or personality) of that day. He concluded that within the personalities of Western Europeans, and especially in the lower-middle class of Germany, was an authoritarian character structure that made possible the cruel efficiency and superhuman willpower of the Nazi regime.

Fromm used the term *authoritarian* to describe the character structure of Germans because the term corresponded to the functioning of authority in Fascist political and social affairs. This authority, in turn, served as the basis for the ideas and emotions forming the nucleus of Nazism. Essentially, the concepts *authoritarian* and *fascistic* were interchangeable under Fromm's formulation. In his words, "By the term 'authoritarian character,' we imply that it represents the personality structure which is the human basis of Fascism" (Fromm, 1941:164).

After the war, Fromm's ideas were studied by Theodor Adorno and his colleagues at the University of California. Known as the Berkeley studies, Adorno et al. (1950) published a series of investigations on fascism in a 990-page volume, *The Authoritarian Personality*. Adorno's work would ultimately create a social psychological paradigm for the study of fascism. That is, research on fascism applies less to superleaders of social and political movements, and more to the broad spectrum of participants in those movements — such as lower-class Germans of the 1930s who came to dominate the ranks of the SS (see Arendt, 1963; Dillehay, 1978; Linz, 1976; Mommsen, 1976).

In essence, this research paradigm is used to unmask and dissect fascist mentality within broad populations. In the view of Adorno and his colleagues, a person with this mentality has (1) a strong need to align him or herself with authority figures and protective in-groups, (2) a strong sense of nationalism, rigid moralism, and definiteness, and (3) a strong tendency to perceive things in absolute terms, that is, as all good or all bad (Rosenthal and Rosnow, 1984).

As any student of social psychology knows, the work of Adorno et al. (1950) led to the creation of the Fascism Scale (or the well-known "F Scale"). The F Scale has proven to be one of the most reliable measures in all of the social sciences (see Dillehay, 1978; Pettigrew, 1981). The F Scale contains thirty-eight questions that are broken down into nine different scales, yet each scale represents a syndrome of factors correlated with the authoritative personality structure. Hence, if "a person displays a considerable amount of one or several of these [factors], he or she is likely to be characterized by others as well" (Dillehay, 1978:93). One set of factors called the authoritarian aggression scale is measured by seven items. Dillehay has defined the seven items like this:

These items were written to measure the tendency of the authoritarian to aggress against out-groups, chiefly minority groups, the weak, people who hold different values, and so on. The items presumably tap the dual aspect of authoritarian aggression: the very narrow limits of acceptance of behavior in other people and the tendency to engage in projection. In regard to the first of these, the authoritarian can be thought of as a kind of *emotional cripple*. (Dillehay, 1978:94, emphasis added).

The Skinhead as an Emotional Cripple

Each skinhead was asked to respond to the seven-item authoritarian aggression scale. Each item was randomly interspersed within a broader series of items, and each subject was asked to indicate agreement, disagreement, or uncertainty with each item by use of the following coding system: agree = 3, uncertain = 2, and disagree = 1. Based on this scoring system, "A low scorer is a person whose psychological universe is relatively wide. . . . He expects differences between people and is tolerant of them. A high scorer, by contrast, is a person who moves in very narrow circles. . . . He does not recognize the existence of a range of values and approaches, and is intolerant of differences" (Kelman and Barclay, 1963:608).

The neo-Marxist theorists would expect terrorists—homogeneous in their musical preference for Skrewdriver—to score higher on this portion of the F Scale than non-terrorists. These findings are reported in Table 7.12 (F Scale Measures). First, subjects were presented with this item: "A person who has bad manners, habits, and breeding can hardly expect to get along with decent people. What do you think of that statement?" Consistent with theoretical expectations, Table 7.12 shows that terrorists scored significantly higher on this item than non-terrorists; hence, they were more fascistic in their attitudes toward minorities. In this vein, the terrorist leader of a Detroit skinhead group reported that, "Niggers can't compete in a modern technological society. They're just fuckin' things up by being here. . . . We ought to send them back to Africa."

Second, subjects were asked to respond to this item: "What the youth needs is strict discipline, rugged determination, and the will to work and fight for family and country." Here terrorist agreement was nearly perfect (91 percent approval), yet their responses did not differ from those of non-terrorists.

The third item, "An insult to your honor should always be punished," also failed to discriminate between subjects. Likewise, no significant differences were found in responses to the fourth item: "Sex crimes, such as rape and attacks on children, deserve more than mere imprisonment; such criminals ought to be publicly whipped or worse." Here the terrorists were in total agreement (100 percent approval). In fact, several subjects called for even more strident forms of punishment for sex offenders. The leader of the Bronx Area Skinheads, for instance, believed that "all sex offenders ought to be castrated." Yet the majority of non-terrorists also agreed with this sentiment.

Responses to the fifth F Scale item also produced insignificant differences. Subjects were presented with the item: "There is hardly anything lower than a person who does not feel a great love, gratitude, and respect for his parents." Table 7.12 shows that terrorist responses were extremely ambivalent; all but eight of them said they were not sure about the item. Although non-terrorists were even less sure about the issue, differences were again insignificant.

Consistent and significant differences between subjects reappear, however, on the final two F Scale measures. The sixth item was "Most of our social problems would be solved if we could somehow get rid of the immoral, crooked, and fee-

Table 7.12

F Scale Measures ($N = 36$)

ITEM: "A person who has bad manners, habits, and breeding can hardly expect to get along with decent people."

Responses of Subjects

	Agree	Not Sure	Disagree
Terrorists	17	5	0
Non-terrorists	4	2	8

$X^2 = 16.36$, $df = 2$, $p < .05$

ITEM: "What the youth needs is strict discipline, rugged determination, and the will to work and fight for family and country."

Responses of Subjects

	Agree	Not Sure	Disagree
Terrorists	21	1	0
Non-terrorists	10	3	1

$X^2 = 4.33$, $df = 2$, $p =$ n.s.

ITEM: "An insult to your honor should always be punished."

Subject Responses

	Agree	Not Sure	Disagree
Terrorists	13	5	4
Non-terrorists	6	7	1

$X^2 = 3.08$, $df = 2$, $p =$ n.s.

ITEM: "Sex crimes, such as rape and attacks on children, deserve more than mere imprisonment; such criminals ought to be publicly whipped or worse."

Subject Responses

	Agree	Not Sure	Disagree
Terrorists	22	0	0
Non-terrorists	12	2	0

$X^2 = 3.22$, $df = 1$, $p =$ n.s.

Table 7.12   (Continued)

ITEM: "There is hardly anything lower than a person who does not feel a great love, gratitude, and respect for his parents."

Subject Responses

	Agree	Not Sure	Disagree
Terrorists	3	14	5
Non-terrorists	2	6	6

$X^2 = 1.80$, $df = 2$, $p = $ n.s.

ITEM: "Most of our social problems would be solved if we could somehow get rid of the immoral, crooked, and feeble-minded people."

Subject Responses

	Agree	Not Sure	Disagree
Terrorists	22	0	0
Non-terrorists	8	6	0

$X^2 = 11.31$, $df = 1$, $p < .05$

ITEM: "Homosexuals are hardly any better than criminals and ought to be severely punished."

Subject Responses

	Agree	Not Sure	Disagree
Terrorists	16	6	0
Non-terrorists	7	0	7

$X^2 = 15.50$, $df = 2$, $p < .05$

ble-minded people." As the table shows, fully 100 percent of the terrorists agreed whereas 43 percent of the non-terrorists were unsure about this issue. Informal comments made by the terrorists on this item left no doubt concerning the identity of those perceived as "immoral, crooked, and feeble-minded people." On several questionnaires, terrorists—after agreeing with the item—crossed out the word *people* and replaced it with the word *Jews;* one left the mark of the swastika to demonstrate the intensity of his views, and a Michigan terrorist reasoned that: "The White man is nature's finest creature who, as the Jews say, 'are cattle ready for slaughter.' "

Last, subjects were presented with this item: "Homosexuals are hardly better than criminals and ought to be severely punished." In this case, terrorists were significantly more homophobic than were non-terrorists.

In summary, terrorists can be distinguished from non-terrorists on three counts. First, terrorists are more likely to focus their hostility against people they perceive to have "bad manners, habits, and breeding." This is the essence of racism, and this finding is consistent with the seminal work of Adorno et al. (1950) who discovered intense levels of intergroup prejudice among criminals.

Second, terrorists are more likely to advocate "getting rid of immoral, crooked, and feeble-minded people." This finding is consistent with the discoveries made by Richard Hofstadter (1967) who argues that those who espouse fascist beliefs are especially responsive to conspiracy theories of social, political, and economic events. In Ronald Dillehay's ever-insightful words, "The essence of conspiracy theories is that they forecast imminent doom for cherished values and institutions, with the impending disaster attributed to a carefully conceived plan of action surreptitiously controlled and conditioned by a diabolical enemy" (1978:112). The diabolical enemy of American skinhead folklore is, of course, ZOG.

Third, terrorists are more likely to hold strong opinions about homosexuals. This finding is also consistent with the Berkeley studies that demonstrate authoritarians typically hold negative attitudes toward a broad range of out-groups (Adorno et al., 1950). It is also consistent with research conducted by political scientists who have found a revolt against the decadence of homosexuality to be an important historical correlate of fascist youth movements in Europe (Linz, 1976).

Neo-Nazism

In order of statistical importance, Table 7.12 indicates that the defining characteristics of terrorist ideology are *racism, homophobia,* and *anti-Semitism.* Taken together, these beliefs comprise the core values of an advanced form of biological determinism. In short, the terrorist skinheads embrace an ideology reminiscent of the German Nazis.

These findings provide strong support for the neo-Marxist perspective: There appears to be a homogeneous musical preference and a coherent ideology among the American skinheads that facilitates the subcultural style of violence. This musical preference is called *Skrewdriver,* this ideology is called *neo-Nazism,* and this subcultural style is called *terrorism.* Terrorists appear to have a rigid moralism and a strong tendency to aggress against racial minorities, gays, and lesbians. Thus, through their political ideology, subcultural members confront their individual problems in a very direct and concrete fashion. Contrary to what some neo-Marxist researchers suggest, the terrorist American skinheads do not appear to seek an abstract or magical solution to their individual problems (Clarke, 1976b; Hebdige, 1979). Rather, they seek answers with baseball bats, guns, knives, brass knuckles, and steel-toed Doc Martens.

This is the essence of skinhead homology. It is confirmed by the statistics presented in Table 7.13 (Homology: Statistical Correlates). Considering the responses of all thirty-six subjects, we see a tight fit between the outstanding terrorist values of neo-Nazism (racism, homophobia, and anti-Semitism), musical preference (white power rock), and traditional skinhead style (self-reported acts of terrorism). All of the correlation coefficients (Pearson's r's) are positive and significant. Moreover, terrorism is empirically homologous with values and music.

Summary

These findings both confirm and refute previous criminological research that is pertinent to our understanding of terrorist youth subcultures. First the confirmations: the findings are similar to the claims made by Lewis Yablonsky who argues that violent subcultures are typically led by youths who exhibit sociopathic personalities (1983:ix). Such sociopathic leaders, it seems, "are unable to experience the pain of violence they may inflict on others, since they have a limited [capacity] to identify or empathize with others" outside their subculture (Yablonsky, 1983:viii).

This discovery is further confirmed by the Berkeley researchers who discovered that the degree of prejudice in a criminal was the result of implicit personality dispositions toward extreme anti-Semitism and general ethnic bigotry (Adorno et al., 1950). Such personality predispositions, according to Adorno and associates, makes such people highly susceptible to Nazi propaganda (e.g., Skrewdriver) with its emphasis on rigid conventionality and the degradation of out-groups, particularly minorities (Dillehay, 1978). In short, there appear to be important individual-level differences between violent and nonviolent skinheads (see Wilson and Herrnstein [1985] for further evidence of such psychological differences between offenders and nonoffenders).

Present findings refute previous research at several levels of analysis. To begin with, the FBI argues that "Skinheads in and of themselves . . . *do not share any common beliefs"* (quoted in Cooper, 1989:263, emphasis added). Yet the present

Table 7.13
Homology: Statistical Correlates ($N = 36$)

F Scale Item	Musical Preference	Acts of Terrorism
Attitudes toward "person who has bad manners, habits and breeding..."	.541*	.627*
Attitudes toward "...immoral, crooked, and feeble-minded people."	.594*	.485*
Attitudes toward "Homosexuals..."	.564*	.440*

$*p < .05$

data clearly imply that the most violent members of the subculture do share common beliefs about racial minorities, Jews, gays, and lesbians.

Similarly, present data refute other research conducted on the far right. After interviewing more than sixty highly prejudiced superpatriots in the midwestern United States, one group of social psychologists concluded that members of the American far right were "pleasant, considerate and law abiding" (quoted in Pettigrew, 1981:104). My data show that other members of the far right are mean-spirited, intolerant of differences, and violent.

Present findings refute claims made by gang researchers on the nature of organized violence. Yablonsky defines gang violence as a senseless act. Like several of the British neo-Marxists, Yablonsky argues that gang violence is "easy, quick and *almost magical"* (1983:viii, emphasis added). My data suggest that skinhead violence is not magical. Rather, it is a concrete and rational behavior that stems from a clearly defined ideology.

COUNTERCULTURE STYLE

Within the neo-Marxist tradition, the linchpin for understanding terrorism is subcultural style. For the neo-Marxists, style—including violence—is a "symbolic resolution offered to the conditions which, for the most part, youths are unable to transcend" (Kingsman, n.d.:2). Under this formulation, style operates as a language, or "a spectacular means of expressing lived relations," in which distinct objects, symbols and rituals (stylistic elements) congeal into a system of meaning for subcultural members (Kingsman, n.d.:2).

These elements of style are, therefore, related to one another as part of the subcultural language. Because terrorism is part of this language, I turn now to other elements of skinhead style to discern the ways in which they support terrorism. I begin by examining the most dramatic stylistic creation of the subculture.

Hairstyle

Historically, the close-shaved head of the skinhead represented a direct flaunting of antihippie sensibilities, working-class solidarity, pragmatism, and an affinity with the Jamaican rude boys of London circa 1969–1972. Because the early skinheads were from white working-class neighborhoods, a shaved head did not offend workers at the loading dock, for instance, or in the factories and pubs of London at the time. Spurred by early reggae artists such as Prince Buster and Desmond Decker—who wore short, rude-boy crops of hair—the skinheads took an item from the real world (a short haircut) and resignified it to celebrate their working-class subcultural style. This style inevitably led to the London paki bashing and queer bashing episodes of the early 1970s. It was then that the skinheads discovered a functional purpose for a shaved head, as well: a bald head cannot be grabbed in a street fight. They gained extraordinary media interest, and in time, the skinheads came to represent a worldwide subculture of hate and violence. Hence, the skinhead subculture is read most effectively in terms of the shaved head.

To assess this defining stylistic element of the subculture, subjects were studied individually in relation to their haircuts. These data are presented in Table 7.14 (Hairstyle). As we see, there are no significant differences between terrorists and non-terrorists. Yet this is a finding of some importance.

The data show that only 32 percent of the terrorists shaved their heads, while more than half of the non-terrorists (57 percent) had shaved heads. The majority of terrorists (68 percent) had hair long enough to comb. In fact, four of the terrorists had long hair reminiscent of the hippie style.

For example, one of the most active terrorists in the sample was a twenty-two-year-old white male from Milwaukee. He referred to himself as a Reverend of the Church of the Creator, and been a skinhead since the age of sixteen. He worked as a full-time pipe-fitter and was also enrolled as a business student at the University of Milwaukee. An avowed neo-Nazi, the Reverend admitted to more than five acts of terrorism against blacks over two years. At all times, he carried a silver Smith & Wesson .357 magnum pistol strapped beneath his leather jacket. He wore Doc Martens and the toes of each boot were painted red, signifying the color of blood that had been shed in his many street battles. His favorite band was Skrewdriver, and the Reverend listened to them daily. And yet, his hair was shoulder length. Here is his explanation. "I wear my hair long because it's a versatile, inconspicuous way to fight ZOG."

Costume

Thus far, the findings suggest that terrorists often do not look like skinheads, yet non-terrorists often do. To further explore this issue, I systematically examined the clothing usually worn by subjects. These findings can be explained without the conventional iteration of a statistical table.

For terrorist males, the usual look was blue jeans, T-shirts, boots, and leather jackets. For non-terrorist males there was a wider variety in clothing usually worn. They were more often dressed in first-generation skinhead clothing: Ben Sherman or Fred Perry shirts, British bobbers, and authentic donkey jackets. The dress of non-terrorist females differed from that of terrorist females, as well. Whereas terrorist females were most likely to wear clothing worn by their male

Table 7.14
Hairstyle (N = 36)

	Traditional (shaved head)	Non-Traditional (long enough to comb)
Terrorists	7	15
Non-terrorists	8	6

X^2 = 2.25, df = 1, p = n.s.

counterparts (jeans, T-shirts, and boots), non-terrorist females were likely to wear clothing reminiscent of the early British skins: Fred Perry shirts, mini-skirts, loafers, fishnet hose, and black and white skirt/blouse combinations. Said a non-terrorist from Detroit: "It's the skinhead girl look; very nice and preppy."

Jewelry and Tattoos

The study proceeds to an examination of the jewelry and tattoos worn by skin-heads. These findings can also be explained without the use of a statistical table. The majority of terrorists (87 percent) wore no jewelry at all. That is to say that the overwhelming number of terrorists did not wear a swastika, an SS badge, or other Nazi regalia; three terrorists wore brass knuckles and one wore a skull and crossbones ring. In contrast, all non-terrorists wore jewelry. For males, these included a variety of rings, swastikas, watches, biker insignias, and chain wal-lets. For females, they included "hope" earrings, bracelets, rings, necklaces, and watches.

Perhaps more instructive is the study of tattoos — whereas jewelry can be re-moved and replaced with other insignias, tattoos represent a sense of permanence and finality in one's beliefs. Although I did not systematically examine tattoos among subjects, through the interviews I did note that terrorists were tattooed with dragons, American flags, Vikings, skull and crossbones, Confederate flags, Dixie, swastikas, the grim reaper, tigers' heads, runes, wolves, and spider webs. I found no evidence of tattooing among non-terrorists.

Artistic Abilities

Similar to the functionalists, neo-Marxists argue that working-class youths ne-gotiate cultural space by refusing to adopt dominant cultural goals. As we have seen, however, this prediction does not stand up when tested among the terrorist American skinheads of this study. In fact, the data strongly suggest that terrorists firmly internalize both the goals and the means of the dominant culture. Yet the neo-Marxists differ from the functionalists in that they predict that youths enter the subculture to attain status via subcultural criteria and, therefore, escape their class and occupation symbolically through the expression of style (Brake, 1985; Hebdige, 1979; Muncie, 1981). One such criteria of subcultural status, accord-ing to the neo-Marxists, is participation in art, music, and literature. Hence, the British neo-Marxists have discovered that punk and skinhead subcultures are typ-ically dominated by working-class artists.

To examine this issue, subjects were questioned about their artistic abilities. These data are presented in Table 7.15 (Artistic Abilities). Two terrorists (10 percent) and four non-terrorists (23 percent) reported that they were musicians in skinhead rock bands. Nearly one-fourth of the terrorists and 42 percent of the non-terrorists reported that they wrote poetry or short stories; and 29 percent of the terrorists and one non-terrorist reported artistic capabilities in painting.

Table 7.15
Artistic Abilities (N = 36)

	Play Music	Writing Poetry or Fiction	Painting	No Abilities
Terrorists	2	5	6	9
Non-terrorists	4	5	1	4

$X^2 = 8.40$, $df = 6$, $p = $ n.s.

On their face, these data do not show significant differences. However, when analyzed for breadth of involvement in the arts, terrorists appeared to be more active than non-terrorists, as a greater percentage of them cited abilities in all three areas: music, literature, and painting. In addition to playing music and writing material for racist rock bands, the terrorists also reported that they wrote book reviews, editorials, and poems for the underground press. Others reported that they drew pictures and cartoons for the underground press, and produced handbills and flyers depicting their beliefs in what they called the white power movement.

CONCLUSIONS

Three central conclusions can be drawn about terrorist American skinheads. First, they are not rebels in the classic sociological sense. Instead, they are working-class conformists with a hyperactive commitment to the goals and means of the dominant American culture. They are often multitalented; they seem to be dedicated workers and responsible students; some are even tattooed with the American flag and listen to Merle Haggard on occasion.

Second, terrorist skinheads prefer the white power rock of Skrewdriver to all other music. Skrewdriver boldly espouses beliefs in neo-Nazism, and terrorists hold neo-Nazi beliefs about blacks, Jews, gays, and lesbians. Music and values, therefore, are homologous with terrorism. In this way, neo-Marxist sociology offers a powerful exegetic tool for understanding the emergence of terrorist youth subcultures.

The third conclusion we can draw is that the traditional skinhead style is in a state of flux in America. Most terrorist skinheads do not look like skinheads at all. It appears that most of them do not "shave-up" as they say within the subculture; none of them wear donkey jackets, red suspenders, or Ben Shermans. They do not wear swastikas or SS badges anymore. Perhaps they are too busy going to school and working at blue-collar jobs. Or perhaps they are too busy dodging law enforcement agents for their unprecedented string of hate crimes. Indeed, perhaps the neo-Nazi look has become too conspicuous for the skinhead subculture, and they have collectively decided to clean up their act.

This raises a compelling question: Why did the skinhead style change so dramatically once it was exported to the United States? Despite the contribution to theoretical discourse on skinheads made by the neo-Marxists, their perspective cannot answer this question. That is, the neo-Marxists treat the subject of style as if it were a static physical property. They cannot explain, for example, why the American skinheads have recently adopted ZOG and the idea that this fantasized political structure ought to be toppled by committing acts of terrorism against disenfranchised out-groups. ZOG is not mentioned in the Skrewdriver text, nor is it manifested in traditional skinhead jewelry, costume, or art. Yet it has become an obvious organizing principle for some of the most violent skinheads in this study. In short, the British neo-Marxists cannot explain changes in skinhead style. I attempt to do so through reference to another anthropological concept, bricolage.

The American Skinhead Bricolage

The word *bricolage* was translated from Late Latin into French about A.D. 1500. Literally translated, *bricolage* means "tinker with something." In colloquial terms, the word has come to mean "odd job," "handyman," or "shit work" among the French working class.

Yet among neo-Marxists, the concept has come to achieve major theoretical importance. Within British sociology, bricolage refers to the transference of meaning or tinkering that must occur with an object before it can be assimilated into subcultural style. Bricolage is, moreover, an extraordinary research paradigm for understanding the changes that have occurred in the American skinhead subculture.

To understand bricolage, let's consider the first generation of London skinheads. They took objects available in mainstream culture (short hair, dockworker boots, stay-pressed trousers, Ben Sherman shirts) and altered their definitions to suit subcultural style. A later generation of London skinheads came along to tinker with the Viking, the swastika, the SS badge, shaved heads, Doc Martens, wolves, and eagles.

Hence, skinheads are bricoleurs by nature. They have taken everything from the Viking and the Nazi to dockworker boots, and shaved heads and resignified these objects to celebrate and reinforce subcultural style. It would follow, then, that American skinheads are bricoleurs as well. In this vein, it seems that terrorists have taken objects available in the extreme far right of American politics, and tinkered with them thereby redefining the skinhead style. Fading quickly from the subculture is the pageantry of the early British and American neo-Nazi skinheads—the shaved heads, the swastika, and other symbols of the subculture. And in their place has come a caricature of Order leader Robert Mathews.

On July 14, 1984, Mathews led thirteen members of the Order in their armed robbery of the Brinks security truck near rural Ukiah, California. The Brink's truck robbery was, moreover, an ingenious crime. Thirteen men had used one machine gun to steal $3.8 million in less than fifteen minutes, leaving no one injured. The Order committed this crime wearing a definite costume. Each member of the group was dressed in blue jeans, a white T-shirt, and tennis shoes or boots. Like Mathews, each member of the Order had hair long enough to comb. They wore no jewelry, and none of them was branded with the swastika. It was, essentially, an inconspicuous way to fight ZOG. Two months later, Mathews and two of his companions assassinated Denver radio personality Allen Berg in another inconspicuous attack against the fantasy of ZOG. Shortly thereafter, Robert Mathews was killed by the FBI. He then became a legend in the white power movement, redefining the American skinhead style.

RESEARCH NOTE

Four issues warrant further explanation: the validity of self-report measures, the operationalization of terrorism, statistical power, and F Scale reliability.

1. *The Validity of Self-Report Measures.* As noted, subjects were asked to report on the total number of fights they had participated in during the previous two years. This raises an obvious question: Why should we expect subjects to be accurate and honest in admitting their violence?

Perhaps the most effective response to this question comes from subjects themselves. One terrorist reported that he was "interested in helping to get rid of all the false myths and stereotypes about the white power movement"; another said that his group "had nothing to hide"; and another said he was "proud of fighting niggers and would gladly do it again." Yet there are more scholarly reasons for utilizing self-report data in the present study.

Most importantly, there is no other systematically collected source of data on skinhead violence available. Although antiracist organizations (particularly the ADL, the John Brown Anti-Klan Committee, the Southern Poverty Law Center and the National Gay & Lesbian Task Force Policy Institute) do keep records on skinhead assaults, these data are collected by different means, and they are categorized in different ways. Essentially, there is no standard method for gathering hate crime statistics.

Furthermore, these data are all incident based. That is, antiracist organizations describe anecdotal accounts of skinhead violence as reported to them by victims, or as contained in police files. Often, researchers do not come in contact with perpetrators of these crimes, and almost never do they record the names or addresses of these offenders. Hence, despite all good intentions, these data do not contain information on the prevalence of violence within the skinhead subculture. Such data are collected for one purpose: To control hate crime. They are not collected for the purpose of understanding hate crime.

Self-report measures are, therefore, an appropriate source of data for exploring the etiology of skinhead violence. Determining the causes of hate crime provides an empirical justification for public policy to control it. Within the field of criminology, efforts to validate self-report measures of delinquency have produced an impressive body of research (Dentler and Moore, 1961; Elliott and Ageton,

1980; Erickson and Empey, 1963; Hindelang et al., 1981; Hirschi, 1969). These researchers have based their successes on two primary research strategies (see Hagan, 1990), both of which were incorporated into the present study.

A. Every subject in this research was examined in relation to others of the same known group (Hardt and Hardt, 1977:82). Thus, responses of one subject ought to reflect, or correlate, with those of another, and the group as a whole. As we have seen, this was the case in the instance of homology.

B. Throughout the empirical analysis, I attempt to measure the internal consistency of questionnaire items by using a total of eighteen interlocking items. Three scales were used including the seven-item authoritarian aggression scale, a five-item alienation scale, and a five-item Satanism scale.

2. *Operationalizing Terrorism.* Within the English language, there is perhaps no more pejorative a term that could be used to describe someone than the word *terrorist.* This emotionally laden concept inspires images of a black-hooded Middle-Eastern extremist who suddenly bombs an airport somewhere in Europe killing hundreds of innocent people. It is hard to imagine applying the term to a fourteen-year-old dishwasher at a Taco Bell Restaurant in Tampa, Florida, or to a sixteen-year-old, female honor-roll student from Austin, Texas, or to a twenty-two-year-old minister from Milwaukee. But together, these three subjects admitted to a total of seventeen assaults against minorities over a two-year period, thus qualifying them for the label *terrorist* as that concept is defined by the FBI (Gurr, 1989).

Yet my measure is deficient in one important aspect: I operationalized terrorism as "fights against people of another race." Therefore, I did not capture data on the incidence and prevalence of skinhead violence against Jews, gays, and lesbians. Indeed, the self-report data revealed that most skinhead violence is not directed against racial minorities, but against other whites. Skinhead violence is primarily a white-on-white phenomena, and some of these victims may have been Jews or white gays and lesbians.

Therefore, this study underestimates terrorism within the skinhead subculture. Yet I committed this mistake knowingly. That is, given my reliance on native field study strategies, I sought a quick and efficient way to ask questions about the sensitive issue of assaults against others. I did not purposefully ignore the Jewish and gay and lesbian communities; rather, I attempted to operationalize the concept in a generic fashion that might be used to understand the criminogenic rudiments of domestic terrorism and hate crime.

3. *Statistical Power.* As previously discussed, a major limitation of studies based on small sample sizes is the inability to generalize findings to other populations or similar groups. Of primary importance in this generalizing process is the consideration of *critical effect size*—a measure of how strong a theoretically derived hypothesis must minimally be to provide conclusive evidence. Critical effect size is important because it determines the statistical power necessary to assess whether observed differences could be due to chance (sampling error), or

if it is highly improbable that the differences have been due to sampling error and thus are considered statistically significant at a given probability level.

Now, recent innovations in statistics have led to the development of detailed instructions for calculating the effect size required by power calculations and for using statistical tables to estimate sample sizes necessary for various test situations. One such table is provided by Helena Kraemer and Sue Thiemann (1987:105–12) in their tract appropriately titled *How Many Subjects? Statistical Power Analysis in Research.*

Inspecting this table in light of the present research, we see that to have a critical effect size of 0.10 (with a value of 0 meaning that the hypothesis is false), it would be necessary to collect data on 616 skinheads to conduct a one-tailed 5 percent test of significance with 80 percent accuracy. (The smaller the critical effect size, the larger the necessary sample size; and the smaller the power, the greater the chance of failure in recognizing significant differences.) Clearly, given the nature of the present research, developing a pool of 616 subjects is prohibitive. However, Kraemer and Thiemann's table also reveals that to have an 80 percent chance of predictive success (power) with a critical effect size of 0.40, we would need only 36 subjects to conduct a 5 percent one-tailed test of significance. And this is what I have—36 subjects.

Therefore, statistical conclusions based on the present sample size are far from perfect. In fact, to achieve a 99 percent level of predictive power (nearly perfect prediction), would require that I recruit and interview more than 150,000 subjects—a figure probably exceeding the number of skinheads worldwide. Instead, my sample size reflects the unique questions, design, and measures used to examine terrorist youth subcultures; therefore, the sample size necessarily affects statistical power. Simply put, my statistical conclusions, reported throughout the study, can be considered 80 percent accurate with a critical effect size of 0.40, meaning that the rejection of null hypotheses is not a chance event at the 5 percent level of confidence.

4. *F Scale reliability.* Reliability is demonstrated through the consistent replication of findings on repeated measures. This consistency is determined by the extent to which a set of survey items used to measure a concept are highly related to one another and tap support for the concept at hand. A statistic (Cronbach's alpha) is generally used to assess the internal consistency of survey items (Cronbach, 1951).

The reliability of the F Scale, on repeated administrations to a wide variety of groups, has averaged alpha $= .90$ (an alpha of 1.0 represents perfect reliability), with a range of .81 to .97 (Dillehay, 1978). Moreover, the F Scale has proven to be a highly reliable psychometric instrument.

In the present study, however, the reliability coefficients were extremely low. For terrorists, the reliability of the authoritarian aggression subscale was only alpha $= .175$, and for non-terrorists it was alpha $= .271$. There are three reasons for this:

First, the high reliability coefficients reported by previous researchers were generally based on the entire thirty-eight-item F Scale instrument. My method of administering the survey required that I employ a shorter version of the instrument, hence I selected a subscale that promised to most effectively measure the beliefs of the highly peculiar subjects in this study.

Second, my method of administering the survey also led me to adopt an abbreviated method of coding data. Whereas previous researchers have asked subjects to indicate their agreement or disagreement with each F Scale item by use of six different categories (ranging from "strongly agree" to "strongly disagree"), I employed a three-point measure ("agree," "disagree," or "not sure"). Not only did this procedure facilitate data collection but it is also consistent with the procedure recommended for administering the well-known alienation scale (Robinson and Shaver, 1973) — the results of which appear in chapter 9. Thus, my procedures — although necessary given the exigencies of the present study — may have artificially constrained subject responses thereby producing low alpha coefficients.

Finally, it is entirely possible that the Fascism or F Scale tapped support for the wrong concept. Indeed, there are important and well-documented differences between fascism and Nazism (Sternhell, 1976). National socialism, also referred to as Hitlerism, assumes love of nation (national) and its people (socialism). Implicit within this definition is a belief in biological determinism or social Darwinism. Fascist regimes, by comparison, are not necessarily committed to this concept. (Benito Mussolini's Italy and Francisco Franco's Spain, though fascist, were not Nazi states.) In this regard, the terrorists in this research appear to resemble a group of neo-Nazis, rather than fascists. Hence, low reliability coefficients on a measure of fascism would be a logical outcome.

8

Terrorism and Racist Media Images

Racism, as distinguished from race, is not a fact of life, but an ideology, and the deeds it leads to are not reflexive actions, but deliberate acts based on pseudo-scientific theories. Violence in interracial struggle is always murderous, but it is not "irrational"; it is the logical and rational consequence of racism.

—Hannah Arendt
On Violence

Nineteen eighty-eight was an important year for the American skinheads. The ADL had recently published a report claiming that neo-Nazi skinhead gangs had sprung up in states other than California. Mulugeta Seraw was brutally murdered in Portland bringing national attention to members of the East Side White Pride, and the FBI had launched a series of investigations into skinhead activity across the nation. Hollywood had released a sensational full-length motion picture on the skinheads, who were also the subject of feature articles in *Time, Newsweek,* the *New York Times,* and *Rolling Stone.* And as announcements for the upcoming Aryan Woodstock began to circulate within the subculture, skinheads were interviewed on national television by Oprah Winfrey, Geraldo Rivera, and Morton Downey, Jr. In many ways, 1988 was the heyday for the American skinhead.

Amid these events, freelance reporter Jeff Coplon interviewed Tom Metzger at his television repair shop in Fallbrook. Pondering this sudden popular interest in the skinheads, Metzger catechized: "The question is, why do these kids feel this way? What has brought them to this position? What is wrong with this system that white kids across the country are joining up with people like me" (quoted in Coplon, 1989:89).

The data presented in the previous chapter suggest that white kids are not joining up with people like Metzger because of problems with the American system. In fact, the most dangerous skinheads appear to be in extreme conformity with this system. They are hard working, industrious, and multitalented in the arts. They have an obvious commitment to postsecondary education and working-class living standards. Many of them, however, are also emotional cripples regarding their tolerance for minorities, Jews, and homosexuals.

Instead, the data presented thus far suggest that certain white youths have entered the skinhead subculture through what appears to be a rational choice based not on socioeconomic disadvantage, but rather, on being drawn to the subculture because of the emotional appeal of white power rock and the skinhead style. During the late 1980s, the unique combination of these two mighty forces appears to have spoken straight to the hearts of certain white children and youth throughout the United States who may, or may not, have started out emotionally crippled.

Whatever their psychological makeup, once these youths inhabited their subculture, the most violent of them — products of working-class backgrounds — redefined various elements of the skinhead style through an act of bricolage. They replaced the traditional skinhead style with the look, language, and behavior of an indigenous American terrorist movement waged by adult neo-Nazis. My hypothesis is that Metzger facilitated (and indeed inspired) this act of bricolage.

THE IMPACT OF TERRORIST MATERIALS ON AMERICAN SKINHEADS

The theory of differential identification-reinforcement predicts that terrorism occurs because some groups have the power and resources to transmit unconventional norms and values from one generation to the next. The theory holds that terrorism is neither unique to nor invented by youths through the development of counterculture ideology. Instead, terrorism is passed on to youths through the skillful use of media images transmitted by in-group role models.

Under this formulation, youths become attracted to and identify with terrorists who live outside of their immediate social world. They do so by identifying with messages transmitted through television, music, and literature. Once this attraction and identification process has been completed, youths join a terrorist subculture embracing its values and style. To paraphrase the oft-quoted axiom of Edwin Sutherland, terrorism exists "because of an excess of definitions favorable to [terrorism] over definitions unfavorable to [terrorism]" (1947:6–7). In this theoretical tradition, I organize the test of differential identification-reinforcement variables around the frequency, duration, and priority of subjects' exposure to Metzger's racist media images.

Terrorism and Cable Television

By 1988, "Race and Reason" had penetrated cable television markets in at least thirty U.S. cities (ADL, 1988b; Klanwatch, 1989). The theory of differential identification-reinforcement predicts that terrorists will exhibit a greater degree of exposure to this program than non-terrorists. To test for this hypothesis, subjects were first asked, "Have you ever seen the cable TV program 'Race and Reason'?" Those who had were then asked to report on the frequency, duration, and priority of their viewing habits.

The first set of findings are reported in Table 8.1 (Exposure to "Race and Reason"). The data show that Metzger's cable program did not have a discriminating effect on terrorists. Roughly equal proportions of terrorists (68 percent) and non-terrorists (72 percent) reported that they had viewed the program. This null-effect was substantiated by the interview data. Several terrorists said that "Race and Reason" was boring; another said the program was too serious; and another called it confusing.

This pattern is repeated in Table 8.2 (Frequency of Exposure to "Race and Reason"). Only two of the terrorists were weekly viewers, one was a bi-weekly viewer, and the remainder watched the program only once a year. As such, these viewing habits were no different from those of non-terrorists.

When questioned about their duration of exposure to "Race and Reason" (Table 8.3), an equal number of terrorists and non-terrorists reported that they had been

Table 8.1
Exposure to "Race and Reason" ($N = 35$)

	Yes	No
Terrorists	14	7
Non-Terrorists	10	4

$X^2 = .743$, $df = 2$, p = n.s.

Table 8.2
Frequency of Exposure to "Race and Reason" ($N = 24$)

	Weekly	Bi-Weekly	Yearly
Terrorists	2	1	11
Non-Terrorists	0	1	9

$X^2 = 1.577$, $df = 2$, p = n.s.

Table 8.3
Duration of Exposure to "Race and Reason" ($N = 24$)

	More than 3 years	Two years	Less than 1 year
Terrorists	6	4	4
Non-Terrorists	6	2	2

$X^2 = .68$, $df = 2$, p = n.s.

viewers of the program for more than three years, and equal proportions had watched the program for two years and less than one year, respectively. Thus, once again "Race and Reason" did not appear to have an effect on the incidence of terrorism.

Last, subjects were asked to report on their priority of viewing. These findings are displayed in Table 8.4 (Priority of Exposure to "Race and Reason"). As we see, none of the subjects reported "Race and Reason" as their top priority for television viewing.

Accordingly, these findings fail to confirm the differential identification-reinforcement predictions. Furthermore, I discovered no evidence to indicate that watching "Race and Reason" had anything to do with changes in counterculture style. All four regular (weekly and bi-weekly) viewers were shaven-headed.

Terrorism and Neo-Nazi Literature

As an American underground publication, *WAR* is a model of vibrant and electric presentations of a particular point of view. *WAR's* photographic work is clear and bold; its Aryan Entertainment Section is resplendent with information about Nazi regalia and Skrewdriver—Ian Stuart's heroic image hovers softly in crucial places of the zine; and it contains "important developments in the white power movement," such as expostulations on Metzger's theory of the Third Position and statements of solidarity with the Order. Yet perhaps the most outstanding feature of *WAR* is its extravagant use of racist cartoons. The purpose of these cartoons, obviously, is to bring humor to the skinhead style of terrorism.

Table 8.5 (Exposure to Racist Literature) shows that only one subject in the entire sample (a terrorist) had never read a racist magazine; two terrorists and seven non-terrorists were readers of only other racist magazines. Yet, a full 86 percent of the terrorists reported that they were readers of *WAR*, whereas less than half of the non-terrorists were *WAR* readers. As such, these differences are statistically significant and provide ostensible support for the differential identification-reinforcement prediction that those youths who closely associate with Metzger will be more dangerous than those who do not.

However, when examined for frequency, duration, and priority of exposure to these racist images, the theoretical predictions are refuted. Tables 8.6 (Frequency of Exposure to Racist Literature), 8.7 (Duration of Exposure to Racist Litera-

Table 8.4
Priority of Exposure to "Race and Reason" ($N = 24$)

	Top Priority	Not The Top Priority
Terrorists	0	14
Non-Terrorists	0	10

Note: X^2 statistic cannot be computed when the number of nonempty rows or columns is one.

Table 8.5
Exposure to Racist Literature (*N* = 34)

	WAR readers	Readers of other extremist literature	Non-readers
Terrorists	18	2	1
Non-Terrorists	6	7	0

$X^2 = 10.59$, $df = 2$, $p < .05$

Table 8.6
Frequency of Exposure to Racist Literature (*N* = 34)

	Weekly	Monthly	Yearly
Terrorists	8	9	4
Non-Terrorists	2	7	4

$X^2 = 2.08$, $df = 2$, $p = $ n.s.

Table 8.7
Duration of Exposure to Racist Literature (*N* = 34)

	More than 3 years	Two Years	Less than 1 year
Terrorists	13	4	4
Non-Terrorists	10	1	2

$X^2 = 1.03$, $df = 2$, $p = $ n.s.

Table 8.8
Priority of Exposure to Racist Literature (*N* = 33)

	Top Priority	Not Top Priority
Terrorists	2	18
Non-Terrorists	1	12

$X^2 = .05$, $df = 1$, $p = $ n.s.

ture), and 8.8 (Priority of Exposure to Racist Literature) show no differences between subjects. We may, therefore, conclude that simply being exposed to *WAR*'s messages—regardless of frequency, duration, and priority of exposure—provides the necessary stimulus for terrorism.

Note that many of the subjects often consumed a broad range of extremist literature. The leader of the Bronx Area Skinheads, for example, was a regular consumer of not only *WAR* but also *New America,* the *Seditionist* (published by former Order confidant Louis Beam), *NAAWP News* (edited by David Duke), *From the Mountain* (edited by Robert Miles), *National Vanguard* (edited by William Pierce, aka William McDonald, author of *The Turner Diaries*), as well as a string of more esoteric newsletters such as the *Racialist, GNOSIS, The Talon, Euro-American Quarterly,* and *Scriptures to the American Common European Home.*

When examined at the level of counterculture change, more than 80 percent of the weekly and monthly terrorist readers of *WAR* had hair long enough to comb, none of them wore jewelry, and all of them typically dressed in T-shirts, blue jeans, and work boots.

Terrorism and Telephone Hate Lines

By 1989, Metzger had established the W.A.R. Hotline in more than thirty U.S. cities. These included major metropolitan areas such as New York City, Los Angeles, Dallas, Miami, Seattle, Portland, Phoenix, San Diego, San Francisco, Detroit, and Washington, D.C. The theory of differential identification-reinforcement predicts that more terrorists will be exposed to the W.A.R. Hotline than non-terrorists. This hypothesis is first tested in Table 8.9 (Exposure to the W.A.R. Hotline).

Here we see that the majority of non-terrorists (71 percent) did not use the W.A.R. Hotline, and the majority of terrorists (71 percent) did. These differences are statistically significant and, once again, provide ostensible support for the differential identification-reinforcement perspective. However, these significant differences disappear, also once again, when examined for Frequency, Duration, and Priority of Exposure to the W.A.R. Hotline (Tables 8.10–8.12). Similar

Table 8.9
Exposure to W.A.R. Hotline ($N = 35$)

	Hotline Users	Non-Users
Terrorists	15	6
Non-Terrorists	4	10

$X^2 = 6.21, \quad df = 1, \quad p < .05$

Table 8.10
Frequency of Exposure to W.A.R. Hotline ($N = 19$)

	Weekly	Monthly	Yearly
Terrorists	1	11	3
Non-Terrorists	1	1	2

$X^2 = 3.25, \quad df = 2, \quad p = \text{n.s.}$

Table 8.11
Duration of Exposure to W.A.R. Hotline ($N = 19$)

	More Than 3 Years	Two Years	Less Than 1 Year
Terrorists	3	9	3
Non-Terrorists	2	1	1

$X^2 = 1.82$, $df = 2$, $p =$ n.s.

Table 8.12
Priority of Exposure to W.A.R. Hotline ($N = 19$)

	Top priority	Not top priority
Terrorists	4	12
Non-Terrorists	2	2

$X^2 = .95$, $df = 1$, $p =$ n.s.

to the impact of the *WAR* zine, it appears that the simple exposure to W.A.R.'s racist messages—regardless of frequency, duration, and priority—provides the necessary impetus for committing acts of terrorism.

Also similar to the impact of *WAR,* the majority of these terrorist hotline users had either a short crop or long hair, did not wear jewelry, and dressed in T-shirts, blue jeans, and work boots.

Terrorism and Computer Bulletin Boards

By 1989, Metzger claimed to have more than 2,000 users of his sophisticated W.A.R. Board (Stills, 1989). The impact of these computerized messages to American skinheads is summarized in Table 8.13 (Exposure to the W.A.R. Board). These findings are also unequivocal. They show that fully 100 percent of the terrorists, and 79 percent of the non-terrorists had never used Metzger's bulletin board, thereby forgoing the need for an empirical examination of the theoretical properties of frequency, duration, and priority of exposure.

Table 8.13
Exposure to the W.A.R. Board ($N = 34$)

	Bulletin board users	Non-users
Terrorists	0	21
Non-Terrorists	2	11

$X^2 = 3.43$, $df = 1$, $p =$ n.s.

TERRORISM AND THE SUBCULTURAL TRANSMISSION
OF IDEOLOGY

More than anything else, the theory of differential identification-reinforcement predicts that Metzger used the emotional appeal of white power rock and the skinhead style to formulate a coherent neo-Nazi ideology among American skinheads. Therefore, the most crucial test of this theory is its ability "to explain *how* meanings that have been transmitted from person to person within a [subculture] can come into conflict with those of another group" (Cressey, 1960:150, emphasis added).

Such an explanation is presented quantitatively in Table 8.14 (Neo-Nazism and Exposure to Racist Images). To make the best use of the data, and to fully examine the processes of transmitting ideology within the skinhead subculture, I again make a temporary shift in the research design and consider terrorists and nonterrorists together.

As noted earlier, the majority of subjects in this study embraced an ideology more closely resembling neo-Nazism, rather than common fascism. Once again, there is a very important and well-documented difference between fascism and Nazism (Sterrhell, 1976). Nazism assumes a belief in biological determinism, fascism does not.

The defining characteristic of national socialism was anti-Semitism. It began and ended with that principle (Sternhell, 1976; Fromm, 1941). Therefore, the litmus test of a belief in Nazism turns on one's attitude toward Jews. Similarly, the litmus test of the effectiveness of a neo-Nazi movement is its ability to transmit such an ideology to its followers. Table 8.14 shows that most of Metzger's propaganda techniques were utter failures in promoting anti-Semitic beliefs among the American skinheads. The correlations between anti-Semitic attitudes and exposure to "Race and Reason," *WAR*, and the W.A.R. Hotline are all puny and insignificant. It appears that white power rock is the only effective means for transmitting anti-Semitic beliefs.

Historically, African-Europeans and African-Americans have occupied no central place in the Nazi agenda. Therefore, to include them into a neo-Nazi be-

Table 8.14
Neo-Nazism and Exposure to Racist Images (Pearson's *r* reported)

	Attitude toward:		
	Jews	Minorities	Homosexuals
Exposure to Race and Reason	.04	.10	-.10
Exposure to WAR	.23	.47*	.11
Exposure to W.A.R. Hotline	.19	.24	.44*
Exposure to Skrewdriver	.59*	.54*	.56*

*$p < .05$

lief system is a perversion of true national socialism, representing an intellectual fetish with Nazi ideology. Table 8.14 reveals that this fetish has successfully implanted itself into the minds of subjects via two primary routes: the *WAR* zine and white power rock. We may suspect that this is due to the emotional appeal of *WAR*'s racist cartoons and Skrewdriver's explicitly racist musical creations such as "Nigger, Nigger," "Race and Nation," "Dead Paki in a Gutter," and "White Power."

The Nazi agenda was also void of specific pogroms against homosexuals. They were not part of an inferior race, and they held no political power in Europe at the time. Including them in a modern-day Nazi agenda is also a perversion of original ideology, representing a carnal morality anchored only in sheer hatred. Table 8.14 suggests that homophobic images are most efficiently transmitted to skinheads via Metzger's W.A.R. Hotline messages about "AIDS-infected queers" and "dirty faggots" and exposure to Skrewdriver's overabsorption with the masculine stereotype represented in such neo-Nazi anthems as "Hail the New Dawn" and "Rudolf Hess (Prisoner of Peace)."

Thus, Metzger's racist messages appear to have a selective impact on the skinhead subculture at large. Among the media creations of his own design, none have significantly contributed to the goal of developing anti-Semitic beliefs—the touchstone of true Nazism—among skinheads studied here. And, his elaborate efforts have contributed only moderately in developing antiblack and antigay/lesbian beliefs (or bastard forms of Nazism). At bottom, Table 8.14 shows that nothing is more important in the subcultural transmission of neo-Nazi ideology than the music of Skrewdriver.

The impotency of Metzger's appeal is confirmed in Table 8.15 (Correlates of Bricolage). Here we see that only one variable—exposure to "Race and Reason"—has a significant impact on the traditional skinhead counterculture style. Contrary to Metzger's invective to "let their hair grow out and melt into the regular scene," the direction of the coefficient indicates that those skinheads who did watch "Race and Reason" were more likely to shave their heads; thereby confirming, instead of rejecting, the traditional skinhead counterculture style.

In summary, a multitude of factors appear to be at work in the transmission of musical preference, values, and the style of terrorism within the skinhead subcul-

Table 8.15
Correlates of Bricolage (Pearson's *r* reported)

	Exhibition of non-traditional style
Exposure to Race and Reason	-.35*
Exposure to WAR	-.09
Exposure to W.A.R. Hotline	-.09
Exposure to Skrewdriver	-.04

*p < .05

ture. Tom Metzger, therefore, cannot be solely blamed for American skinhead terrorism. Nor is he responsible for the act of bricolage. Things are more complicated than this. As such, the theory of differential identification-reinforcement offers minimal explanatory power. Furthermore, as examined thus far, the theory cannot explain variances in the impact of W.A.R. materials on subjects. Why did "Race and Reason" have such a limited appeal among terrorists, and why did the *WAR* zine enjoy a more widesweeping transmission? Why did the majority of terrorists use the W.A.R. Hotline, while fully 100 percent of them rejected the W.A.R. Board?

To answer these questions, I now turn to a research strategy established in the field of criminology by Edwin Sutherland (1937) in his classic work, *The Professional Thief.* Sutherland argued that "in themselves, statistics are nothing more than symptoms of unknown causal processes" (1947:61). To probe more deeply into these unknown processes, Sutherland advocated the use of case studies. In this tradition, I consider four case studies in an attempt to disentangle the complex ways in which music, values, and terrorism are transmitted within the skinhead subculture.

Phen and the Raging White Rhino II

We begin with a sixteen-year-old white male from Milwaukee who goes by the street name of Phen (for the Phenomenon). Phen's dad is a welder who lives at home with his wife, Phen, and another son. Phen gets along with his parents; he is a high school junior and makes *A*'s and *B*'s in his classes. Upon graduation, Phen plans to pursue a career in labor management. He hopes to one day attend the University of Milwaukee and graduate with a degree in sociology or political science.

Phen is also a part-time janitor at a local Burger King restaurant. For this job, he is required to wear a white T-shirt, jeans, and work boots. Most of the Burger King cooks are black, and Phen's job is to clean up after them. Moreover, Phen is a working-class white kid from the streets of Milwaukee. When he was fifteen years old, Phen learned how to play rhythm guitar and has since fronted a skinhead garage band at his parents' home.

Phen became a skinhead at the age of fourteen, when he was an eighth grader. He was recruited into the local skinhead collective by the Reverend referred to in the preceding chapter. At the time, the Reverend was a regular reader of *WAR,* the *Seditionist, From the Mountain,* and the *National Vanguard.* For more than three years, the Reverend had been a frequent user of the W.A.R. Hotline. Between 1988 and 1990, the Reverend received a variety of free recruiting materials from Tom Metzger including racist stickers and copies of *WAR.* In fact, Metzger had paid for the Reverend's airline ticket to San Francisco so that he could attend the historic Aryan Woodstock in the winter of 1989. On his return, the Reverend recruited more than 200 youths into Milwaukee's growing white power movement.

Today, Phen usually carries a 9-mm Glockenspeil pistol when he is out with his skinhead friends; he wears no jewelry nor is he tattooed with the mark of the swastika or the Viking. Phen's hair is long enough to comb and he does not use drugs. Between 1989 and 1990, Phen committed seven attacks against blacks in Milwaukee's expansive working-class neighborhoods. Each time, he was drunk on beer. Here is his explanation for this terrorism: "Sometimes they provoke it. Like they'll say some shit about white power. That's when we throw down. I beat one nigger in the head with a beer bottle. Fucked him up good! Just goin' berserk!"

When asked to further explain why he did such things, Phen replied: "It's working-class style." In his bedroom at home, Phen listens to Skrewdriver every day. His parents don't seem to mind. When Phen was in the seventh grade, he was introduced to the band by the Reverend. His other favorite bands now include Brutal Attack, No Remorse, and White Noise.

Although Phen has never seen "Race and Reason" and has never used the W.A.R. Board, for the past two years he has been an avid reader of *WAR* and the *National Vanguard*. These are the only magazines that interest Phen. He is also a monthly W.A.R. Hotline user and has been for a year. Yet Phen uses another racist telephone hotline as well; and the W.A.R. Hotline is not the top priority for Phen's hotline usage. Not surprisingly, Phen is a high scorer on the F Scale. To be more precise, Phen is a full-throttled neo-Nazi.

The second case study is Phen's companion in the Milwaukee group; this eighteen-year-old white male calls himself "The Raging White Rhino II" (presumably, there was a "Raging White Rhino I"). Like Phen, the Rhino's father is a factory worker, and the Rhino himself is currently employed as an assemblyman in a rubber plant where he dresses in a T-shirt, blue jeans, and work boots. He lives at home, has few problems with his parents, does not use drugs, is a recent high school graduate, and plans to attend trade school to improve his lot in life. Although the Rhino does not play music, he paints pictures for his own amusement.

When the Rhino was seventeen years old, he was also recruited into the skinheads by the Reverend. Since then, he has carried a silver .357 magnum Smith & Wesson pistol. His hair is cut short, but not shaved, and he usually wears his factory costume when he associates with friends. Yet the Rhino does wear one piece of jewelry. As he walks the streets of Milwaukee, the Rhino wears a set of brass knuckles as a visual display of his bad-ass presentation of self (see Katz, 1988). Along with Phen and the Reverend, the Rhino was involved in four racial assaults over the two-year period. Each time, however, he was sober.

The Rhino listens to Skrewdriver every day. He was introduced to the band a year ago by the Reverend. He now listens to other white power acts such as Brutal Attack, White Noise, and GBH. Like Phen, the Rhino has never seen "Race and Reason." There is good reason for this. "Race and Reason" has not yet penetrated the Milwaukee cable TV market, and Phen and the Rhino have never left Milwaukee. Yet unlike Phen, the Rhino has only read *WAR* once in his life, and has never called the W.A.R. Hotline number. Essentially, the Rhino prefers zines such as *Maximum Rock 'N' Roll* over political literature. Yet he was also a high scorer on the F Scale—a neo-Nazi.

Summary   In the end, there are no differences between Phen and the Raging White Rhino II. They are both terrorists. There are also similarities in the means to their crimes. Both were recruited by the Reverend who was associated with Tom Metzger; both were intense listeners of Skrewdriver; and both were neo-Nazis. Yet there are also differences in the means to their violence. Whereas Phen committed his terrorism while intoxicated, the Rhino was sober. And whereas Phen was a regular user of W.A.R. materials, the Rhino was not.

Elizabeth and Ronald

The next two cases were selected because of their group affiliation. One subject was a member of the Portland, Oregon, American Front (AF) and the other belonged to the Orlando, Florida, chapter of the American Front. I do not know the names of these two skinheads, so I have given them the pseudonyms Elizabeth and Ronald.

Elizabeth is a nineteen-year-old history major at the University of Oregon. Her father is an attorney and she is now living by herself in an apartment near the university. She has typically gotten along with her parents, and she does not use drugs. Elizabeth plans to enter law school and eventually become a labor attorney. In her spare time, she writes poetry and draws cartoons for the American Front newsletter and other white power publications.

Elizabeth joined the American Front when she was fifteen years old. She was recruited into the group by other skinhead girls associated with Tom Metzger. Associating with these girls has given Elizabeth high self-esteem and a sense of belonging. Today, she keeps a 12-gauge pump-action shotgun in her bedroom closet for protection.

Reminiscent of the popular rock star Sinead O'Connor, Elizabeth's head is shaved bald and she wears a paramilitary jumpsuit to her university classes and AF meetings. She sets this costume off with a delicate pair of hope earrings and a small diamond pierced through her nostril. She is not tattooed with swastikas or Vikings. Yet, everyday Elizabeth listens to Skrewdriver, Last Resort, and the Midtown Boot Boys. Between 1988 and 1990, she was involved in seven attacks against blacks on the streets of Portland. Each time, she was drunk on beer. In her words, "I fight for pride in my race. And for pride in my womanhood."

Since becoming a skinhead, Elizabeth has watched "Race and Reason" on a weekly basis. She is also an avid reader of *WAR* and other white power literature. In fact, she devours this literature. Each week Elizabeth pores through copies of *War,* David Duke's *NAAWP News,* and Pierce's *Vanguard.* Elizabeth also regularly phones the W.A.R. Hotline but has never used Metzger's computer bulletin board.

Since 1988, Metzger has supplied Elizabeth with complimentary copies of

WAR so that she may distribute them to other students on the University of Oregon campus and to youths on the streets of Portland. Not surprisingly, Elizabeth is also a neo-Nazi as measured by the F Scale.

The final case study involves Ronald, a fourteen-year-old terrorist from Orlando, Florida. Ronald's father works in a factory, and he and Ronald do not get along. Therefore, Ronald has recently moved out of the house and into the living quarters of the American Front. Ronald has also recently dropped out of high school and the local truant officers are seeking his whereabouts. To survive, Ronald washes dishes under an alias at a local Taco Bell restaurant. In the future, Ronald plans to return to high school and eventually graduate. But for now, he is into other things.

At the AF headquarters, Ronald spends his free time painting pictures. He does not use drugs because they are forbidden on the premises, and he cannot afford them given his meager wages. There are seven women (skinhead girls) who are also members of the Orlando American Front, and two of them live in bedrooms down the hall from Ronald. In fact, Ronald is in love with a fifteen-year-old skinhead girl we call Rhonda. And it was Rhonda who recruited Ronald into the AF back when he was a sixth-grader.

Like Elizabeth, Ronald's head is clean-shaven. Unlike her paramilitary dress, however, Ronald's style is more clean-cut as he says. Both at work and after the job, Ronald is usually dressed in a T-shirt, freshly laundered blue jeans, and highly polished Doc Martens. He wears only a skull and crossbones ring and is not tattooed. Every day, Ronald listens to Skrewdriver, Last Resort, War Zone, Brutal Attack, and Danzig. He has listened to these bands since Rhonda introduced him to them when they fell in love back in the sixth grade. Together with Rhonda and other AF members, Ronald has engaged in seven street fights against Orlando blacks over the two-year period. Each time, he was drunk on vodka.

Because Ronald lives in an area of the country that carries "Race and Reason," he watches this program every two weeks. Yet Ronald has only read *WAR* twice in his life. He is also more interested in *Maximum Rock 'N' Roll*. Likewise, Ronald has only used the W.A.R. Hotline once in his life, and found it boring. Instead, Ronald is a regular user of a telephone hotline operated by the Florida Klavern of the Ku Klux Klan. Yet like Elizabeth, Ronald receives regular complimentary copies of *WAR* to distribute to youths in his hometown (even though he is not a regular reader himself). And also like Elizabeth, Ronald is a neo-Nazi as measured by the F Scale.

Summary   Once again, the end product of these two case studies is the same. Elizabeth and Ronald are both terrorists. And also like before, these two skinheads operated from similar means. Both belonged to the American Front; both were intensive listeners of Skrewdriver; both were neo-Nazis; both were recruited by their peers; and both were intoxicated at the time of their hate crimes. Yet again, there are important differences in their means to violence.

First, Elizabeth was more intensive in her use of W.A.R. materials than was Ronald. And second, during the course of this study, Ronald began to have romantic problems with Rhonda. This, in turn, spilled over to his relationships with other AF members. Therefore, unlike Elizabeth who enjoyed a great sense of camaraderie with her companions, the Orlando American Front had no real effect on Ronald's self-esteem and sense of belonging. In fact, Ronald was experiencing great conflict with his subcultural companions at the time of his terrorist activities.

TERRORISM AND REWARDS

The theory of differential identification-reinforcement also holds that terrorism is a response to rewards and punishments. As rewards increase following a terrorist incident, and as threats of punishment decrease, the frequency of terrorist behavior increases. Therefore, terrorist behavior is learned and maintained when it is followed by such rewards as money and social prestige.

The test of rewards given to skinheads for their terrorism began with responses to this item: "Have you ever heard of the organization known as W.A.R.?" Of the 35 subjects who responded to this question, 34 (or 97 percent) indicated that they had knowledge of Metzger's organization. This is a finding of some importance. It means that Metzger is a well-known figure throughout the subculture. Yet it means only that. This does not necessarily imply that "thousands of American white youths became skinheads because of Metzger's deliberate attempt to recruit them into his army subculture."

Next, I asked subjects to respond to a checklist of items they had received from W.A.R. Findings are presented in Table 8.16 (The W.A.R. Reward System). The most frequently received item was a copy of the *WAR* zine. Sixteen terrorists and ten non-terrorists received complimentary copies of *WAR*. In some cases, members of both groups received multiple copies. Four terrorists received racist stickers from W.A.R. and five non-terrorists received stickers. Two terrorists and one non-terrorist received racist books from W.A.R. One non-terrorist received a racist video from W.A.R. and one terrorist (the Reverend) received an airplane ticket to a white power rock concert.

Table 8.16
The W.A.R. Reward System (*N* = 35)**

	No. Terrorist Receiving	No. Non-Terrorist Receiving
Reward		
Stickers	4	5
WAR zine	16	10
A book	2	1
Name Printed in WAR	0	0
Invitation to Appear on TV	0	0
A Record, Tape, or Video	0	1
Travel to Convention/Rock Concert	1	0
Chance to Make Rock Album	0	0
Chance to Meet "Rock Star"	0	0

None of the subjects had ever had their names printed in *WAR* as a result of their terrorism. Nor were any of them ever invited to appear on "Race and Reason," or some other television talk show. None of the musicians in the sample were invited to the West Coast to record a racist rock album. Finally, Table 8.16 shows that none of the subjects were afforded the opportunity to meet a rock star.

As such, there appears to be no coherent organizational method of rewarding skinheads for their terrorism. That is, rewards were administered to skinheads at random. There was essentially something for everyone regardless of an individual's battle record. Yet what is perhaps most instructive in this regard is the overwhelming skinhead reaction to Metzger and his reward system.

For example, a twenty-one-year-old terrorist from the East Coast said, "Metzger's a joke. His whole thing is naive. He's using people to do his dirty work. I think that's really wrong." Another East Coast terrorist reported that "The job done on European-Americans will not be cleared up over night. It will take a racialist struggle. The vast majority in the racial right only want skinheads to do their dirty work. . . . I am a national socialist. I am not a Tom Metzger follower. I am a European-American with strong family ties."

A midwestern terrorist said simply, "Metzger gives me a headache." A serious West Coast terrorist claimed that "Metzger is slow. He's bringin' people backwards. He should be ignored." And a Southern terrorist reported that

W.A.R. and the Klan are associated. I don't believe they are well organized, however. They only deal with the ignorant people. . . . Did you hear about that meeting in British Columbia? The meeting of the British National Party? Metzger's people were thrown out. They're a joke!

And finally, these observations were made by the Reverend: "I think Metzger's a good guy, but his organization is a polyglot of other organizations that don't work. They are not prepared for the long struggle and they have no clear-cut vision of what to do in the future."

In summary, these findings refute theoretical predictions. Differential identification-reinforcement holds that there will be a tight fit between acts of terrorism and rewards given. There was none. Yet this is not so much a problem of theory as it is a problem of practice. In other words, despite his elaborate attempts to do so, Tom Metzger failed to develop a coherent subculture that would respond to his material incentives.

CONCLUSIONS

These findings imply that skinhead homology—music, values, and the style of terrorism—are propped-up and sustained by racist literature and telephone hotlines only in selective instances. Exposure to *WAR* is associated only with antiblack attitudes, and exposure to the W.A.R. Hotline is associated only with antihomosexual beliefs. Indeed, the case study research indicates that music, values, and the style of terrorism are transmitted through the skinhead subculture in varied and complex ways. That is, a myriad of causal processes—peer group pressure, alcohol use, and economic marginalization—also seem to be operating in the construction of homology. Although there is evidence to suggest that those youths who differentially identify with a terrorist role model will be more likely to commit terrorism than those who do not, there are also important differences in the means to this identification process.

Therefore, the findings adduced in this chapter suggest that Tom Metzger is not, as hypothesized earlier, solely responsible for the spectacular increase in the number of racist skinheads in the United States during the late 1980s. Instead, there seem to be other factors at work in the culture that drive American working-class white youths into the neo-Nazi skinhead movement.

9

The Social Organization of Terrorist Youth Subcultures

In order to understand the dynamics and the impact of racism, we must view it as a faith—and, for the American society, a permanent belief system rather than a transient apparition. Its longevity has been tried and tested. It now occupies a place in the American value pantheon alongside such concepts as democracy and liberty, though one would ordinarily view this combination as contradictory.

—Rutledge M. Dennis
"Socialization and Racism"

Geraldo Rivera: "Look, you did time in prison for beating a poor black kid. Don't you think that's terrorism?"
Anonymous Klansman: "It was self-defense. Everything the Ku Klux Klan does is in self-defense. What's wrong with that?"

—"Geraldo"
July 15, 1991

Two unexpected findings have emerged from this analysis. First, there is a diversity to the patterns of terrorism. Some skinheads have committed acts of terrorism and others have not. Second, there are also diverse patterns regarding subcultural values, musical preference, and counterculture style. Influenced by racist media images, terrorists embrace neo-Nazi values and non-terrorists do not embrace these values. Terrorists are homogeneous in their preference for white power rock, and non-terrorists prefer a wider variety of music. In their dress, non-terrorists still embrace the British-skinhead style, while terrorists have rejected this style and replaced it with the hard prototype of an indigenous American terrorist of historical proportions.

These findings suggest that factors in the social organization of skinhead groups and processes of affiliation and cohesion either encourage or discourage the act of terrorism. Hence, an analysis of the diverse patterns of organization, the role of the group, and group processes may produce knowledge about the complex etiology of terrorism and the different ways in which values, music, and style are transmitted within the skinhead subculture.

NORMS OF THE SKINHEAD SUBCULTURE

The understanding of group norms has been a critical concept for scholars in their attempts to delineate theories of organized violence in gangs. To the extent that American skinheads represent a true threat to public safety, an understanding of the microsocial processes of their norm transmission networks can be viewed as crucial to the theoretical discourse on terrorist youth subcultures and essential for public policy.

Historically, researchers have focused on four microsocial processes that constitute the norms of a gang. These norms are derived from the criminological principles advanced by Edwin Sutherland (1947) in his theory of differential association and by Travis Hirschi (1969) in his seminal work on social control theory.

First, there is the role of deviant peers in facilitating criminal values and behaviors. Second, there is the role of social bond formation in the domain of the neighborhood. The third process involves the role of these neighborhood influences on the propensity of a gang member to use drugs and alcohol. The fourth, and most recent, process involves the role of religious influences in the social development of violent subcultures (see Fagan, 1990b; Flynn and Gerhardt, 1989; Hagedorn, 1988; Linedecker, 1989; Moore, 1978; Short and Strodtbeck, 1965). In the next four chapters, I examine each of these processes in an attempt to unmask the norms of the skinhead subculture.

THE ROLE OF DEVIANT PEERS

The theory of differential association holds that deviant peers play an important role in teaching terrorist values and behaviors to other youth. Certainly, this was implied in the case studies of Phen and the Rhino, and Elizabeth and Ronald. These teaching processes are seen as providing instrumental value or meaning to group violence, which leads to the acquisition of a group definition of violence. This, in turn, creates opportunities for practicing violence in comfort and security with other group members standing nearby. Violence then becomes an act of imitation, and group reinforcement for this behavior comes to define violence as acceptable in the minds of organizational members (see Fagan, 1990b; Sutherland, 1947).

The skinhead norm of violence is summarized in Table 9.1 (Prevalence of Skinhead Violence). Here I consider both racial and nonracial assaults committed by subjects over the two-year observation. We see that the norm differs significantly between subjects. The majority of terrorists engaged in more than five fights, while half of the non-terrorists did not engage in fighting. (Yet there was

Table 9.1
Prevalence of Skinhead Violence (N = 36)

	No fights	1-2 fights	3-4 fights	5 or more fights
Terrorists	0	6	4	12
Non-Terrorists	7	4	3	0

X^2 = 18.68, df = 3, p < .05

violence committed by non-terrorists: four had been in at least two fights and three had been in four fights.) Thus, violence is the norm among terrorists; it is a fundamental part of subcultural style. Non-violence is, therefore, a form of deviancy within a terrorist youth subculture.

The interviews suggested that this violence is largely defensive in nature. For example, a Virginia terrorist indicated that his problems came mainly from anti-racist skinheads: "Last year I got into a fight with SHARP [Skinheads Against Racism]. But they instigated it by saying things about white power, callin' us Nazis and shit like that. They instigate most of the problems down here."

Other terrorists reported that fights had been waged against them because of their dramatic presentation of style. Especially instructive are the experiences of the leader of the Bronx Area Skinheads. This twenty-five-year-old man was well-known in his community as a white power activist. He published and disseminated his own white power zine and his Bronx apartment became the headquarters for his group's meetings and activities. There, he and his fiancée—a skinhead girl—had assembled a rich collection of white power rock, classical and country western music, and a veritable library on racist literature. A stonemason by trade, this young man was physically fit, wore his hair short, and typically dressed in a white power T-shirt, jeans, and Doc Martens. His arms were covered with bold and colorful tattoos including a dragon, the grim reaper, the American flag, a tiger's head, skull and crossbones, and runes. He explains the skinhead norm of violence like this: "Every fight I've ever been in has been started by other people. The color of another person's skin is not relevant. They can't deal with the way I look, and I defend myself."

Further insights into the skinhead norm of violence are provided by the Reverend:

I grew up in the suburbs of Milwaukee. I was always encouraged to read a lot by my parents. Even though I was the victim of hate crimes when I was growing up, this didn't have much of an effect on me.

Through reading, I learned that this stuff about the "poor oppressed minorities" was all lies. Blacks are just not equipped to live in a modern technological society. It's impossible for them to melt in. I became racially active in high school, and joined the skinheads [at age 16].

I've never started a fight against anyone, white or black. Every fight I've been in was to defend myself and my beliefs in the eternal laws of nature.

The biggest misperception people have about us [skinheads] is that we speak through evil or ignorance. I would like for the public to know that this is not true.

As noted in Chapter 7, the majority of fights reported by subjects (58 percent) were not acts of racial violence; rather, they were white-on-white assaults. Taken together with these interview data, we may tentatively conclude that the skinhead norm of violence is, in the minds of skinheads themselves, a defensive behavior waged against outside antagonists. Therefore, violence is not predatory. As seen by subcultural members, it is a necessary means of protecting group values. As such, the role of the deviant peer seems to be an inconsequential factor in the formulation of this norm. In other words, there is nothing sociologically or legally deviant about self-defense. Instead, self-defense is a cherished value of American nationalism.

Because this conclusion stands in such stark contrast to conventional wisdom about the American skinheads, it deserves further interpretation and analysis. Such a task, however, demands another brief digression.

The Impact of Perceptions on Definitions of Violence

There appear to be important differences between popular and subcultural perceptions of violence. These differences, as I demonstrate in a moment, have an important impact on attempts to define the skinhead norm of violence. Whereas popular opinion holds that skinhead violence is predatory and terroristic, skinheads themselves view violence as necessary for defending their subculture.

Analogous to this distinction are the various meanings applied to the traditional costume of the Ku Klux Klan. To the general public, the white sheet and pointy hat of the Klan is a symbol of racial hatred and terrorism. Within the Klan, however, this costume represents a sense of racial superiority, racial pride, and group cohesiveness. Therefore, the Klan costume means different things to different people, and these differences are determined by whether one is a member of the subculture. It all depends on where you stand. In simple terms, the Klan uniform is perceived as a positive symbol by Klan members, and as a negative symbol by outsiders.

Similar processes are at work in formulating definitions of skinhead violence. The following case study exemplifies the subtle interplay between perceptions of violence, and the resulting definitions of violence. This case study also points the way for coming to an informed conclusion about the skinhead norm of violence and the role of the deviant peer in the formulation of that norm.

The Patio Club Incident

The case study involves an incident that I witnessed during the winter of 1988 at an Indianapolis nightspot called the Patio Club. The Patio Club was then a well-known hang out for local motorcycle gangs, drug dealers, and heavy metal enthusiasts. It was also the favorite nightspot for a local collective of neo-Nazi skinheads.

The incident began on a Saturday night at about 2:00 A.M., when three neo-Nazi skinheads, who had been drinking heavily all night, were confronted by an equally intoxicated antiracist skinhead wearing a T-shirt with a swastika and a line drawn through it over the logo "Nazi Punks Fuck Off." Loud words were exchanged through the extraordinary din of late-night heavy metal. Then, one neo-Nazi stepped forth to square off against the antiracist. Harsh words were exchanged at a vein-bursting level of intensity. At this point, the two skinheads looked hatefully at one another and walked toward the restroom. I followed.

Once inside the restroom, the antiracist stunned the neo-Nazi with a hard blow to the face. "Fuckin' Nazi!" he shouted. The neo-Nazi staggered against the porcelain sinks of the lavatory, and his nose began to bleed. Then he sprang forth and shoved his opponent backwards saying, "Don't mess around. I mean it!" Then the antiracist shouted, "Give fuckin' peace a chance, will ya! There's no need for all your racial shit. Give the shit up, alright?" Then an important thing happened. The antiracist shoved the neo-Nazi a second time. The neo-Nazi then calmly uttered the words, "Okay, if that's how you want it."

The neo-Nazi then opened the door of the lavatory stall, entered, and closed the door behind him. A moment passed and nothing was said. Then suddenly the stall door opened, and the neo-Nazi stood in the middle of the restroom holding the thick white porcelain commode tank cover.

He made two moves. Using the commode cover, he faked a blow to his opponent's midsection. When the opponent went for this, the neo-Nazi regained his composure for a split second, and then with savage force bludgeoned the antiracist in the forehead. Then he walloped him again on the side of the head, making an ungodly thud as the porcelain smacked against tissue and bone.

The neo-Nazi stepped back. The victim staggered and said something incoherent. He then began to bleed from the ears, and turned deathly pale. The neo-Nazi looked at me, and I looked back without saying a word. The neo-Nazi turned to look at his victim. Drunk and suffering obvious internal injuries to his skull, he is still standing, though barely. The neo-Nazi said, "I warned you, man." He then drops the commode cover and leaves the restroom. With his two skinhead companions, he immediately exited the Patio Club. I phoned the local paramedics and then left the club myself.

This case study exemplifies the important differences in perceptions of skinhead violence. From the antiracist's point of view, he saw himself as a defender of counterculture democracy — a heroic warrior in the fight against racism. The neo-Nazi, by contrast, perceived his violence as a necessary means of self-defense, and as a defense of his own subcultural value system. From this perspective, violence is rational. It is not predatory, nor is it inspired by a deviant peer.

Two additional lessons can be gleaned from this case study. The first is practical. That is, violence could have been avoided. Had the antiracist not worn such a confrontational piece of clothing (Nazi Punks Fuck Off) and had he not gone looking for a confrontation in his inebriated state, there would have been no need for the neo-Nazi to resort to violence.

Accordingly, the second lesson is criminological. It seems that finding valid, consistent, and reliable information as to why skinheads engage in violence defies any standard method of gathering data on human behavior. Skinhead violence appears to be a result of a unique set of social events and circumstances that are perceived in vastly different ways by the parties to each incident. Skinhead violence — and by implication, skinhead terrorism — is therefore read as an interactive process based on individual value-laden assumptions about human nature. Criminologist Albert Cohen eloquently describes this process:

The history of a [violent] incident is the history of an interaction process. The intention and the capacity for violence do not pop out, like a candy bar out of a vending machine. They take shape over time. One event calls forth, inhibits, or deflects another; it invites, provokes, abets, tempts, counsels, soothes, or turns away wrath. Every violent episode, whether it is an altercation between friends, a mugging, or a riot is the product of such an interactive history. (1976:8)

Rites of Passage

The foregoing discussion implies that the skinhead norm of violence is rational and instrumental. It is not irrational or meaningless. Neither is it magical. This conclusion is confirmed by an analysis of the initiation rites used by the subjects. In this vein, experts from the Center for Democratic Renewal have written that "gay-bashing is an initiation rite for certain Nazi skinhead groups" (Sears, 1989:24).

Each subject was presented with the following item: "All of us, no matter what group we belong to, have to endure a 'rite of passage' in order to gain membership into our selected groups. Did you have to use violence in order to gain membership into your group?" Results are presented in Table 9.2 (Rites of Passage). Here we witness the most unequivocal finding of the research. Fully 100 percent of both groups — terrorists and non-terrorists — denied taking part in an initiation rite of violence. Once again, violence appears to be an instrumental behavior of the

Table 9.2
Rites of Passage ($N = 33$)

	Violence used as initiation rite	
	Yes	No
Terrorists	0	20
Non-Terrorists	0	13

Note: X^2 statistic cannot be computed.

subculture; and the role of the deviant peer seems to be an irrelevant sociological abstraction.

Gun Ownership

Additional knowledge about these issues can be achieved from an examination of gun ownership. Gun ownership has been found to be widespread among gangs in Milwaukee (Hagedorn, 1988) and Los Angeles (Maxson and Klein, 1990), and has been at the center of recent criminal justice policy debates on American street gangs (Huff, 1989). Likewise, investigations of the American far right have led Rex Gatewood (1989), Morris Dees (1991), Kevin Flynn and Gary Gerhardt (1989) and James Coates (1987) to conclude that gun ownership and membership in the National Rifle Association and the American Pistol and Rifle Association are standard practices within the American racist underground. Indeed, experts from the ADL have warned that "there is something especially troubling about the possession of weapons of death by volatile youngsters filled with racial and religious hatred. All the more reason why the dangers posed by neo-Nazi Skinheads warrants . . . urgent attention" (1989b:4).

Accordingly, we would expect gun ownership to be the norm among terrorist skinheads—signifying the defensive and instrumental nature of their violence. Findings are reported in Table 9.3 (Gun Ownership). We see that terrorists were significantly more likely to own guns than non-terrorists. These weapons included a variety of hunting rifles, shotguns, and handguns. The most frequently owned weapon was a Smith & Wesson .357 magnum pistol. Like the gang leaders interviewed by John Hagedorn, terrorists were often owners of multiple unlicensed firearms; like their reasoning for street fights, they viewed gun ownership as largely a defensive strategy to protect themselves against antagonists.

When further examined under a sociological microscope, gun ownership can be read as a metaphor. That is, the presence of firearms represents a group process serving to heighten the aggressive effect on subjects' behavior, thereby entrenching violence as a subcultural norm (see Yablonsky, 1990). Yet, how is this norm transmitted through the subculture? The data examined thus far offer thin support for the differential association hypothesis that violence is transmitted through the subculture by a deviant peer. In the case of the neo-Nazi skinheads, a deviant peer would be one who did not fight to defend the subculture, did not own

Table 9.3
Gun Ownership ($N = 36$)

	Yes	No
Terrorists	16	6
Non-Terrorists	1	13

$X^2 = 14.76$, $df = 1$, $p < .05$

a gun, but engaged in predatory violence as an initiation rite. Furthermore, gun ownership — like self-defense — is not considered deviant under any sociological or legal definition used in the United States today. Hence, there are obviously other forces operating to support the norm of violence.

The Network of Violence

These forces are summarized in Table 9.4 (Violence Transmission Matrix). (Because half of the non-terrorists admitted to fighting, once again I include them in the analysis.) The table shows a tight fit between violence and the primary transmitters of terrorist values. In order of importance, the most influential correlates of violence are gun ownership, exposure to Skrewdriver, exposure to the *WAR* zine, and exposure to the W.A.R. Hotline. More than any other factors considered thus far, these tell us the most about the causes of skinhead violence. And each of these factors — gun ownership, white power rock, and racist media images — are all safely protected by the U.S. Constitution. Hence, these protections play a crucial role in the development of policies to control domestic terrorism.

The network of violence is also defined by the remainder of correlates in Table 9.4. As such, these variables represent a package of transmission sources. Each variable is positively and significantly related to the prevalence of violence, and for the most part, each variable is significantly related to all others. Thus, the skinhead norm of violence is supported by forces both indigenous to the subculture (gun ownership) and external to the subculture (the activism of the NRA, the legacy of gun ownership within the racist underground, white power rock, and racist media images).

In the final analysis, Table 9.4 reveals that the backbone of this transmission process is Skrewdriver. Thus, white power rock, guns, and racist media images — not a deviant peer — are the factors that support the skinhead norm of violence. This norm is rational. This is because the skinhead style of violence is rational. And it is rational, as we have seen, because it is grounded in a form of neo-Nazism born in Britain under the administration of Margaret Thatcher and subsequently transported to North America during the Reagan years.

THE ROLE OF THE NEIGHBORHOOD IN SOCIAL BOND FORMATION

The theoretical framework used to formulate contemporary U.S. gang control policy assumes that certain deviant social bonds develop in the domain of the local community, or neighborhood. Under this formulation, gangs are seen as a natural product of advanced urbanization. Gang members are viewed as underclass youth struggling to live in communities that have experienced severe demographic transformations and extreme structural changes in the local economy. Sociologist William Julius Wilson attributes these developments to a "shift from

Table 9.4
Violence Transmission Matrix ($N = 36$) (Pearson's *r* reported)

	Prevalence of Violence	Gun Ownership	Exposure to Skrewdriver	Exposure to WAR	Exposure to W.A.R. Hotline
Prevalence of Violence	---	.721*	.648*	.450*	.360*
Gun Ownership	.721*	---	.595*	.291*	.266
Exposure to Skrewdriver	.648*	.595*	---	.639*	.600*
Exposure to WAR	.450*	.291*	.639*	---	.579*
Exposure to W.A.R.	.360*	.266	.600*	.579*	---

*$p < .05$

goods-producing to service-producing industries, the increasing polarization of the labor market into low-wage sectors, technological innovations, and the relocation of manufacturing industries out of the central cities" (1987:39).

Youths who live under these economic circumstances are thought to experience extreme social alienation. Once these youths become alienated, contemporary criminologists and criminal justice policymakers assume that certain young men will come to affiliate with each other in their neighborhoods and develop a subcultural value system that permits organized violence as a solution to their socioeconomic plight (see Fagan, 1990b; Hagedorn, 1990; Huff, 1989; Short, 1990; Spergel, 1990; U.S. Department of Justice, 1991).

Accordingly, three questions emerge, the answers to which are important for understanding terrorist youth subcultures and their norms. First, are skinheads truly alienated from mainstream society? Antiracist researchers point to a profound sense of alienation as the major cause of violence committed by the American neo-Nazi skinheads (ADL, 1989b; Klanwatch, 1991).

Second, if skinheads are found to be alienated, do they bring these concerns to their local neighborhoods and, like street gangs, formulate their violent collectives within the neighborhood domain? And third, do skinheads develop strong and meaningful social bonds within the domain of the neighborhood, or do they develop them otherwise?

Alienation

Like fascism, alienation is one of the most intriguing concepts of the social sciences. In the most general sense, alienation refers to "a separation between self and others, a fundamental failure to achieve reciprocity thinking" (Nash, 1985:124). Over the years, at least twenty-five scales, subscales, or indices of alienation have appeared in the journals of political science, sociology, and social psychology (Babbie, 1989; Robinson and Shaver, 1973). The original conceptualization and operationalization of the construct was performed by Leo Srole (1956) in an *American Sociological Review* article that has since been designated a citation classic by the American Institute for Scientific Information.

Srole began to formulate his reckonings on alienation as an undergraduate student at Harvard University during the mid-1930s. Srole's mentor, Professor Alfred Radcliffe-Brown, had carried on a lively correspondence with the great French sociologist Emile Durkheim, prior to Durkheim's death in 1917. After reading Durkheim's *Le Suicide,* Srole became fixated on the concept of anomie, or normlessness. In his words, Srole was "moved by Durkheim's preoccupation with the moral forces of the interpersonal ties that bind us to our time, place, and past, and also his insights about the lethal consequences that can follow from shrinkage and decay of those ties" (1989:116).

Srole later served with the United Nations Relief and Rehabilitation Administration helping to rebuild Europe in the wake of World War II. This led Srole to visit the Nazi concentration camp at Dachau. Says Srole, "There I saw first-hand the depths of dehumanization that macro-social forces, such as those that engaged Durkheim, could produce in individuals like Hitler, Eichmann, and others serving their dictates at all levels in the Nazi death factories" (Srole, 1989).

Moreover, Srole had begun to ponder the complex relationship between anomie and Nazism. Returning to his faculty post at Columbia University, Srole set out to develop a psychometric instrument that could measure the dynamics of disintegrated social bonds experienced at the individual level of analysis. This construct he called *anomia,* representing a psychological condition of an individual caused by macrosocial forces, or the sociological equivalent of alienation (Babbie, 1989; Wilson, 1981). Similar to the Berkeley social psychologists working on a theory of fascism at the time (Adorno et al., 1950), Srole was seeking to discover the structural forces that led thousands of German working-class youth into the ranks of the Nazi movement.

By the mid-1950s, Srole had tested, expanded, and refined his measurement of social disintegration through the study of several thousand bus drivers and other citizens of Springfield, Massachusetts, and New York City in the well-known Manhattan Project. The result of Srole's work was a five-item scale in which subjects were asked to either agree, disagree, or state their uncertainty with each item.

By 1982, the Science Citation Index and the Social Science Citation Index had listed some 400 scholarly publications in the United States and abroad that had cited Srole's simple yet classic research instrument. In the opinion of one scholar, Srole's scale represents "a seminal piece of work . . . [and] has undoubtedly been the most often referenced measure of alienation proposed to date" (Wilson, 1981:14). Down through the years, however, Srole's instrument has never been administered to a group of former Nazis or neo-Nazis. Therefore, the relationship between alienation and extremist ideology has never been estimated.

These issues are initially taken up in Table 9.5 (Alienation). Each subject was administered Srole's five-item anomia scale (Cronbach's alpha = .599 for all subjects) and each item was randomly placed within a broader list of items. Social control theorists and antiracist researchers would predict that terrorists would be more alienated than non-terrorists.

Subjects were first presented with the item: "Most public officials (people in public office) are not really interested in the problems of the average man." A full 100 percent of both groups agreed with this item. Hence, there is no difference between terrorists and non-terrorists. Both groups appear to be profoundly alienated.

Yet this certainty disappears when we examine responses to the second item: "Nowadays a person has to live pretty much for today and let tomorrow take care of itself." The overwhelming majority of terrorists and non-terrorists disagreed with this statement, indicating that their alienation might be limited only to feelings about public officials.

We learn more about the causes of alienation from an examination of responses

Table 9.5
Alienation ($N = 36$)

ITEM: "Most public officials (people in public office) are not
really interested in the problems of the average man."

| | Responses of Subjects | | |
	Agree	Not Sure	Disagree
Terrorists	22	0	0
Non-Terrorists	14	0	0

Note: X^2 statistic cannot be computed.

ITEM: "Nowadays a person has to live pretty much for today and
let tomorrow take care of itself."

| | Responses of Subjects | | |
	Agree	Not Sure	Disagree
Terrorists	4	1	17
Non-Terrorists	3	0	11

$X^2 = .68$, $df = 2$, $p = $ n.s.

ITEM: "In spite of what some people say, the lot of the average
man is getting worse, not better."

| | Responses of Subjects | | |
	Agree	Not Sure	Disagree
Terrorists	21	1	0
Non-Terrorists	14	0	0

$X^2 = .65$, $df = 1$, $p = $ n.s.

ITEM: "It's hardly fair to bring children into the world with
the way things look for the future."

| | Responses of Subjects | | |
	Agree	Not Sure	Disagree
Terrorists	3	0	19
Non-Terrorists	0	1	13

$X^2 = 3.52$, $df = 2$, $p = $ n.s.

ITEM: "These days a person doesn't really know whom he can count
on."

| | Responses of Subjects | | |
	Agree	Not Sure	Disagree
Terrorists	7	1	14
Non-Terrorists	10	2	2

$X^2 = 8.50$, $df = 2$, $p < .05$

to the third item: "In spite of what some people say, the lot of the average man is getting worse, not better." Here, 97 percent of the terrorists agreed, yet a full 100 percent of the non-terrorists also agreed. Therefore, both groups again appear to be profoundly alienated.

Yet once again our doubts are raised in reference to the fourth item: "It's hardly fair to bring children into the world with the way things look for the future." Both groups seem to have great expectations about the future as an overwhelming number of terrorists and non-terrorists rejected this pessimistic view of the world.

Last, subjects were presented with this item: "These days a person doesn't really know whom he can count on." This item elicited the only significant difference between subjects. That is, terrorists differ in only one way from non-terrorists. As the data show, terrorists are more likely to find someone in this world whom they can count on. Therefore, terrorists are less alienated than non-terrorists.

The association between neo-Nazism and alienation is displayed in Table 9.6 (Alienation and Neo-Nazism). The original theoretical expostulations of Srole would lead us to predict that there will be a tight fit between neo-Nazi beliefs and alienation. Such predictions are soundly refuted by the data in Table 9.6 (considering terrorists and non-terrorists together). The strongest coefficient is between the alienation item measuring attitudes toward "people you can count on" and the F-Scale item measuring antiminority attitudes. The direction of the coefficient shows that a low level of alienation is strongly associated with a high antiminority attitude—a blatant contradiction of alienation theory (see Srole, 1989).

This finding is confirmed by the association between attitudes toward "people you can count on" and anti-Semitic beliefs. Again, low alienation is associated with high anti-Semitism. Last, Table 9.6 shows that the remainder of the aliena-

Table 9.6
Alienation and Neo-Nazism ($N = 36$) (Pearson's r reported)

Alienation Scale Items Measuring attitudes toward:	F Scale Items Measuring Attitudes Toward:		
	Jews	Minorities	Homosexuals
"public officials"	.000	.000	.000
"letting tomorrow take care of itself"	.234	.152	.321*
"lot of the average man"	-.075	.074	-.117
"bringing children into the world"	.152	.265	.235
"people whom you can count on"	-.298*	-.843*	-.198

$*p < .05$

tion items uniformly fail to predict neo-Nazi beliefs, with one exception. Those who believed that they should "let tomorrow take care of itself" were more likely to hold antigay/lesbian attitudes.

These findings can be interpreted at several levels of analysis. Perhaps most importantly, the data reveal that terrorists are no more alienated than non-terrorists. Therefore, alienation does not appear to be a causal factor in the formulation of terrorist youth subcultures. Second, the data indicate, however, that both terrorists and non-terrorists have strong feelings of alienation in matters related to politics and economics. Third, both groups are clearly not alienated in their attitudes toward the future. Fourth, terrorists differ from non-terrorists on only one count: Terrorists are more likely to have faith in their fellow men or women than non-terrorists. This means that terrorists are less alienated than non-terrorists; a finding that social control theorists and antiracist researchers fail to predict. Finally, the findings show that alienation is not a necessary antecedent for the development of extreme political beliefs. The transmission of neo-Nazism, as demonstrated in chapter 8, is accomplished through white power rock and racist media images.

Neighborhood Influences

Thus, alienation is not a driving force behind the organization of terrorist youth subcultures. Nor is it a driving force behind the emergence of American neo-Nazism. Hence, there is no reason to believe that alienation plays a role in the development of skinhead norms. In fact, the data point in the opposite direction. If anything, the terrorist neo-Nazi skinheads appear to be socially integrated and well shielded from the extreme levels of bitterness and social estrangement noted by scholars in their analyses of urban minority gangs.

Thus, contrary to social control theory predictions, we have no reasons to expect terrorists to take their concerns to the neighborhood for resolution with other nonalienated white youth. This expectation is tested and confirmed in Table 9.7 (Neighborhood Organization). Here, subjects were asked "Do members of your group live in the same neighborhood?" They were given three response op-

Table 9.7
Neighborhood Organization ($N = 36$)

	All from same neighborhood	Some from same neighborhood	None from same neighborhood
Terrorists	0	16	6
Non-Terrorists	0	9	5

$X^2 = .28$, $df = 1$, $p = $ n.s.

tions: "They all live in the same neighborhood," "Some live in the same neighborhood, others don't," and "Nobody lives in the same neighborhood."

Overall, the table shows that neighborhood influences have no impact on the development of terrorist youth subcultures. None of the groups were made up of youths who all came from the same neighborhood. In fact, the table shows that nearly one-third of all groups were composed of youths who came from outside the neighborhood. Therefore, terrorist youth subcultures are not neighborhood-based. They are not interstitial. Rather, they are part of an international extremist movement that embraces a coherent system of values, music, and style. This system is called homology. And this homology ultimately constitutes the skinhead norm of violence.

Further insights into the decrepit power of neighborhood influences can be gained from an inspection of the methods used by the various skinhead collectives to recruit their members. Each subject was asked, "How were you brought into your group?" They were given two response options: "I was recruited," or "I jumped into the group on my own." Results are presented in Table 9.8 (Methods of Recruitment). Again, these results show no significant differences between terrorists and non-terrorists.

The majority of subjects reported that they "jumped into the group on their own." Hence, their decisions to become skinheads appear to be rational choices.

Social Bond Formation

Regarding the organization of violent youth subcultures, the logic of social control theory runs as follows: Harsh economic conditions cause some inner-city youths to experience ruptures in their bonds to conventional social institutions. The most important are the family, the school, and the labor market. As a result, these youths come together in the neighborhood and form their own community—a youth subculture. In time, this subculture adopts a set of deviant values permitting the emergence of organized violence as a reaction to extreme alienation. Finally, because these groups have their roots in a deviant value system, their group social bonds are weak. These weak bonds then produce unorganized collectives of ragtag youth. This logic has moved control theorists to believe that

Table 9.8
Methods of Recruitment ($N = 35$)

	Recruited by Others	"Jumped into" Group on Their Own
Terrorists	7	14
Non-Terrorists	3	11

$X^2 = .58$, $df = 1$, $p = $ n.s.

gangs . . . are better characterized as unorganized than as organized . . . there is, at best, an informal structure of *friendship*, but no hint of formal organization. *Gang members do not care much for one another. They do not trust one another. [G]ang members do not come together because they share positive interests or values*, but because they share poverty, unhappy homes, and social disabilities. (Gottfredson and Hirschi, 1990:207–8, emphasis added)

Present findings refute a number of these claims. The data do not support the notion that groups of violent youth share poverty. Only one subject in the entire sample had a father who was unemployed. Most terrorists came from blue-collar backgrounds, and the majority (77 percent) held down blue-collar jobs themselves. In fact, two terrorists were white-collar workers.

The majority of terrorists did not come from unhappy homes and few of them experienced social disabilities related to education and unemployment. Moreover, alienation was not found to be a common theme underlying the formation of terrorist youth subcultures. The analysis also revealed that terrorists do, indeed, "come together because they share interests or values." Their interests include the skinhead counterculture style, guns, violence, white power rock, and racist media images. Terrorists share a common value system rooted in neo-Nazism. And from their point of view—psychological predispositions notwithstanding—this value system is positive.

Yet, several issues do remain regarding the implications of social control theory for understanding terrorist youth subcultures. These relate specifically to the social bonds formed between skinheads, and the organizational structures that result from these bonds. Social control theorists center their argument around two conflicting propositions. On one hand, they argue that "gang members do not care much for one another [and] . . . they do not trust one another." Yet on the other, social control theorists claim that gangs represent "an informal structure of friendship." Thus, gangs are made up of friends; but these friends do not care for each other, and do not trust each other. One does not need to be a criminologist to appreciate the faulty logic of social control theory.

I began the examination of social bonds by asking a question about self-image. Criminological evidence shows that an individual's self-image is often boosted by close friendships; and when these friendships fall apart, violence is often the result (Chambliss, 1962). Each subject was presented with the following item: "All of us have certain people we hang out with. We do this because it makes us feel wanted, and we improve our self-images by being around these people. Among the people you hang out with, which best describes your feelings?"

Subjects were given three response options: They either indicated that their group affiliation gave them a high self-image, had no effect, or gave them a low self-image. Results are presented in Table 9.9 (Self-Image). Consistent with social control theory predictions, most terrorists appear to be friends with each other. Friendship is the norm within terrorist youth subcultures as nearly 90 percent of the terrorists indicated that their group affiliation gave them a high self-

Table 9.9
Self-Image ($N = 35$)

	High Self-Image	No Effect	Low Self-Image
Terrorists	19	2	0
Non-Terrorists	10	4	0

$X^2 = 2.14$, $df = 1$, $p =$ n.s.

image. Yet the same holds true for non-terrorists. Thus, something in the quality of these friendships must support and sustain the skinhead norm of violence — something that has been overlooked by social control theorists in their discourse on violent youth subcultures.

The Dynamics of Skinhead Friendships   We gain an initial understanding of the dynamics of skinhead friendships from the data presented in Table 9.10 (Subcultural Conflict). Subjects were presented with the item, "No matter what group we join, this group will have problems. Someone will always disagree with another over things like power and control of the group. What are the problems of your group?" Three response options were given: "We have no problems, there is a low level of conflict, We have a few problems, there is a moderate level of conflict, or We have a lot of problems, there is a high level of conflict."

Using these measures, social control theorists would predict that terrorists would display a high level of conflict. Table 9.10 refutes this expectation. The data show that none of the terrorists experienced high conflict in their groups, nor did any of the non-terrorists. In fact, 40 percent of the terrorists reported that they experienced low conflict and more than 90 percent of the non-terrorists reported low conflict. Skinhead friendships, therefore, do not lead to high levels of conflict.

However, Table 9.10 also shows that something in the quality of skinhead friendships leads to modest amounts of group conflict. And this finding confirms social control theory predictions at a level of statistical significance. The majority of terrorists (59 percent) experienced moderate conflict in their groups, and only one non-terrorist reported moderate conflict. Hence, moderate conflict is the norm within terrorist youth subcultures.

Table 9.10
Subcultural Conflict ($N = 36$)

	Low Conflict	Moderate Conflict	High Conflict
Terrorists	9	13	0
Non-Terrorists	13	1	0

$X^2 = 9.71$, $df = 1$, $p < .05$

This finding should cause concern among theorists, policymakers, and community activists. Such conflict is an indication that something may be fundamentally wrong within the American neo-Nazi skinhead subculture. If something is inherently wrong within a youth subculture, then we may assume that the subculture is prone to self-destruction under the sheer weight of its own ideological and organizational dynamics. If so, it would follow that the neo-Nazi skinheads will one day fade away into obscurity. They will do so naturally. They will simply go the way of other largely defunct British and U.S. subcultures—the beats, teddy boys, mods, hippies, rockers, new wavers, punks, casuals, and so forth. Part and parcel of counterculture living is experiencing the birth, life, and death of a movement.

In this way, the statistical correlates in Table 9.11 (Sources of Social Bond Formation) can be read as a thermostat of skinhead organizational mental health. Here, all subjects are studied in terms of their self-images and group conflicts. (I examined all of the bivariate correlations for the entire range of variables analyzed thus far in the research. Only the significant correlations appear in Table 9.11.) As we see, several factors currently undermine group bonding among American skinheads.

A Portrait of the Unfriendly Skinhead   There are four factors that affect a subject's self-image: The most important is the attitude that there are people you can count on. The direction of the coefficient shows that if a skinhead has no one to count on, this leads to the group having no effect on the subject's self-image. The next most influential predictor in the direction of a decreased self-image is artistic ability. It appears that the more varied a subject's artistic capabilities, the more likely the group will have no effect on self-image. The final two predictors are drawn from responses to the F scale. Those who embrace strong traditional views about the family are likely to experience no group effect on their self-

Table 9.11
Sources of Social Bond Formation ($N = 36$) (Pearson's r reported)

	Individual Self-Image	Group Conflict
Occupational goals	.12	-.45*
Family friction	.17	-.25*
Educational goals	-.26	.29*
Artistic abilities	.37*	.22
Recruitment methods	.11	-.29*
Terrorism	.19	-.39*
Exposure to Skrewdriver	.15	-.36*
Frequency of viewing Race and Reason	.08	-.35*
Anti-black attitudes	.29*	-.48*
Attitudes toward the family	.33*	-.30*
Anti-Semitic attitudes	.20	-.35*
Attitudes toward "people you can count on"	-.47*	.20

*$p < .05$

images. And those who embrace strong antiminority attitudes are more likely to experience no effect on their self-images.

Taken together, these findings allow for the construction of a stochastic portrait of the subcultural member whose bond has been weakened within the group. In effect, this is a portrait of the unfriendly skinhead. These persons are more extreme than other subcultural members in their hatred of blacks and are more traditional in their attitudes toward the family. These attitudes are heightened by an overindulgence in racist artistic endeavors. Combined, these forces appear to push other skinheads away leaving the subject to believe, most importantly, that they have been abandoned—they have no one to count on.

A Portrait of a Skinhead Who Can't Be Trusted   The majority of terrorists reported moderate group conflict. Yet Table 9.11 also shows that this conflict comes from a variety of sources. As such, these findings allow us to create a composite picture of the skinhead who, in the language of social control theorists, "cannot be trusted." This person is the agent of group conflict. Table 9.11 indicates that this person is recruited into the group and did not join of his own volition. This person comes from a family where there was more than the normal amount of conflict. And today, strong opinions about the traditional family continue to dominate this person's thinking.

The agent of conflict has also set inordinantly high occupational goals. Whereas most skinheads aspire to a blue-collar job in the future, our protagonist hopes to land a white-collar job, thereby blatantly rejecting the working-class roots of the skinhead subculture. In fact, the protagonist hopes to one day earn a college diploma. This aspiration further sets the agent of conflict apart from the authentic working-class brothers and sisters of the skinhead subculture.

The agent of conflict is the most violent member of the subculture, committing acts of terrorism at a level exceeding that of his peers. This person is a troublemaker of the first degree; and therefore, the group experiences conflict.

The agent of conflict does not listen to Skrewdriver more than other white power bands. Perhaps this person does not understand the words of Skrewdriver. Perhaps Skrewdriver represents hidebound beliefs about Vikings and Nazis, and the agent of conflict envisions something beyond this for transmitting revisionistic theories of national socialism. Our skinhead who can't be trusted then turns to the media for the transmission of this oddball form of Nazism. And in this regard, the cable television program "Race and Reason" has an important effect on our protagonist. In turn, this person adopts extremist beliefs about Jews and African-Americans.

Thus, we can make two conclusions about the skinhead who can't be trusted—the agent of conflict. First, this person may cause a terrorist youth subculture to buckle under the weight of its own obsessions. The agent of conflict is, therefore, an important player in the geometry of public policy to control the spread of domestic terrorism in the United States. If allowed to run his course, the agent of conflict may inevitably send the neo-Nazi skinheads into subcultural oblivion. The second conclusion we can draw is that this person, in many ways, represents a caricature of Tom Metzger.

10

Antifeminism and the Orthodoxy of Domestic Terrorism

Control theory assumes that the bond of affection for conventional persons is a major deterrent to crime. The stronger this bond, the more likely the person is to take it into account when and if he contemplates a criminal act.

—Travis Hirschi
Causes of Delinquency

The Hammer Skins are strong into family values. . . . There are eleven women in our group and eight are pregnant. This is the most important way we can carry on with the white power tradition.

—Sherry
Confederate Hammer Skins

The American gang literature is divided on the issue of organization. On one hand, scholars describe the internal structure of a gang as age-graded and pyramidal in shape (Hagedorn, 1988; Mieczkowski, 1986; Moore, 1978; Thrasher, 1963; Vigil, 1988; Yablonsky, 1983). The picture emerging from this explanation is one in which a gang is founded and organized by a core group of older violent youth, and its ranks are made up of a fringe group of less violent youth. Members are, therefore, thought to be arranged in a hierarchical or paramilitary order with chiefs or seniors at the top; officers or lieutenants in the middle; and juniors, peewees or wanna-bes at the bottom. Advancement through the ranks is thought to come primarily from bold acts of violence perpetrated against rival gang members. This is the stereotypical image of violent gangs popularized in such films as *Colors, New Jack City,* and *Boyz N the Hood.*

On the other hand, social control theorists postulate that "gangs of adolescent *males* are better characterized as unorganized than as organized . . . [they have] no hint of formal organization" (Gottfredson and Hirschi, 1990:207, emphasis added). From this perspective, gang members do not care for each other and do not trust each other. Therefore, they form weak social bonds based on "an informal structure of friendship" (Gottfredson and Hirschi, 1990:207).

Research conducted on the skinheads is also split in its depiction of organizational structure. The FBI has published information suggesting that skinheads are organized into a subcultural army (Clarke, 1991). These conclusions have been confirmed by the investigative reporters from ABC's "20/20" who discovered that Metzger's W.A.R. was organized into such paramilitary ranks where lieutenants were issued report cards and were rewarded for bashing somebody, as former W.A.R. Lt. David Mazzella has testified ("20/20," December 15, 1990).

Alternatively, however, research conducted by the ADL indicates that skinheads are organized into small communes:

Skinhead gangs, like all street gangs and cults, provide their members with a substitute family composed of their peers. This is particularly true for those Skinheads who live communally, in rented apartments or houses, as many do. . . . This sense of kinship is strengthened even further if the gang has been involved in violence together. (ADL, 1989b:29)

My research findings are consistent with those of the ADL. Through the interviews, I noted that a number of skinhead leaders were married or engaged. Others reported that they had children or planned to start a family in the near future. For example, the leader of the Bronx Area Skinheads (who lived with his fiancée and two other skinheads) said, "There's no central organization among the East Coast skins. Each group is made up of friends who believe in the struggle. No one gets recruited."

A Louisville skinhead reported that his group was "just like a big family . . . everybody works together." And I found that several of the more violent subjects (including Ronald) did share communal living arrangements with other subcultural members. Perhaps the most insightful lesson on the organization of skinhead groups comes from a musician in the study.

This twenty-one-year-old non-terrorist was a popular guitar player and singer in an East Coast skinhead band. His head was shaved, his ears were pierced, and he dressed in traditional skinhead garb—Doc Martens, a white power T-shirt, red suspenders, and a donkey jacket. Essentially, he was a strong advocate of skinhead music and style, but did not embrace a neo-Nazi value system. In fact, he was quick to say, "I am not a national socialist!" He lived communally with other skinheads, and over the two-year period he had not been in one fight. In fact, he had never committed a crime in his life—not even a traffic violation.

Between 1987 and 1989, his band traveled across the United States, Canada, and Great Britain playing gigs at bars and pubs, and visiting local skinhead collectives. In London, he met a skinhead girl and she returned to the States with him where they began to arrange their wedding. About the organization of American skinheads he says,

There are two levels in the U.S. It varies from region to region depending on who you deal with. There are groups, like mine, that believe we have been discriminated against because of the color of our skin. But we only take it so far. Then there are political groups, and they have a lot of influence especially in California. I've seen a lot of good people getting mixed up with political groups. . . . The political groups have exploited the skins. They're not interested in the true skinheads, they only use these kids for their muscle. [These] skins have become front men for the Klan and W.A.R.

Following these insights, we may first conclude that the most beneficial course of analysis is to examine the organization of skinhead groups from the perspective of the family. In this way, we can then determine whether political groups (i.e., terrorists) are organized differently from non-political groups (i.e., non-terrorists). Yet, using this family model to explain skinhead organization demands that we ignore hypotheses advanced by other researchers. This means that I focus on neither group stratification nor age. And unlike social control theorists, I assume that these groups are composed of both males and females.

THE ROLE OF WOMEN IN TERRORIST
YOUTH SUBCULTURES

The word *family* is based on the Middle English *familie* that was derived from the Middle Latin *familia* and translated from the early Latin *famulust,* or "servant." In its current usage, family is defined by the *American Heritage Dictionary of the English Language* as "The most instinctive, fundamental social or mating group in man and animal, especially the union of man and woman through marriage and their offspring."

We are, therefore, led to ponder this most instinctive of all social groups and its impact on the internal structure of terrorist youth subcultures. Centuries worth of historical evidence shows that women have played a major role in creating the family as a social institution. Because the American skinheads appear to be family-based, we would expect women to play a major role in the internal organization of such groups.

We gain our baseline of knowledge about the role played by women by looking back on the findings. The historical and case study data revealed two intriguing cases: First there was Ronald, the Orlando terrorist. Ronald indicated that he was going through a romantic crisis with his girlfriend during the latter days of his two-year spree of racial violence. And then there was Clark Martell, who used a knife to mutilate his girlfriend after their falling out. In addition, the quantitative analysis revealed that conservative attitudes toward the family led to a significant weakening of social bonds between subjects.

Further in this vein, I interviewed several skinhead girls who reported moderate conflict in their groups over the issue of sexual promiscuity. For example, an Austin, Texas, skinhead (also a high-school honor student) reported, "I would say that we have a moderate level of conflict in our organization. The only time a problem came up was when this guy [who was married] got caught sleeping with another girl. . . . She got her ass kicked."

On this basis, we may tentatively hypothesize that the presence of women in a skinhead group somehow serves to promote terrorism. Such an hypothesis is considered in Table 10.1 (Presence of Women). As we see, the data suggest that the majority of terrorist and non-terrorist groups included women. Thus, the presence of women in a skinhead collective appears to have no direct effect on the proclivity of its members to engage in terrorism.

Social Roles and Gender Differences

To gain further insights into the role of women in the organization of terrorist youth subcultures, I examined the individual differences between men and women in the sample. These findings are displayed in Table 10.2 (Gender and the Skinhead Subculture). (Here I consider all subjects, yet examine only the significant bivariate correlations associated with the previously discovered differences between terrorists and non-terrorists.) The significant differences between skinhead men and women are as follows:

1. Men are more likely to own guns than women.

2. Men are more violent than women.

3. Men are more terroristic than women.

Table 10.1
Presence of Women ($N = 35$)

	Women in group	No women in group
Terrorists	21	1
Non-Terrorists	12	1

$X^2 = .15$, $df = 1$, $p =$ n.s.

Table 10.2
Gender and the Skinhead Subculture ($N = 36$) (Pearson's r reported)

	Gender
Gun ownership	.28*
Prevalence of violence	.39*
Terrorism	.46*
Exposure to Skrewdriver	.36*
Exposure to WAR	.28*
Anti-minority attitudes	.48*
Anti-semitic attitudes	.43*
Attitudes toward "people you can count on"	-.45*

*$p < .05$

4. Men are more frequently exposed to Skrewdriver than women.

5. Men are more frequently exposed to *WAR* than women.

6. Men are more racist than women.

7. Men are more anti-Semitic than women.

8. Women are less alienated than men.

Thus, terrorist youth subcultures are primarily male-oriented. Women, it seems, take a secondary or subservient role in the internal structuring of skinhead groups. They do not play a central role. Perhaps this explains why they are less alienated than men (see Pettigrew, 1981, for a discussion of racism and mental health among white Americans). Such findings are not surprising. They are consistent with studies on the development of German national socialism showing that the early Nazis "exalted masculinity and could in many ways be characterized as anti-feminist" (Linz, 1976:87).

The Impact of Women in Sustaining Homology

Perhaps a more important issue relates to the role played by women in sustaining subcultural homology—the wellspring of terrorism. This issue is examined quantitatively in Table 10.3 (Impact of Women on Skinhead Homology). (Here I consider all subjects and report only significant coefficients from the entire range of variables examined thus far.)

It appears that women have their strongest impact in the area of attitudes toward family and country. This correlation represents the association between the presence of women in a group and responses to the F-Scale item, "What the youth needs is strict discipline, rugged determination, and the will to work and fight for family and country." Although the association is significant, as we have seen, such a belief was not part of the terrorist value system (i.e., neo-Nazism).

Similarly, women have an influence on group attitudes toward raising children. This conclusion is based on the bivariate relationship between presence of women and responses to the alienation item, "It's hardly fair to bring children into the world with the way things look for the future." The direction of the coefficient

Table 10.3
The Impact of Women on Skinhead Homology ($N = 36$) (Pearson's r reported)

	Presence of Women
Attitudes toward respect for parents	.31*
Attitudes toward raising children	-.34*
Attitudes toward family	.73*
Exposure to W.A.R. Hotline	.25*
Exposure to WAR	.53*
Frequency of exposure to Skrewdriver	.45*

*$p < .05$

indicates that the presence of women in a group is significantly associated with the rejection of that attitude. However, once again this positive attitude toward the future was not an identifiable feature of the terrorist value system; that is, non-terrorists were equally as positive about raising children.

Women also have a strong effect on group attitudes toward respect for parents. This association is based on the bivariate correlation between presence of women and responses to the F Scale item, "There is hardly anything lower than a person who does not feel a great love, gratitude, and respect for his parents"—an attitude that also had no impact on terrorist values.

I have just reviewed three ways in which women influence the organization of skinhead groups. Each relates to the family, though none relate to neo-Nazism. Thus, women seem to play a small role in sustaining homology. Yet Table 10.3 shows that women impact skinhead groups in three additional ways, and each relates to transmitting the style of terrorism:

First, the presence of women in a group is strongly correlated with the propensity of group members to read *WAR*. And exposure to *WAR* was found to be an influential correlate of gun ownership, violence, exposure to Skrewdriver, exposure to the W.A.R. Hotline, and a primary source of transmitting neo-Nazi beliefs about racial minorities.

Second, (and consistent with the previous finding), Table 10.3 shows that the presence of women in a group is significantly associated with the frequency of exposure to Skrewdriver—found to be the major source for transmitting neo-Nazi values and the style of terrorism. Finally, the table shows that women seem to facilitate exposure to the W.A.R. Hotline. And exposure to the W.A.R. Hotline was found to be an important correlate of violence, exposure to Skrewdriver, exposure to *WAR,* and a major source of transmitting neo-Nazi beliefs about gays and lesbians.

In summary, the role of women in the transmission of terrorist values, music, and style is subtle and complex. Women play a major role in providing traditional family values that may encourage the processes of affiliation and cohesion in a terrorist youth subculture. The presence of women in the subculture appears to elicit strong attitudes toward family, child raising, and respect for parents. Not only are these traditional family values but they are traditional conservative values as well.

Because women play a major part in legitimizing and institutionalizing traditional family values within the subculture, they seem to create conditions conducive to the frequency of exposure to white power rock and exposure to racist media images. These conditions, in turn, lead to terrorism. Therefore, women sustain skinhead homology primarily through their role as wives, girlfriends, and/or mothers—not through their role as terrorists. We may therefore conclude that women have an important yet indirect impact on the transmission of terrorism, and a conservative and distinctly antifeminist impact on the internal structure of groups that appears to support the recent American skinhead bricolage.

ANTIFEMINISM, BRICOLAGE, AND TERRORISM

The relationships between antifeminism, bricolage, and terrorism are more easily understood through an analysis of the interview data. The following four case studies demonstrate these relationships. The first two studies examine the leadership of non-terrorist groups, and the second two examine the leadership of terrorist organizations.

The Detroit Case Study

The first case study involved a twenty-year-old woman from the Detroit area. She had a steady boyfriend who owned his own computer consulting business and was the leader of a local skinhead collective. He was also a minister in the Church of the Creator, an avowed national socialist, and a non-terrorist who claimed that the members of his group did not engage in violence against anyone. Again, the starting point for understanding the skinhead subculture is hairstyle. Says our Detroit subject,

I wear my hair long and naturally curly. I feel that it becomes me, so naturally I like it. I usually wear conservative business clothes during the workday and casual or dressy clothes at other times. *I am not trying to make any fashion statement.* I wear rings, watches, and a bracelet which has sentimental value [emphasis added].

Her favorite band was Aerosmith; she did not hold neo-Nazi beliefs; nor had she committed any acts of terrorism or violence over the two-year period. She did not own a gun, did not read *WAR,* nor did she use the W.A.R. Hotline. She worked as a secretary and planned to marry her boyfriend in the near future and start a family.

The Point Pleasant Case Study

Our second case study involved a twenty-one-year-old woman from Point Pleasant, New Jersey. She is now married to the skinhead musician who earlier made the insightful comments about political and nonpolitical groups. He is not a neo-Nazi; neither he nor members of his group engage in terrorism. Once more, we begin with hairstyle. Says our subject, "My hair is shaved on top in skinhead girl style, but long on the sides. I usually wear jeans, Fred Perrys, Doc Marten shoes, and a flight jacket. I also wear a silver wedding ring."

Her favorite band was the Jam, and according to my measures, she was a neo-Nazi. She had been in four fights during the two-year period (two in her native London), yet none were against racial minorities. Thus, she was not a terrorist. An occasional reader of the racist publications *National Vanguard* and *The Thunderbolt,* she did not read *WAR* nor use the Hotline. She was unemployed, did not own a gun, and held strong opinions about the media's portrayal of skinheads. She said

I don't like to work at all. I just want to be a housewife and raise my kids in the white power movement because it's a positive culture. . . . It's typical of people in the U.S. to laugh at us skinheads, but we really stand for strong family ties. In England, skinheads are more readily accepted.

The Milwaukee Case Study

Now we turn to case studies of terrorist groups to assess the influences of anti-feminism and bricolage on the internal structure of skinhead organizations. The first case study involved a nineteen-year-old woman from Milwaukee. She was married to the Reverend. And the Reverend, in my opinion, is a model of American skinheadism. Says our subject, "I wear my hair long, layered, and curled because I think it's an attractive style. I usually wear very feminine preppie clothes; sometimes a Fred Perry tennis shirt. It just means I take pride in my appearance. *It means nothing really*" (emphasis added).

Her favorite group was the Canadian skinhead band Ra Ho Wa. She does not hold neo-Nazi beliefs about minorities, nor is she anti-Semitic. Yet she is homophobic. Over the two years studied, she engaged in no fights and no acts of terrorism; neither did she own a gun. An occasional reader of *Racial Loyalty*, she did not read *WAR* nor does she use the Hotline.

During the research, this young woman became pregnant. And in 1990, she gave birth to their daughter. Because the Reverend is drug free, employed, and committed to his future educational and occupational goals, he is able to provide for his family, and they are relatively happy. They are far from alienated. And this, in turn, inspires the Reverend to even greater heights of white power activism. Accordingly, Milwaukee now has one of the fastest growing skinhead groups in America.

The Dallas Case Study

Our final case study involved a twenty-year-old woman from Dallas, Texas. She was the founder of the Confederate Hammer Skins (CHS). During the late 1980s, CHS came under the scrutiny of U.S. Attorney General Dick Thornburgh (1990). At issue was the severe desecration of the Jewish Community Center of Dallas. Moreover, members of CHS had spray painted swastikas and other anti-Semitic graffiti on the walls of the center. But that was not all. One Hammer Skin male had climbed to the roof of the center and placed a cyanide gas pellet into the air-conditioning system. And this had incurred the wrath of the Texas attorney general, the U.S. attorney general, and later, the president of the United States. There was good reason for their concern. Had this young man succeeded in his crime that was foiled by Dallas police, it would have represented the most horrendous act of domestic terrorism in the American twentieth century.

The identity of this terrorist is well-known. For several weeks during 1989, he occupied a position on the FBI's Ten Most Wanted Criminals List. The *New York Times*, the *Nation*, and the ADL had told his story in some detail. Yet he is married to the woman who is the subject of this case study; and her name I cannot reveal. Therefore, ethics dictate that I not reveal his name either. Suffice it to say that he is now serving a ten-year federal prison sentence for a string of hate crimes. And, because of his avowed neo-Nazi beliefs, he is currently having a difficult time adjusting to prison life.

For the sake of expediency, I call this young woman Sherry, and her husband, Rick. We begin with Sherry's upbringing.

I had very little conflict growing up. My dad was in the U.S. Coast Guard, and I liked him. Me and my mom always got along. Then they got divorced, and I went to live with my mom. She belongs to the Ku Klux Klan.

Then I met Rick. He was into white power, too. We got married in a Klan ceremony, up north. When we came back from our honeymoon, I started the Hammer Skins because I wanted to express my opinions about the white race.

At this point, Sherry also started playing bass guitar in a skinhead garage band fronted by Rick. Because of her mother's association with the West Coast Klan, Sherry became exposed to *WAR,* "Race and Reason," the W.A.R. Hotline, Skrewdriver, and the W.A.R. Board. Moreover, Sherry was in love with Rick, and Sherry was in love with her mother. Rick got along just fine with Sherry's mother, and everybody was positive about the future of the Confederate Hammer Skins. In essence, organized terrorism was being structured in the family – the most instinctual social group known to man and animal.

By the Fourth of July 1989, the Confederate Hammer Skins numbered approximately sixty, making them one of the largest skinhead collectives in the United States (ADL, 1989b). Sherry, supported by her family, was the titular head of this group (and "none of the CHS members," according to Sherry, "came from the same neighborhood"). She was drug free, unemployed, and carried a 12-gauge pump-action shotgun and a .36 caliber pistol in full view on the dashboard of her pick-up truck. In fact, together with other CHS members, Sherry had stockpiled a small cache of shotguns and handguns buried in a vacant lot near her mom's house (ADL, 1989b). She says,

I wear my hair like a skinhead girl. It's blonde, and I wear it in a short crop on top with a long fringe of red dyed hair in back. I usually wear Doc Martens, miniskirts, fishnet hose, white power T-shirts, or Fred Perry tennis shirts to be preppy.

Sherry's favorite band was Brutal Attack. She also listened to No Remorse, Condemned 84, and Skrewdriver on a daily basis. Sherry reported that she had listened to these bands for seven or eight years. (During my interview with Sherry, I realized that this was impossible. Sherry was interviewed on February 14, 1990. If she started listening to this music seven or eight years ago, this means she was introduced to white power rock in 1982 — when Sherry was twelve years old. Yet Skrewdriver records were not available in the United States until around 1985. Brutal Attack and the others followed.)

So I repeated the question: "How long have you listened to these bands?" She again responded, "seven or eight years." Since this is impossible, I began to think that perhaps Sherry lives in what forensic psychologists refer to as a separate reality (see Lillyquist, 1980). I am also reminded of the social psychology literature that shows extreme racism breeds distortions in reality (Kushnick, 1981).

Sherry said that she watched "Race and Reason" once a week, and had done so for more than three years. I asked how many years, and she again replied "about seven or eight." Yet Metzger made the Dallas cable TV hookup in 1988, the heyday of the American skinhead movement. It was not in operation seven or eight years ago. "How many years?" I repeated. "Seven or eight," she replied.

Sherry reported that she was a regular reader of *WAR, From the Mountain,* and *National Vanguard.* She said she had read *WAR* for more than three years. "How many years?" I asked. "Seven or eight," she replied. The first edition of *WAR* appeared in 1985, approximately the same year that white power rock was introduced into U.S. record stores.

Sherry also reported that she was a frequent user of the W.A.R. Hotline. "How often do you use it?" I asked. "I use it every day," she responded. I then called the Dallas W.A.R. Hotline for seven days and discovered that Metzger's message was the same every day. Sherry, apparently, had used the Hotline in this obsessive fashion since its establishment in 1988, and it was the only hotline she used.

In 1988, her mother purchased a computer; in 1989 Sherry became a user of Metzger's W.A.R. Board. By this time, Sherry herself was familiar with Metzger. He had sent Sherry copies of *WAR* for distribution to the CHS membership, and a video of "Race and Reason" classics. One night as she was using the W.A.R. Board, Sherry saw the announcement for an upcoming white power rock concert called the Reich 'N' Roll Festival to be held in Oklahoma on Memorial Day. She called Rick immediately.

According to my measures, Sherry was a neo-Nazi. But she was not a terrorist. Over the past two years, she had only been in one fight, and that was against another skinhead girl who had gotten pregnant by a married man in the Hammer Skins.

On Memorial Day weekend 1989, Rick, Sherry, and fourteen other Hammer Skins traveled to the suburbs of Tomahawk, Oklahoma, for the Reich 'N' Roll Festival — billed by John Metzger as a historic Aryan event. Based on what has been discovered in this research, we may surmise that the Hammer Skins were well-armed and blasted white power rock from the tape decks of their pickup trucks as they made their journey across the flatlands of north Texas.

Two important events transpired at the festival. First, Sherry and Rick, because of their white power activism in Dallas, were reportedly offered a portion of the Order money taken from the Brinks truck robbery of 1984. It is alleged that Tom Metzger made this offer himself, though he denies the charge. According to FBI documents obtained by the John Brown Anti-Klan Committee, Sherry and Rick accepted this money (John Brown Anti-Klan Committee, 1990c).

Next, Rick met someone (identity unknown) at the festival who exposed him to a cache of cyanide pellets. Several of these pellets were handed over to Rick. A week later—inspired by the emotions he felt at the Tomahawk music festival—Rick inserted one of these pellets into the air-conditioning system of the Dallas Jewish Community Center (Thornburgh, 1990).

Today Rick is incarcerated at the U.S. Federal Penitentiary, Terre Haute. Sherry has her things stored at her mom's house in Dallas; but Sherry herself is on an extended visit with family members, as her mother recently told me. In short, Rick, Sherry, and her mom have begun to drift apart. Their family bond, and the internal structure of CHS, has been weakened by the brute forces of the American criminal justice system. Before going underground Sherry told me that

There are so many misperceptions about us. What people don't know is that the Hammer Skins are strong into family values and strong antidrug. There are eleven women in our group and eight are pregnant. This is the most important way we can carry on with the white power tradition.

[Rick] is being treated very unfairly and is being made an example of by our government. His codefendants were all moved to prisons which are basically close to their families. My main concern is for my husband's safety. He is so far from me, and I feel very out of touch.

I have no control over anything that happens to him. I'm desperate! (*Beginning to cry*) I need help from someone and everyone keeps slamming their doors! . . . [Rick's] association with the skinheads has blacklisted him! (*Sobbing*) Can you help me . . . please?

CONCLUSIONS

There appears to be no difference between the organizational structure of political and nonpolitical skinhead groups. Both are family-oriented, and both include women who serve a number of important functions. Women bring to the internal structure of skinhead groups a respect for traditional family values. They encourage attitudes toward childbearing and parenting. And this gives the group a positive outlook on the future, and "someone they can count on."

As a consequence, women encourage group attitudes of antifeminism. The German Nazis were antifeminists, and terrorist skinhead men hold strong neo-Nazi beliefs. This transmission process can be read through hairstyle. The women involved with both terrorist and non-terrorist leaders referred to their hairstyle with the term *skinhead girl*. This is common parlance across the subculture. However, the term *skinhead boy* does not exist. Skinhead groups, both political and nonpolitical, are family-oriented organizations that are male-dominated. Women are servants within this family. They purposefully act like girls (i.e., they usually do not perform acts of terrorism) and they allow themselves to be treated like girls.

In this way, women become agent provocateurs in the American skinhead bricolage and contribute to an American orthodoxy of neo-Nazism and terrorism. The leadership of both political and nonpolitical skinhead groups have become involved with women who were not trying to make fashion statements. Moreover, they were meek women. They looked and behaved like the girl next door. And with their strong beliefs about childbirth firmly communicated to their lovers, these men gained the family support to indulge themselves in political ideology. As a result, women sustained homology by creating a family space that allowed skinhead men to increase their exposure to white power rock and W.A.R. materials. This led to acts of terrorism.

Yet taken to its extreme, Sherry has taught us that terrorism can destroy the family. And as we saw in the previous chapter, indulgence in terrorism can also weaken social bonds. Hence, skinhead women not only serve the goals of terrorism but their antifeminism also undermines the cohesion of the family unit itself.

This is the norm of skinhead terrorism. It is fraught with contradiction. On one hand, women support a traditional family; yet on the other, they allow the transmission of terrorist values, music, and style. The result is the destruction of their own families — institutions to which they are mere servants to begin with.

This norm defines the internal structure of terrorist youth subcultures for better or worse. The norm has nothing to do with age or group stratification. It has nothing to do with group status ascriptions, alienation, or paramilitary training. Terrorist youth subcultures are not comprised of people who dislike and mistrust one another.

Rather, the American skinheads appear to love and value one another. The skinheads are rooted in the most instinctive social group known to humankind — the family. Throughout the history of American white supremacism, extremist activity has always been based on an us versus them mentality. The skinheads have institutionalized this mentality within the domain of the family. And terrorism bleeds over into the family and destroys it.

Thus, the American neo-Nazi skinheads represent a nonliterate, nontechnical tribe of primitive men who respond to the world around them with a rational form of violence. This violence involves a political science of the concrete, not an abstract science of the civilized. These skinhead men, supported by their wives and girlfriends, then carefully and precisely order and arrange into the family structure the minutiae of the concrete world by means of a convoluted logic not of their own creation. Terrorism is then constructed from the heart of this logic.

RESEARCH NOTE

The women referred to in the Detroit, Point Pleasant, and Milwaukee case studies are not part of the study sample of thirty-six skinheads.

11

Beer, Bonding, and the Ceremony of Berserking

Under every scientific and pharmacological constraint existing today for the protection of society, alcohol most certainly would be a class 2 narcotic and would be available only with a Government Narcotic Registry Number.

—Howard Abadinsky
Drug Abuse

We just started out as a bunch of guys who liked to drink beer.

—Joe
Portland's East Side White Pride

The relationship between criminal and drug-using behavior is one of the most thoroughly examined relationships in criminology. Research shows that some drug-intoxicated individuals commit crimes because they have lost their natural inhibitions while under the influence. Other studies show that crime is the result of drug dealing; and still others show that crimes arise from economic necessity, because users need money to purchase more drugs (see Brownstein and Goldstein, 1990; Johnson et al., 1990). However, these patterns are not corroborated by gang scholars. Although many cities have reported a dramatic increase in gang- and drug-related murders and other violent crimes, the gang literature fails to tell us whether this phenomenon is due to the pharmacological intoxication of gang members, disputes over drug sales, and/or from economic necessity.

For example, James Vigil (1988) reports an increase in intergang warfare based on access to and distribution of crack cocaine. Moreover, Vigil's gang members engaged in both the use and sales of crack and other drugs in the neighborhood context of a subculture that valued violence. Yet the research of Jeffrey Fagan (1989) demonstrates many gang members avoid using drugs while dealing or avoid them altogether. Fagan does, however, point to a linear relationship between drugs and violence. "Drug use," he writes, "is intrinsic to gang life among more violent gangs" (1989:645). Such violence, according to Fagan, serves to strengthen the social bonds between gang members.

To the extent that Fagan is correct, such a relationship between drugs and violence ought to transcend the various origins and subjective meanings of collective violence across social contexts of criminal subcultures. That is, drug use and/or sales should also be intrinsic to the violent skinhead subculture as well. And, accordingly, such behavior should serve to strengthen the social bonds between subcultural members.

Yet, such propositions seem to carry little freight among antiracist researchers. The ADL, for one, contends that

There is no denying that the Skinheads, unlike such criminal gangs as the Crips and Bloods, have not been found to engage in wholesale drug dealing. At the same time, there are indications that some Skinheads use drugs and have been engaged in some low level dealing (1989b:30).

But instead of strengthening social bonds, the ADL reports that drug use weakens the internal structure of skinhead groups. They argue that "the Skinhead gangs have severe internal problems. There is substantial evidence of drug use" (ADL, 1988c:28).

DRUGS AND TERRORISM

The prevalence of drug use among the skinheads in this study is reported in Table 11.1 (Frequency of Drug Use). Subjects were asked, "How often do you use illegal drugs?" They were given three response options: "I never use drugs," "I use drugs several times a week," or "I use drugs every day."

Table 11.1 boldly suggests that drug abstinence is the norm throughout the skinhead subculture. Only one subject in the entire sample (an imprisoned terrorist) admitted to using drugs (i.e., marijuana). The interview data revealed numerous corroborations of this finding. Sherry, for example, said the Confederate Hammer Skins were "strong antidrug." A California terrorist said bluntly, "I hate drugs, they fuck up your mind." As previously mentioned, a Wisconsin subject reported that he "used to be into drugs, and really depressed. But now I'm into

Table 11.1
Frequency of Drug Use ($N = 36$)

	Never Use Drugs	Use Several Times A Week	Daily Use
Terrorists	21	0	1
Non-Terrorists	14	0	0

$X^2 = .543$, $df = 1$, $p = $ n.s.

white power and I'm making *A*'s in school and I've got a girlfriend." And the Reverend offered the following insights:

Most of the youth in the white power movement are involved in salubrious living. Salubrious living is part of our religion of Creativity. It means to have a clean mind, body, and soul. Most of these kids [in the white power movement] actually look more like Young Republicans than skinheads. Nobody uses drugs. We're more positive. We go by the eternal laws of nature.

Contrary to Fagan's discoveries, these findings indicate that drugs are not necessarily "intrinsic to gang life among more violent gangs" (1989:654). Hence, drugs do not necessarily strengthen or deteriorate social bonds between violent youth. In other words, there appear to be vastly different meanings of organized violence across various social contexts of criminal subcultures. For terrorist skinheads, the norm of violence is drawn from the internal structure of the conventional American family which provides the social basis for their reliance on neo-Nazism. Thus, drug abstinence represents something of a revolt against cultural decadence.

Modern drug use in the United States is, for all intents and purposes, a manifestation of the hippie counterculture ideology of the late 1960s (see Hamm, 1986; Trebach, 1982). In this social context, drugs—especially marijuana and LSD—were used to seek an instant humanism in an unconventional family arrangement wherein hippies explored eroticism, mysticism, and altruism. Therefore, the drug-oriented hippies offered youth of the late sixties a nontraditional cult of feeling, emotion, tolerance, and love. The salubrious neo-Nazi skinheads, by contrast, appear to have offered youth of the late eighties a traditional cult of feeling, emotion, intolerance, and hatred.

Such a revolt against cultural decadence is not without historical precedent. National socialism and earlier forms of European fascism also echoed this theme. Writing on the French neo-fascist movement of the 1930s, Leon Degrelle observed that neo-fascism was the reaction of a younger generation to a Europe whose

morals are in decay, whose faith is debased, and which is sick to the teeth of individualism, fanaticism and arrogance. [A Europe] slowly expiring of manifold ills: . . . syphilis; towns full of cinemas and cafes, brothels, [and] newspapers; a Paris that had become a centre of bohemian intellectuals, fast livers and homosexuals; *drugs,* music halls, Catholic writers, Jews, [and] Picasso's paintings (1938:151, emphasis added).

Perhaps the most important neo-fascist tract of the World War II era was Pierre Drieu La Rochelle's *Gilles,* a 1943 novel that takes decomposition as a theme and abounds with images of death, annihilation, and putrefaction. Influenced by Hitler's *Mein Kampf,* La Rochelle viewed the world as a place incapable of producing a virile and involuntary reaction to the forces that sought to tear Europe apart at the time (e.g., massive unemployment among the working class). Instead, the world had become dominated by self-satisfied heirs and descendants of old bourgeois Europe. The French neo-fascists, and the German Nazis, rebelled against this world. In so doing, they offered their followers an alternative conceptualization of man. Rather than promoting the image of a degenerate man of a stay-at-home civilization who found physical labor to be repugnant, they offered the cult of the body, health, and outdoor life—salubrious living.

ALCOHOL AND TERRORISM

Historically, the literature bearing on the relationship between alcohol use and crime has been drawn from studies of adult alcoholics. In the main, this research supports the notion that alcohol use is associated with violence (White, 1990). Moreover, among adult alcoholics the psychopharmacological effects of alcohol intoxication are viewed as the primary cause of violent behavior.

Criminologists working in the area of juvenile delinquency have attempted to confirm this alcohol-violence model, yet have generally failed to do so. For example, in their national study on the etiology of substance abuse, Delbert Elliott, David Huizinga, and Suzanne Ageton (1985) discovered strong support for social control theory: Adolescents who are not well-bonded to their parents, to their teachers, or to school are likely to engage in delinquency and in substance abuse. Simultaneously, the researchers discovered support for differential association theory: Adolescents who associate with deviant peers are also likely to engage in delinquency and substance abuse.

However, Elliott and his associates did not attempt to disentangle the independent effects of alcohol use on delinquency. Rather, they concluded that alcohol and marijuana use—together—belong to a general deviance syndrome involving a wide range of relatively minor criminal acts. As such, their national study failed to confirm the alcohol-violence model.

Four years later, Elliott and associates (1989) published the results of a second wave of national surveys of American youth that, in fact, blatantly refute the alcohol-violence model. They found a strong connection between progressive stages of substance use and stages of delinquency. In essence, drug-abstainers and alcohol-only users were most likely to be nondelinquent. Those who used alcohol and marijuana as compared to only alcohol were more likely to be delinquent, and those who had progressed to the use of other drugs, as compared to those not involved with other drugs, were most likely to have also progressed to involvement in more serious forms of delinquency.

On balance, there is little reason to believe that alcohol use is associated with violence among American youth. This conclusion has recently been confirmed in what is perhaps the most exhaustive review of the literature ever conducted on the alcohol-violence model. After examining the results of more than 280 published articles, books, and reports on the relationship between intoxication and aggression, Jeffrey Fagan concluded that

There is only limited evidence that ingestion of substances is a direct, pharmacological cause of aggression. The temporal order of substance use and aggression *does not* indicate a causal role for intoxicants. Research on the nexus between substance use and aggression consistently has found a complex relation, mediated by the *types of substance* and its psychoactive effects, *personality factors* and the . . . *situational factors* in the immediate settings where substances are used, and *sociocultural factors* that channel the arousal effects of substances into behaviors that may include aggression. (1990a:241, emphasis added)

Not surprisingly, the American gang literature is equally void of solid evidence indicating an alcohol-violence model. John Hagedorn, for example, mentions nothing about drinking among Milwaukee gang leaders. The research of James Short and Fred Strodtbeck (1965), Jeffrey Fagan (1989), Lewis Yablonsky (1983), and Joan Moore (1978) also does not substantiate the alcohol-violence model.

In fact, my review of the literature discovered only one study that even marginally supports the model. This is the work of James Diego Vigil (1988). In his analysis of Southern California Chicano gangs, Vigil found that alcohol and drugs—when taken together—were valued for enhancing the fun of partying and as a means of demonstrating machismo. Moreover, if a gang member drank and used drugs substantially more than others at a gang party, then he demonstrated his machismo to other members of the gang. Vigil then discovered that gang members combined their intoxication and machismo to engage in an act of *locura* (to "go loco" or "go crazy") against rival gangs. Therefore, going loco became a core value of Chicano gangs.

Yet, as with drug use, such phenomenon do not appear to transcend the origins and subjective meanings of collective violence across social contexts of gangs. The alcohol-violence model does not stand up when tested within the African-American gangs. In an extremely unique study, Fagan (1990b) compared the alcohol-using behaviors of his sample of predominantly black gang members from Chicago, Los Angeles, and San Diego with those of a general (nongang) sample of youths drawn from the same areas of these three cities. Consistent with the extant literature on the alcohol-violence model, Fagan discovered that alcohol use played only a small role in gang activity. Fagan found that "gang and nongang youths differed little in their involvement in alcohol and marijuana use" (1990b:202). Furthermore, Fagan discovered that "Few youths confined their substance use to alcohol" (1990b:202).

In summary, these findings can be synthesized to form a set of testable propositions about the connection between alcohol and terrorism. First, and most importantly, we would expect alcohol to play a small and insignificant role in the commission of self-reported acts of racial violence. The alcohol-violence model has little credibility within the discipline of academic criminology; therefore, it should have little credibility as an explanatory paradigm for understanding terrorism.

Second, the research of Vigil (1988) and Fagan (1990b) has taught us that there may be important differences across the various social contexts of violent youth subcultures. That is, alcohol use may mean vastly different things to youths depending on their social and cultural heritage. And finally, drawing from Fagan's (1990a) meticulous review of the research on intoxication and aggression, these vastly different perceptions about the use of alcohol may be influenced by (1) personality factors, (2) situational factors, and (3) sociocultural factors.

THE ALCOHOL-VIOLENCE MODEL RECONSIDERED

The literature of American criminology shows that the alcohol-violence model is without credibility: Intoxication does not consistently lead to aggression. Yet this research is primarily based on studies of the general public. Most members of the general public, however, do not embrace a belief in neo-Nazism. They do not shut themselves into their bedrooms every day where they listen to Skrewdriver, Brutal Attack, No Remorse, White Noise, and Doc Marten. They do not voraciously read racist literature, and they do not use racist telephone hotlines. Most members of the general public know nothing about salubrious living; and they do not commit acts of violence against racial minorities.

Because skinheads are so extremely deviant to begin with, we should not be surprised if their alcohol use and its resulting behaviors also deviate from mainstream social norms. We gain our baseline of knowledge about these issue from the ADL. In a 1989 publication entitled *Skinheads Target the Schools,* the ADL wrote: "Much more common [than drugs] has been the abundant use of alcohol, especially beer drinking seems to be virtually required at all Skinhead gatherings. . . . The heavy consumption of beer very likely has contributed to the Skinhead propensity toward violence" (1989b:30).

Beer and Terrorism

Table 11.2 (Alcohol and Terrorism) confirms the ADL research quantitatively. To establish a baseline for temporal ordering, subjects were first asked, "How many fights have you been in during the past two years?" (Responses ranged from none to five or more.) Then they were asked, "How many of these fights were against people of another race?" Responses were coded "none, about half of

Table 11.2
Alcohol and Terrorism ($N = 22$)

	Substances used prior to racial assaults:					
	Beer	Liquor	Marijuana	PCP/Cocaine	Speed/ Barbituates	Sober
Terrorist	16	1	0	0	0	5

them, or all of them." As noted earlier, only those who responded either half or all were considered terrorists.

Then, terrorists were asked this question with five response options: "Before these fights, were you (circle all that apply): "Drinking Beer; Drinking gin, vodka, or other liquor; Smoking Marijuana; Taking PCP or Cocaine; Taking Speed or Barbiturates." Those who did not report intoxication were coded as sober.

The table shows that sixteen of the twenty-two terrorists reported that they were intoxicated on beer during their self-reported acts of racial violence. One terrorist (Ronald) was intoxicated on vodka and five were sober. No subject reported drug use. Hence, it appears that marijuana, PCP, cocaine, amphetamines, and barbiturates have nothing to do with domestic terrorism. Rather, it is beer—and only beer—that seems to fuel the neo-Nazi skinheads in their commission of political violence.

Beer and Personality

Fagan (1990a) argues that the nexus between alcohol use and aggression may be mediated by certain personality factors. If so, we would expect that the more beer a terrorist consumes, the more intoxicated he becomes. The more intoxicated he becomes, the more likely he is to undergo a personality transformation. Or, conversely, we might assume that his personality structure (and we do mean his—terrorism is an explicitly male-dominated affair) leads to an overindulgence in beer. Whatever the temporal ordering of these things, Fagan's research would predict that the confluence of these two factors—beer and personality—provide the necessary impetus for acts of terrorism.

As such, beer drinking before acts of terrorism should be empirically linked to the authoritarian personality structure. This hypothesis is examined in Table 11.3 (Beer and Neo-Nazism). The table shows, however, that there is no relationship between beer drinking and neo-Nazism (alternatively referred to as the authoritarian personality structure, see Fromm, 1941; Dillehay, 1978). The correlations between beer drinking at the presenting offense and antiblack and homophobic attitudes are only −.12, respectively; the correlation between beer drinking and anti-Semitic beliefs is absolutely zero. Thus, personality factors—as measured here—do not appear to mediate the nexus between alcohol use and violence.

Table 11.3
Beer and Neo-Nazism ($N = 22$) (Pearson's r reported)

	Alcohol Use Prior To Racial Assaults
Anti-minority attitudes	−.12
Anti-Semitic attitudes	.00
Homophobic attitudes	−.12

Beer and Situational Factors

Fagan's (1990a) analysis of the research shows that there may also be situational factors in the immediate setting where intoxicants are used that precipitate acts of aggression. The previous discussion on the skinhead norm of violence revealed that violence was perceived by subcultural members as a self-defensive and instrumental behavior. The case studies showed that each act of violence is the result of an interactive process that emerges from a unique set of social events and circumstances that are perceived in vastly different ways by the actors in a scene of violence.

This was substantiated by the leader of the Bronx Area Skinheads, who reported that every fight he had ever been in was started by other people, and by the Reverend, who indicated that he had "never started a fight against anyone, white or black," and that all of his assaults were committed "to defend myself and my beliefs in the eternal laws of nature." From the intoxicated neo-Nazi skinhead point of view, the brutal Patio Club beating was a necessary act of self-defense. And, Phen explained his beer-induced terrorism like this: "Sometimes they provoke it. Like they'll say some shit about white power. That's when we throw down!" He then spoke of going berserk with a beer bottle on the skull of a black youth.

This interactive process appears to represent the situational factors that mediate the nexus between beer drinking and terrorism. Similar to Vigil's barrio gangs, the neo-Nazi skinheads seem to value beer drinking as a means of demonstrating their machismo, or masculinity. Skinheads then combine their intoxication and masculinity to engage in an act of berserking whenever they feel that others are agitating or provoking a situation. Going berserk behind the psychoactive effects of beer is therefore read as an instrumental stylistic creation of the subculture.

Beer and Sociocultural Factors

About the alcohol-violence model, Fagan further argues that there may be certain "sociocultural factors that channel the arousal effects of substances into behaviors that may include aggression" (1990a:241). In essence, certain features of a violent subculture may "channel the arousal effects" of beer into acts of terrorism.

Such an hypothesis is considered in Table 11.4 (Beer and Subcultural Factors). Based on the findings produced thus far, we would expect beer drinking before an act of terrorism to be strongly related to a subject's exposure to white power rock. Historically, white power rock has its roots in Oi music borrowed from drunken pub sing-alongs about the glories of the British state. White power rock is, moreover, a musical form that was quite literally born within a state of beer intoxication. Most terrorist skinheads listen to white power rock daily, exposure to white power rock is the most potent transmitter of neo-Nazism, and most neo-Nazis are intoxicated on beer at the time of their terrorism. Yet the coefficients in Table

Table 11.4
Beer and Subcultural Factors (Pearson's *r* reported)

	Alcohol Use Prior To Racial Assaults
Exposure to Skrewdriver	-.05
Gun ownership	.30
Self-image	.68*
Frequency of exposure to WAR	.58*
Duration of exposure to WAR	.45*
Frequency of W.A.R. Hotline use	.46*

*p < .05

11.4 do not empirically confirm this relationship between beer drinking, terrorism, and white power rock. Perhaps there is good reason for this.

Skrewdriver and the other white power bands do not write songs about such forms of recreation. Neither do they sing about sex, love, or the pathos of romance. They transmit only images of masculinity, neo-Nazism, and violence. White power rock is a music of carnal morality – without sex and without other pleasures of the human condition. Therefore, white power rock does not transmit images of beer drinking.

We might also assume that gun ownership would play an important mediating role between beer drinking and terrorism. Gun ownership was found to be the most influential correlate of all forms of skinhead violence. And from the field observations, I have taken great and serious notice of the fact that a beer drinking neo-Nazi skinhead, angry and armed with a loaded .37 Smith & Wesson, is a frightening sight to behold.

Yet guns, per se, do not seem to raise the aggression potential for skinheads when they are intoxicated on beer. Table 11.4 shows that the relationship between gun ownership and beer drinking prior to a racial assault produces an insignificant statistic. There is, perhaps, also good reason for this. Gun ownership is perceived by skinheads through the lens of the National Rifle Association, and the survivalist movement led by heroic men of the Order. The NRA does not transmit images of beer drinking, and neither does the survivalist movement. It is led by rugged outdoorsmen like Robert Mathews – who was a teetotaler (Flynn and Gerhardt, 1989). He was also committed to a form of salubrious living.

Accordingly, there appear to be other sociocultural forces at work that take precedence over music and gun ownership in the violence-alcohol model of terrorist youth subcultures. These forces are explained by the remainder of the coefficients in Table 11.4. Among all of the variables examined thus far in the research, we see that beer drinking before a terrorist incident is most strongly correlated with an individual's self-image. Beer drinking prior to a racial assault serves to strengthen the social bonds between skinheads.

Yet, other sociocultural variables also enter the alcohol-violence model at a level of statistical significance. Moreover, the coefficients suggest that Tom

Metzger recognized this connection between beer drinking, bonding, and terrorism. And he capitalized on it in his political campaign to transmit his messages of neo-Nazism to the skinhead subculture. Metzger has made public comments, intended to be humorous, about the skinheads and their beer drinking. He has told skinheads that racialism should be fun. He has published and disseminated racist cartoons, stickers, and a poster of white children *Seig Heiling* alongside Mickey Mouse at Disneyland. Metzger has essentially created an amusement park atmosphere for transmitting messages of hate.

Table 11.4 shows that beer drinking before a terrorist incident is strongly related to both the frequency and duration of exposure to the *WAR* zine. The table shows that frequency of exposure to the W.A.R. Hotline also enters the model with statistical significance. Therefore, the more a skinhead indulges himself in beer drinking and racist images, the more likely he is to bond with others and commit an act of terrorism. These appear to be the immediate, street-level antecedents of berserking—beer, bonding, and racist media images. Skrewdriver is only background music at this point. And the Smith & Wesson revolver is reduced to a vacant symbol of masculinity—a sex pistol.

CONCLUSIONS

These findings both refute and confirm previous research on the alcohol-violence model. Like the research conducted on adult alcoholics, it appears that the psychopharmacological effects of beer intoxication are a primary cause of violent behavior. Yet such a discovery does not confirm the theoretical predictions made by social control and differential association theorists.

For the most part, terrorists are well-bonded to their parents and teachers. They are often employed and achieve high self-images within their own highly conventional subcultural family units. Like all families throughout history, this one values childbirth, respect for parents, and love of the family circle. Moreover, the skinheads are well-bonded to conventional systems. There is nothing deviant about this at all.

Drug abstinence is the norm within terrorist youth subcultures, and there is nothing deviant about this either. In the wake of the current war on drugs, drug abstinence is often seen as a cherished virtue of American nationalism.

The average age of the typical skinhead in this study was almost twenty years old. He lived away from home, was employed, and often lived in a state where he was permitted by law to purchase beer. There is nothing illegal, or deviant, about buying beer and drinking it.

As a result, there is no deviant peer operating within the skinhead subculture. The skinheads are "strong antidrug and strong into family values," as Sherry said. Among the neo-Nazi skinheads, a deviant peer would be one who used marijuana or cocaine, but abstained from beer. He would rebel against the family, but would fail to take part in acts of terrorism. He would be seen as a coward and a manifestation of cultural decadence. I found no such deviant peer in this study.

Therefore, present findings are inconsistent with national surveys on the etiology of substance use and delinquency. Elliott and associates (1989) discovered that drug abstainers and alcohol-only users were most likely to be nondelinquent. My findings show that there are young people in America who while abstaining from drugs have progressed to an extreme form of delinquency.

These findings are also inconsistent with Fagan's hypothesis that "There is only limited evidence that ingestion of substances is a direct, pharmacological cause of aggression" (1990a:241). The temporal order of beer use and terrorism does suggest a causal role for intoxicants. However, consistent with Fagan's hypothesis, I did discover important mediators in the nexus between alcohol and violence. Yet these mediators were not located in the personality structures of terrorists. Rather, they were located in the situational factors associated with the subcultural norm of violence, and to sociocultural factors located in group bonding and exposure to racist media images.

When examined in relation to the gang literature, these findings suggest important differences in the social meanings ascribed to substance use across contexts of violent collectives. Whereas Hispanic gangs use alcohol, cocaine, marijuana, PCP, and barbiturates in a ceremony to go loco against rival barrio gangs (Vigil, 1988), African-American gangs do not use drugs and alcohol more often than non-gang members, and very few black gang members confine their substance use strictly to alcohol (Fagan, 1990b).

By contrast, the skinheads are hard-core drug abstainers. They despise drugs for social, political, and religious reasons. Instead, they confine their substance use to beer. Skinheads integrate the psychoactive effects of beer with close social bonding. Then they expose themselves to racist and homophobic media messages that are not of their own creation. Riding the powerful waves of beer intoxication, family bonding, and bizarre forms of social learning, skinheads develop the emotional capacity to go berserk on outsiders who agitate them.

12

Chaos in the Soul: Nazi Occultism and the Morality of Vengeance

religion, *n.* 3. An objective pursued with zeal or conscientious devotion.
—*American Heritage Dictionary*

Unlike the drug-crime connection, the relationship between religion and criminal behavior is one of the least understood in all of criminology. Traditionally, this relationship has been interpreted through the prism of social control theory that assumes the existence of a single value system in society premised on a universal set of moral beliefs. Travis Hirschi has described the complex relationship like this.

The idea of a common (or, perhaps better, a *single*) *value system* is consistent with the fact, or presumption, of variation in the strength of moral beliefs. *We have not suggested that delinquency is based on beliefs counter to conventional morality;* we have not suggested that delinquents do not believe delinquent acts are wrong. They may well believe these acts are wrong, but the meaning and efficacy of such beliefs are contingent upon other beliefs and, indeed, on the strength of other ties to the conventional order. (1969:26, emphasis added)

Over the years, Hirschi's ideas about morality and delinquency have received extensive research attention (e.g., Albrecht et al., 1977; Burkett and White, 1977; Elifson et al., 1983; Hirschi and Stark, 1969; Jensen and Erickson, 1979; Johnson et al., 1987; Nagin and Paternoster, 1991). Similar to Hirschi's approach, these studies have been based on school records, police records, and questionnaire responses gathered from large samples of juveniles.

In the main, this body of research has confirmed social control theory predictions: Instead of looking for causes of delinquency, it is more fruitful to look for the causes of conformity. And rather than looking for some motivation toward delinquency, delinquency is best understood as merely an absence of the causes of conformity (Beirne and Messerschmidt, 1991). In other words, delinquency has no moral life of its own. Instead, social control theorists work from the proposition that "Delinquency *is not* caused by beliefs that require delinquency" (Hirschi, 1969:198, emphasis added).

For the most part, research conducted in the social control theory tradition has examined the issue of morality by focusing on church attendance. Several researchers have also used attitude scales measuring such diverse concepts as religious participation (frequency of prayer), religious attitudes (beliefs in God, Jesus, and the Bible), and religious beliefs about a supernatural life. Rarely has a study employed more than a two-item scale, and never has a study measured moral concepts that lie outside traditional Judeo-Christian doctrine. Finally, few studies have focused solely on the problem of violence.

Similarly, the gang literature appears to be totally void of research on the role of religion and its relationship to violence. Religion has gone unexamined in the native field studies conducted by William Chambliss (1973) and Stephen Baron (1989). It has gone unexamined by the Birmingham scholars (Hebdige, 1979; Muncie, 1981); and John Hagedorn (1988), Joan Moore (1978), James Vigil (1988), Lewis Yablonsky (1983), James Short and Fred Strodtbeck (1965), and Jeffrey Fagan (1989, 1990b) have all chosen not to examine this issue.

As such, the core principle of social control theory—Hirschi's basic assumption about human morality—is undemonstrable in the extreme case of crime and delinquency.

RELIGION AND THE POLITICS OF
DOMESTIC TERRORISM

In what is, no doubt, one of the most remarkable claims made in the entire corpus of U.S. antiracist literature, the ADL has written that

the young Skinheads have been embraced by the veteran racist activists in the hope they will contribute to the movement's regeneration. While the Skins have indeed brought some renewed strength to the far-right, their long-run impact is uncertain. . . . Skinhead gangs have severe internal problems. There is substantial evidence of . . . Satanism. (1988c:28)

If this is true, it signals an unprecedented transformation in the religious character of American hate groups and an unprecedented development within the skinhead subculture itself. Throughout the American twentieth century, white extremists have used bizarre forms of Christian fundamentalism as moral justification for their political violence. But there has never been an American hate group organized around the principles of Satanism, including the Ku Klux Klan, the Order, and Tom Metzger's W.A.R. Nor is there any evidence that Satanism has been practiced by skinheads in other countries, including Great Britain. Indeed, the worship of Satan seems to contradict an essential premise of Nazism. During the Holocaust, the Nazis destroyed most of the religious shrines in German-occupied Europe. They destroyed religious symbols of both Judaism and Christianity. They replaced them with the swastika. They did not replace them with the universal symbol of Satanism — the inverted pentagram.

Yet the ADL is not alone on this issue. The link between skinheads and Satanism has been incorporated into a number of recent police training programs in the United States. For example, the National Information Network (NIN) — a private police training firm dedicated to "aiding police investigators and authorities who may come in contact with the occult" — have published information that connects skinheads to what they call Heavy Metal Satanism. Quoted verbatim, these materials say that

Heavy metal Satanists [are] referred to as "stoners," "self-stylists," "punkers," "skinheads," or "heavy metalists." . . . Their philosophy is "Do what you will." The end is soon so live for today. They often appear to be anti-authority and show disrespect for shock effects. They may spit alot, urinate publicly, display sexual tattoos, display sexual activities openly. They appear anti-elderly and sacrilegious (sic). These students usually are involved in drugs, alcohol, sadomasochism and threaten suicide frequently. (NIN, 1989: unpaginated document)

Another law enforcement trainer, Jonathan R. White, has made similar claims in his recent textbook entitled *Terrorism: An Introduction:*

The Skinheads are a relatively new movement in the United States. . . . To date their violence has been random. Their most noted activity was the beating and crucifixion of a former leader. . . . *The greatest future danger* [of American terrorism] is the increasing number of skinhead groups, *cult-like* groups of young men and women aged 15–20, generally centered in urban areas. These young neo-Nazis are establishing patterns of . . . *religious violence.* (White, 1991:28–29, 188, 191, emphasis added)

The link between skinheads and Satanism has even been alluded to in an award-winning piece of criminology. Writing on the *Seductions of Crime,* essayist Jack Katz explains skinhead violence as a spiritual chaos. After reading an angry poem written by a British skinhead, Katz reflects:

The person who is most fearsomely beyond social control is the one who does not appear to be quite in control of himself because his *soul* is rooted in what, to us, is *chaos.* . . . The suggestion is that chaos is at the very source of one's spiritual being. (1988:102, emphasis added)

CHAOS IN THE SOUL

To test for the presence of Satanic beliefs among skinheads, I created a five-item religion scale (Cronbach's alpha = .408 for all subjects) based on the principles set forth in Anton Szandor LaVey's *The Satanic Bible.* As envisioned by LaVey (1969), Satanism is an eclectic theology that traces its origins to classic voodoo, the Hell Fire Club of eighteenth-century England, the drug and sexual magick of Aleister Crowley, and the Black Order of Germany—a pre-Nazi cult of Satanists from Berlin.

According to *The Satanic Bible,* Satan is not visualized as an anthropomorphic being. Instead, Satan represents the forces of nature. To the Satanist, the self— and self-indulgence—is the highest embodiment of human life and is considered sacred. Therefore, the Golden Rule of Satanism is "Do What Thou Wilt Shall Be the Full of the Law." Simply put, Satanism is a direct blasphemy of Judeo-Christian principles. It represents a religious belief system which, in the words of Hirschi, is "based on beliefs counter to conventional morality" (1969:26).

The religion is based on "Nine Satanic Statements" set forth in *The Satanic Bible.* I examined skinhead beliefs in five of these religious principles and report findings in Table 12.1 (Religious Beliefs).

The first principle is this: "Satan represents indulgence instead of abstinence!" To examine subjects' beliefs, I presented them with the following item: "All of us want the good things in life: Money, laughter, sex. We want all kinds of pleasure. Which best describes your attitude about pleasure?" They were given three response options: "I believe that 'anything goes,' I'll do what I have to in order to get my pleasure"; "I believe it is more important to control my desire for pleasure than to take an 'anything goes' attitude"; and "I'm not sure."

Table 12.1 shows that fully 100 percent of the sample rejected this religious principle, and that there were no differences between terrorists and non-terrorists. Therefore, regarding the most essential Satanic belief—self-indulgence— skinheads do not appear to be Satanists; nor is there any evidence of a religion-terrorism model.

The second principle is "Satan represents vital existence, instead of spiritual pipe dreams!" To tap support for this belief, I presented the item: "Some people believe only in the here-and-now of life. Others believe that there is something more than here-and-now, and they look forward to a spiritual afterlife. Which best describes your beliefs?" Response options were: "There is no afterlife for us," "There is an afterlife for us," and "I'm not sure."

The vast majority of subjects were sure about their beliefs in this area. Nine terrorists believed in vital existence, and nine believed in omnipotent existence. Even though there are no significant differences between terrorists and non-terrorists, this finding does suggest that some skinheads embrace religious beliefs that run counter to conventional morality.

The third Satanic principle, "Satan represents kindness to those who deserve it, instead of love wasted on ingrates!" was measured by the item: "Some people believe we should offer kindness to everyone. Others believe we should offer kindness to only those who deserve it. Which describes your belief?" Response options were: "We should offer kindness to everyone," "We should offer kindness to only those who deserve it," and "I'm not sure."

The table shows that the majority of terrorists and non-terrorists endorsed the Satanic principle. Kindness and compassion, it appears, should only be offered

Table 12.1
Religious Beliefs ($N = 36$)

ITEM: "Belief in indulgence, instead of abstinence."

	Agree	Not Sure	Disagree
Terrorists	0	5	17
Non-Terrorists	0	1	13

$X^2 = 1.43$, $df = 1$, $p = $ n.s.

ITEM: "Belief in vital existence, instead of spiritual pipedreams."

	Agree	Not Sure	Disagree
Terrorists	9	4	9
Non-Terrorists	2	1	11

$X^2 = 4.91$, $df = 2$, $p = $ n.s.

ITEM: "Belief in offering kindness to those who deserve it, instead of love wasted on ingrates."

	Agree	Not Sure	Disagree
Terrorists	14	3	5
Non-Terrorists	10	4	0

$X^2 = 4.24$, $df = 2$, $p = $ n.s.

ITEM: "Belief in vengeance instead of turning the other cheek."

	Agree	Not Sure	Disagree
Terrorists	12	6	4
Non-Terrorists	1	8	5

$X^2 = 7.63$, $df = 2$, $p < .05$

ITEM: "Belief that man is just another animal who can be the most vicious animal of all."

	Agree	Not Sure	Disagree
Terrorists	13	2	5
Non-Terrorists	4	2	6

$X^2 = 3.04$, $df = 2$, $p = $ n.s.

to members of their own protective in-group. Compassion is not something that is freely given to all people in need. Although differences between subjects were insignificant, this level of agreement provides another indication that some skinheads do embrace religious beliefs that run counter to conventional morality.

The fourth Satanic principle is "Satan represents vengeance instead of turning the other cheek!" Subjects were presented with this item: "All of us have problems with other people. Some believe that vengeance is the best way to solve these problems. Others believe that forgiving is the best way. Which do you believe in?" Response options were: "I believe that vengeance is usually the best way to solve my problems," "I believe that forgiving is usually the best way to solve my problems," and "I'm not sure."

The table shows that more than half of the terrorists preferred vengeance over forgiveness, and only one non-terrorist embraced this principle. As such, this finding is statistically significant. There is, therefore, an empirical link between a religious belief and terrorism. And this link is defined by an individual's capacity for vengeance.

The final Satanic principle is long and complex. It reads: "Satan represents man as just another animal, sometimes better, sometimes worse than those that walk on all-fours, who, because of his 'divine spiritual and intellectual development,' has become the most vicious animal of all!" Subjects were presented with this item: "Some believe that man is just another animal who, at times, can be the most vicious animal of all! What do you think of this statement?" Response options were: "I agree," "I disagree," and "I'm not sure."

The table reveals that the majority of terrorists also agreed with this principle, yet their responses did not differ from non-terrorists. Thus, once again we have a case where a number of skinheads do embrace a religious belief that runs counter to conventional morality, yet we have only minimal confirmation of the religion-terrorism model.

Skinheads, Satanism, and the Nazi Occult

Three conclusions can be drawn from these data: First, a number of skinheads do embrace religious beliefs that defy conventional morality. This belief system values vengeance over forgiveness; selective compassion over unconditional compassion; and conceives of man as a potentially vicious animal rather than a spiritual being. Second, the heart of the religion-terrorism model appears to be located in the morality of vengeance. And last, because of their unequivocal lack of faith in self-indulgence, the skinheads cannot be considered Satanists. The skinheads may be neo-Nazis and terrorists, but they are not hedonists.

In its most basic form, Satanism looks on self-indulgence—pleasures of the flesh and soul—as sacred. Perverse sex magick (including orgies, homosexuality, and pedaphelia) was an essential feature of Aleister Crowley's Ordo Templi Orientis, and sex magick is considered sacred by LeVay's Church of Satan. Rampant drug use, especially cocaine, was also a standard feature of these evil cabals (see Kahaner, 1988). In contrast, the skinheads are devoted to conventional family values of monogamy, childbirth, and parenting; and they are hardcore drug abstainers.

These conclusions were verified by the field investigations. I encountered no skinheads who displayed jewelry or tattoos of the inverted pentagram, the Mark of the Beast (666), the Inverted Cross, the Cross of Nero, or any other Satanic symbol. None of the subjects indicated that they had sold their souls to Satan as required by neophytes in the religion. Skinheads are not Satanists. Yet they are religious. In America, many of them are devotees of *Nazi Occultism.*

THE CHURCH OF THE CREATOR

A total of seven skinhead leaders in the sample, from various parts of the nation, referred to themselves as reverends of the Church of the Creator. They were all neo-Nazis; they all embraced beliefs in vengeance, conditional compassion, and viewed man as an animal. They all had strong family ties, led salubrious lifestyles, and (with one exception) they were all terrorists who had committed their acts of violence while intoxicated on beer. They were also daily listeners of white power rock, regular users of the W.A.R. material, and owners of multiple firearms.

During the summer of 1991, the terrorist I have referred to as the Reverend hosted a Milwaukee convention for followers of the Church of the Creator. The event was attended by more than 250 young white power activists from across the midwestern United States and various parts of Canada. (It was an event that did not go unnoticed by the FBI.) I interviewed other subjects who reported that "Creativity" is at the very core of the American skinhead subculture. Accordingly, I now turn to a brief discussion of this religion to decipher the theological justification for a belief in vengeance.

The White Man's Bible

The Church of the Creator is an offshoot of the Christian Identity movement. Its major text is *The White Man's Bible,* published in 1971 by a longtime extremist named Ben Klassen (ADL, 1983). The book was used by Metzger in his days as an Identity preacher, and was later read by members of the Order. *The White Man's Bible* can be ordered by mail through David Duke's *NAAWP News, National Vanguard, WAR,* and from dozens of Klan and neo-Nazi groups in the United States (Wallace, 1985).

The White Man's Bible begins with a reinterpretation of the Book of Genesis. It maintains that God created all races, except one, on the third day of Creation. These races were seen as inferior in the eyes of God, however, and not an embodiment of God's true imagination and splendor. It was on the final day of Creation, according to this scenario, that God succeeded in making the perfect man. This was Adam, a white man.

This is the essence of Creativity. It is a religion based on a reinterpretation of Creation. Never mind the fact that the King James Version of the Bible says nothing about races of people being created on different days. Never mind the fact that God is believed to have rested on the final day of Creation. And never mind the fact that Genesis refers to Adam as a "red man." All of this means nothing to the devotee of Creativity. He lives in a separate reality. He believes, with all his heart, that Aryan supremacy is an eternal law of nature. Robert Mathews died for this belief, with no quarter asked for, and none given; this has made Mathews a martyr among modern-day devotees.

In addition to *The White Man's Bible,* Creativity relies on a variety of supplementary readings. These include such texts as *The Negro: A Beast, The Origins of the Jews, The International Jew, The Turner Diaries,* and *The Holy Book of Adolf Hitler*—a work that elevates Hitler to sainthood. Creativity sermons are preached in the comfort of homes. This allows Creativity's born-again men and women to practice with clear moral consciences the bigotry, hatred, and violence that has traditionally been defined to them as sinful (Coates, 1987).

And herein lies the essence of morality within the Church of the Creator. Like the Ku Klux Klan of the 1920s, the eighth-century Vikings of Europe, and the Nazis of twentieth-century Germany, the Church of the Creator allows its followers to redefine the meaning of sin as it relates to violence. Through this redefinition process, the devotee conquers his moral self and comes to believe that violence is not a sin. Under certain circumstances, it is an exalted virtue.

This is what is needed for a belief in vengeance. As targets for their vengeance, devotees have a host of enemies. Foremost among them is the African-American male who is considered an animal, a beast, or a monkey within the church. Specifically at issue is his sexuality. According to Creativity doctrine, race mixing is the most sinful act known to mankind. Yet, it is allowed to happen by the United States government. Hence, they become the second target of vengeance.

Allowing the ultimate sin is a firm indication that the United States is being administered by men of a Zionist Occupied Government. Thus, race mixing is viewed by devotees as a state-organized Jewish effort to dilute the sacred white progeny, and inevitably turn the Aryans into a race of mongrels.

Gay men are the third target of vengeance. To the devotee, gays represent a putrefaction of human morality. They are also looked on as animals and are referred to by a number of pejorative terms. Gays are seen as blasphemous in their treatment of the sacred male stereotype. In this regard, devotees are strongly influenced by their neo-Nazi beliefs in cultural decadence. They are also influenced by their identity as skinheads. Since the London spring of 1972, skinheads have traditionally engaged in queer bashing as part of their subcultural style. In the United States, however, this style has become politicized by people like Robert Mathews, David Duke, and Tom Metzger who have (somehow) sewn this violence into the very fabric of Nazi Occultism.

The American Jewish community is the final target of vengeance. Influenced by the anti-Semitic doctrine of British-Israelism, *The White Man's Bible* interprets the events of history as follows: First, the true chosen people—the descendants of Abraham, Moses, Isaac, Jacob, and Jesus Christ—were all thought to have once lived on the British Isles. They represented one of the so-called lost tribes of ancient Israel, the Tribe of Manasseh.

Having spent centuries traversing the European continent, the Tribe of Manasseh crossed the mighty Caucasus Mountains and settled in London shortly after the life of Christ. Jews, according to Creativity doctrine, are considered a race of Mongolian-Turkish "Khazars" thought to be descended from the seed that Satan planted in the womb of Eve at the Garden of Eden. Years later, descendants of the Chosen People of the British Isles are thought to have sailed aboard the *Mayflower*. And their descendants supposedly went on to write two holy documents: the Constitution of the United States of America and the Bill of Rights.

Creativity promotes strong conventional family values of matrimony, monogamy, and childbirth. Bearing children is viewed as a woman's supreme and holy task in life and is sacred. Hence, immediate family members—along with others who follow the teachings of Creativity—are the only ones deserving of compassion and love. To pass on the healthiest Aryan seed possible, devotees are urged to keep strict dietary laws. These laws are considered to be "anti-Semitic kosher" and they forbid pork, shellfish, and catfish. This is called salubrious living, and drug abstinence is considered part and parcel of this dietary regime.

This is the religion of Creativity. It has been described by one theologist as "a religion by sociopaths, for sociopaths. It turns their sickness into virtue" (quoted in Coates, 1987:92). The Reverend, on the other hand, refers to Creativity as the "nature of eternal religion." They clearly live in separate realities.

CONCLUSIONS

Social control theory is based on the assumption that "delinquency is not caused by [moral] beliefs that require delinquency" (Hirschi, 1969:198). In the Western world, conventional morality is grounded in Judeo-Christian principles of unconditional love and compassion, forgiveness, and divine existence. To be sure, these beliefs do not require delinquency.

However, these beliefs do not represent the religious orientation of violent American skinheads. Their beliefs run counter to conventional morality. They believe in vengeance, selective compassion, and they often look on other men as animals. They worship Nazis and are devoted to the vitriolic hatred of black males, gays, and Jewish institutions. Their souls are full of chaos. Their morality requires violence, and violence is delivered.

Part III

Conclusions and Recommendations

Each time the community moves to censure some act of deviation . . . and convenes a formal ceremony to deal with the responsible offender, it sharpens the authority of the violated norm and restates where the boundaries of the group are located.

—Kai Erikson
Wayward Puritans

13

The Criminology and Control of Domestic Terrorism

You've contacted WAR! White Aryan Resistance.

Don't think that with the recent court proceedings levied against the White Aryan Resistance in Portland, Oregon, that our activities will cease! In fact, this case has convinced us to go the extra mile, take the extra step. We will create a revolution in this country. We will put the blood on the streets like you've never seen. And advocate more violence than both world wars put together. We're putting the system on notice that if you want to play hard ball with the big boys you better be prepared to pay the piper. We will no longer waste time talking about the niggers, the gooks, or the wetbacks. We have a new set of targets to play with. So if you're white and work for the system, watch your step. Whether you be a system cop, a control judge, or a crooked lawyer, your ass is grass. The next time you run across a white cop, a white judge, or a white lawyer, don't hesitate to act. A fight to the death and nothing less. And just remember, Morris, you will soon experience your own dog day afternoon. And this is WAR.

—W.A.R. Hotline Message
October 24, 1990

On October 21, 1990, the Multnomah County, Oregon, Circuit Court found that Tom and John Metzger had intentionally incited Portland skinheads to provoke confrontations with minority groups and should therefore be financially liable for the death of Mulugeta Seraw. The jury ordered Tom Metzger to pay $5 million in punitive damages, his son to pay $1 million, and Kenneth Mieske and Steven Strasser to pay $500,000 each. (Mieske is currently on death row for Seraw's murder and Strasser is serving a twenty-five-year sentence.) The jury also awarded $3 million in punitive damages and $2.5 million in compensatory damages against W.A.R. (London, 1990). In total, the Metzgers were saddled with a $12 million fine, indenturing them for life.

This law suit, waged by famed civil rights attorney Morris Dees, represented the latest and most important use of a strategy to control the spread of right-wing domestic terrorism in the United States — bankrupting white extremist groups with extraordinary civil judgments. Four years earlier, Dees had won a $7 million award in a wrongful death suit in Mobile, Alabama, against the United Klans of America on behalf of a woman whose teenage son had been hanged to death by members of the Klan. As a result, the Mobile chapter of the Klan was disbanded. Dees had effectively destroyed them (Dees, 1991).

Yet, other strategies have been used to control the spread of domestic terrorism. On December 1, 1991, Tom Metzger appeared before Superior Court Judge J. D. Smith in Los Angeles to answer for his part in the 1983 Keagle Canyon cross burning. Metzger's codefendants included three members of a Southern California neo-Nazi group called the National Socialist American Workers Party. For his part in the crime, Metzger received a six-month prison sentence.

Bankrupt, humiliated, and on his way to prison, Metzger has called for "blood on the streets like you've never seen." This is the state of affairs in U.S. strategies to control domestic terrorism: Civil rights attorneys go after extremist leaders, bankrupting and humiliating them; in response, extremists cry louder for violence and revolution. A compelling question emerges. Is this the most effective way to prevent future acts of domestic terrorism?

THE CRIMINOLOGY OF TERRORIST
YOUTH SUBCULTURES

Figure 13.1 (A Theory of Terrorist Youth Subcultures) presents a summary of the findings adduced from the present research. This theoretical model is based on the significant statistical differences between terrorists and non-terrorists and is organized into two parts: immediate causes of terrorism and motivations toward terrorism. Immediate causes are defined as those of the individual's own creation. That is, skinheads themselves played a hand in making these events part of their reality. Motivations toward terrorism are defined as those not of the individual's own creation.

The theory begins with a postulate drawn from functionalist sociology: Terrorist youth subcultures are a product of working-class families. These families assume the existence of a dominant ideology that stresses the achievement of economic goals. Youngsters who grow up in these families conform to this achievement ideology and as they mature, they set highly realistic goals that are well within their reach.

These youths are successful high school students and aspire to enter universities in the future. Drawing from their working-class heritage, however, they are highly committed to the tradition of blue-collar employment. Thus, on graduation from high school, they turn not to the ephemeral abstractions of higher education but to the rugged realities of working-class life. They become common laborers, carpenters, steamfitters, and construction workers. They are not frustrated by this. They do not set their sights on a white-collar job in the future.

Instead, they plan only to confirm their working-class roots by continuing their life on the factory floor, on the construction site, and on the loading dock. They are not upwardly mobile in the traditional sense. Rather, they are deeply committed to their occupations, and they unabashedly lay claim to a working-class consciousness because it is a natural and logical reaction to their upbringing.

At this point, these young people are no different than millions of working-class youth throughout the world. But unlike their peers on the stage of world events, our youths go on to become self-styled terrorists in their local communities. Their path to terrorism begins to take shape and form when they are introduced to white power heavy metal.

White power rock exposes these youths to the raw and vitriolic language of racial and ethnic hatred. It does so by presenting an elaborate fantasy wherein minorities and Jews are portrayed as agents in a conspiracy to threaten the well-being of the average blue-collar worker. And it will do so with such powerful emotion that youths will begin to link musical messages to their focal concerns about employment. Through almost daily exposure to songs such as "Nigger, Nigger," and "Race and Nation," these youths are transformed into adherents of a bizarre form of Nazism.

This transformation process occurs at a metaphysical level through a sort of seat-of-the-pants shamanism. That is, players in white power bands transform themselves from ordinary musicians to extraordinary ones through the expression of highly forbidden messages and symbols that are part of a larger and widely known consciousness. Listeners of this music, in turn, seek to transform themselves from their ordinary realities to something wider, something that enlarges them as people. They become skinheads.

Neo-Nazism is the ideology of the international skinhead subculture. At the basis of this ideology operates a well-developed paranoia that working-class whites will have their self-respect, power, and economic wealth usurped by racial and ethnic minorities. This paranoia not only has a well-developed musical expression but also a vibrant underground press. Daily exposure to white power rock serves as a springboard for youths to discover this underground literature.

In the United States, the most influential radical publication is *WAR*. Exposure to *WAR* entrenches neo-Nazism in the minds of youth. This is accomplished primarily through extravagant cartoons depicting grotesque images of young black males refereed to as "Black-Assed Coons" and "Monkeys." Yet this underground press has capitalized on advances in technology; and as a result, neo-Nazism is supported and sustained by W.A.R. telephone hotline messages about "AIDS-infected queers," "faggots," and lesbians.

Once youths have become inspired by this ideology, they come to embrace an occult-oriented morality that supports a belief in vengeance. And vengeance is the soul of Nazism. It is a soul, however, that is deeply rooted in chaos.

Nevertheless, drawing from these abstractions created by others, youths then carve out a social world of their own that is a literal and imaginative representation of Nazism. These devotees of vengeance form strong family-type bonds.

Figure 13.1
A Theory of Terrorist Youth Subcultures

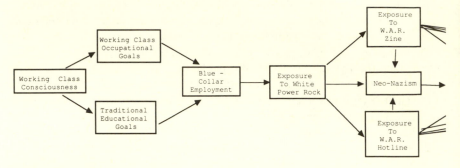

They are not besieged by anomie. In fact, by this point our youths are syn-anomic—they are hyperactively bonded to the dominant social order and to one another.

During this period of development, skinheads become fascinated with fire-arms. They select the Smith & Wesson .357 magnum revolver as their subcul-tural symbol. Riding the powerful waves of guns, synanomia, ideology, heavy metal, vengeance, and group bonding, these youths then mix in the most power-ful elixir contained within this theory of terrorist youth subcultures—beer. And it is beer, and only beer, that triggers a terrorist act against individuals perceived as threats to the skinhead way of thinking. In the United States, the most obvious threats are black males in the company of white women, gays who unabashedly display their sexual orientation, and immigrants who are awkward in their public attempts to fit into American society.

THE CONTROL OF TERRORIST YOUTH SUBCULTURES

Thus, the civil rights strategy of bankrupting and humiliating white extremist leaders portends to offer an effective and scientifically justifiable strategy to con-trol the spread of domestic terrorism in the United States. By legally seizing the Metzgers' assets and property, Morris Dees singlehandedly closed down W.A.R.'s printing presses, mail-order marketing of white power rock and Nazi regalia, telephone hatelines, and computer bulletin boards. This strategy goes straight to the heart of terrorist youth subcultures by dismantling piecemeal its prime transmitters of ideology and morality. However, this strategy does not con-trol for several important cultural forces deeply ingrained in the American way of life that may promote neo-Nazism and terrorism in the years to come. These forces are considered next.

THE CULTURAL LEGACY OF REAGANOMICS

This research discovered that the American neo-Nazi skinheads emerged in an era of relative economic prosperity. Ostensibly organized by young mentally in-

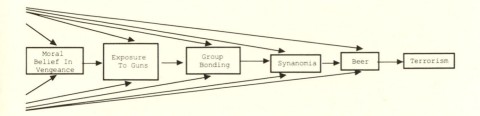

firmed bigots and criminals, the skinheads came to national attention largely through the efforts of Tom Metzger and those media personalities who followed him in their attempts to inform the public about this chilling wave of Nazism during the mid-to-late 1980s.

Since then, the United States has undergone the second presidential term of an aged former movie star so ignorant of modern and contemporary history as to assert in the late 1980s that very few living Germans even remembered World War II and the Nazi rise to power. Reaganomics left the United States with deep cuts in domestic programs coupled with massive defense buildups. In this way, Ronald Reagan led the nation from inflation through recession into prosperity, and was the commander-in-chief when America won the Cold War at decade's end.

Yet this president also left behind an American culture that was, in the words of cultural anthropologist Paul Fussell, "inflated by hyperbole and gilded with a fine coat of fraud" (1991:16). Under the presidency of Ronald Reagan, the United States spent nearly $2 trillion on military weapons while millions of its poor and hungry slept in the streets like the beggars of some Third World nation. Instead, Reaganomics nurtured the values and fiscal practices that brought America the shopping mall explosion, the new Atlantic City, and the pathological narcissism of Donald Trump, Jim and Tammy Faye Bakker, Leona Helmsley, Ivan Boesky, Michael Milken, Charles Keating, and the great savings and loan disaster. This orthodoxy of narcissism laid testament to the need of Americans during the Reagan years to believe that everything is attainable through slick opportunity and fraud.

Thus, Reaganomics created the decade of greed in which tens of millions of American white youth became so culturally, intellectually, and spiritually vacant that their main way of defining themselves and achieving self-respect was to "go to the mall." The value of profit-grabbing and the full-scale publicity fraud of the savings and loan debacle left behind a plethora of charmless and hugely blunt architectural designs in American shopping malls that are, in the words of Fussell, "Hitler-resonant: brutal and despotic" (1991:32).

Thanks to Ronald Reagan, many Americans also turned to the occult seeking spiritual guidance for everyday problems. It must be remembered that Nancy Reagan's reliance on astrology in advising the president led to a situation where national affairs were predicated on occultism; thus drawing the national psyche into self-deception, and provoking a lust for wonders far beyond the avenues of conventional religion.

Although Reaganomics expanded opportunities for the education of white youth, the quality of that education has become highly suspect. Among the participating countries in the United Nations, the United States currently ranks near the bottom in literacy in reading and math. One-fourth of American bachelor's degrees are now awarded in business. These degrees, it is argued, do not measure the quality of the intellect but the rude command of techniques likely to fit college graduates uncritically into the ready-made niches of American middle-class society where money, sports, entertainment, and fashion are valued over human compassion, service, and love—where the outside of a person is valued over the inside; the appearance over actuality. Hence, America manifested a generation of white youth who exalt such ostentatious phenomena as Ronald Reagan, Trump Plaza, Madonna, stretch limousines, $150 Nike basketball shoes, Troop jackets, gold chains, Rolex watches, and Mike Tyson.

Young whites now graduate from American schools and automatically join the labor force "without the capacity to wonder what they're doing or whether their work is right or wrong, noble or demeaning" (Fussell, 1991:71). And, concomitant with the decline of American education came the escalation in military spending. Hence, military culture—not academic culture—came to serve as a model for social arrangements among American youth, thus creating a space—along with Reagan's emphasis on the occult—for grand theories of social and political affairs having no relation to reality whatsoever.

Central to the formulation of such theories, of course, is a language that by design is meant to deceive. During the Reagan era, like no time before in American history, the quest for social, cultural, and political significance came through a language aimed to "elevate the worthless to the wonderful via extraordinary verbal pomposity" (Fussell, 1991:71).

So it is that Americans have witnessed the flourishing of magazines aimed to promote grand theories of accumulating wealth (e.g., *Money, Inc.,* and *Fortune*); underground publications promoting grand theories of militarism and white working-class revolt (e.g., *WAR* and David Duke's *NAAWP News*); movie actors and rock bands promoting grand theories of paramilitarism and fake patriotism (e.g., Niggers with Attitude, Skrewdriver, Brutal Attack, No Remorse, Public Enemy, Slaughter, Vengeance, Megadeath, Metallica, Arnold Schwarzenegger, Sylvester Stallone, and Chuck Norris); and blockbuster movies (e.g., *Batman, Dick Tracy, Teenage Mutant Ninja Turtles, Terminator II*) that have relied solely on overstated comic-book motivations and special effects. The object of such enterprises has been to reconstitute adult audiences as children. "The obvious effect," argues Fussell, "has been the 'infantilization of the electorate,' resulting in, among other things, the election[s] of Ronald Reagan and George Bush" (Fussell, 1991:124).

It is within this context that we can come to truly understand the proclivity of American white youth to embrace the ideology of neo-Nazism and formulate strategies to prevent domestic terrorism in the future. Once more, Fussell: "Actual American life as experienced by most [young] people is so boring, uniform, and devoid of significant soul, so isolated from resonances of European culture, that it demands to be 'raised' and misrepresented as something wonderful" (Fussell, 1991:198).

From this perspective, the American skinheads can be viewed as a small, self-contained subculture whose rituals and symbols reveal a basic truth about the values of society at large. That is, the skinheads are both a product of, and an understandable reaction to, the national emptiness, dullness, self-deceit, and fraud of Reaganomics. And from the perspective of several thousand working-class white youth, the skinheads represent a quest for at least the illusion of personal distinction and value in a nation seeking to destroy these traits.

THE FUTURE OF AMERICAN NEO-NAZISM AND DOMESTIC TERRORISM

The primary cause of domestic terrorism, according to Figure 13.1, is neo-Nazism—attitudes that are antiblack, antigay, and anti-Semitic (in that order). The development of this ideology is a necessary prerequisite for acts of vengeance against black males, gays, and Jewish institutions. Although President Bush has taken a stand against "racism, anti-Semitism, bigotry, and hate," he actually rode into the White House on a platform that was one of the most racially biased in American history. In fact, some analysts contend that it was the use of campaign photos of black murderer Willie Horton that provided the necessary political grist to catapult George Bush into the American presidency. This event, combined with the cultural legacy of Reaganomics, racially polarized the nation and fostered a climate ripe for the continuation of American neo-Nazism well into the 1990s. Since then, certain events have made this climate even more conducive to the spread of right-wing extremism.

The Economic Recession

Figure 13.1 shows that neo-Nazism begins with a well-developed working-class consciousness. Since George Bush took office, economic prosperity among the working-class has become a thing of the distant past. By October of 1991, the national rate of unemployment stood at 6.8 percent. The majority of these 4.5 million unemployed Americans come from blue-collar occupations in manufacturing, retail sales, and construction (Hershey, 1991). Yet the economic forecast is even darker.

Research in economics suggests that if present trends continue, only the best trained of the working-class will prosper in the future, while others will remain stuck at current living standards or fall behind into extreme economic marginalization (Peterson, 1991). For the first time in history, the vast majority of American working-class youth can anticipate a future in which their standard of living will not be as high as their parents'. Figure 13.1 implies that such working-class bitterness over the economy can make conditions ripe for American youth to embrace extreme political beliefs.

Modern Developments in Unified Germany

The American skinheads, it must be remembered, are part of an international youth subculture. Were it not for the ascendancy of European skinheads onto the stage of world events during the mid-1980s, skinhead violence would have never become a problem in the United States. Therefore, modern developments abroad are important for predicting future trends at home.

On November 6, 1991, the *New York Times* reported that a German court ordered construction workers to lop off the head of a sixty-three-foot statue of Vladimir Lenin in Berlin Square. At least symbolically, the democratization of Germany had come full circle. Yet freedom has its costs. Once a country so economically powerful that it influenced political events throughout Europe, Germany has begun to suffer a severe financial slump. Today Germany faces massive spending commitments including an estimated $58 billion a year price tag to bring the former East German infrastructure up to Western standards. With unemployment in the east at 15 percent in the summer of 1992, Germany—quietly mindful that an economic depression and hyperinflation in the 1920s fueled the Nazi rise to power—has begun to experience an unprecedented upswing in violence committed by neo-Nazi skinheads across the nation (Tamayo, 1991).

There are important symbols of this development as well. On November 9–10, 1938, Nazi stormtroopers beat and murdered Jews, ransacked their homes and businesses and destroyed synagogues. The night is called *Kristallnacht,* or "Crystal Night," because of the shattered glass that filled the streets of German cities and villages. It is considered the beginning of the extermination of 6 million European Jews and hundreds of thousands of others. By extraordinary historical accident, on November 9–10, 1989, the Berlin Wall fell ushering in the demise of communism and the unification of Germany. And on November 9–10, 1991, more than 300 neo-Nazis marched through the Eastern German cities of Halle and Leipzig in celebration of *Kristallnacht,* as tens of thousands of marchers in more than 100 German cities protested skinhead attacks on foreigners that marked the anniversary of the savage 1938 Nazi pogrom against Jews.

Meanwhile, reports of violence have begun to escalate in Spain, Switzerland, Sweden, Denmark, and France where skinheads have mounted attacks on immigrants and foreign students (*Economist,* November 16, 1991: Ward, 1991). Such dramatic and widely covered events, combined with working-class frustrations over a stagnant U.S. economy, may entrench the international context of American neo-Nazism well into the twenty-first century.

Permissive Gun Control

Figure 13.1 shows that gun ownership is an important consequence of neo-Nazism and a necessary antecedent of terrorism. However, the United States already has the most liberal gun control policies in the world and recent developments in the U.S. Congress have made it easier for more and more young Americans to arm themselves. On October 17, 1991, the U.S. House of Representatives, at the urging of NRA lobbyists, approved an amendment to remove from recent crime legislation a ban on the purchase and ownership of semiautomatic assault weapons (Shaw, 1991). Meanwhile, the Bush administration, also at the NRA's urging, opened the door to the import of thousands of cheap semiautomatic assault weapons from former communist countries. For example, between March and September of 1991, the U.S. State Department authorized commercial import permits to be issued to Czechoslovakia and Hungary for more than 280,000 semiautomatic pistols and rifles (*Bloomington Herald Tribune,* October 21, 1991). These weapons—including various clones of the Uzi, the MAC-10 semiautomatic machine pistol and AK-47 assault rifle—are now available for purchase over-the-counter in gun shops or through mail-order outlets advertised in obscure paramilitary magazines and newsletters (Tomb, 1991).

The Ascendancy of David Duke

Last, Figure 13.1 shows that racist media images play an important role in the nexus between neo-Nazism and terrorism. Yet, mainstream media images of neo-Nazism have never been so prevalent in America as they are today. During April and May of 1991 alone, skinheads, Klansmen, and other avowed neo-Nazis were the subjects of two PBS specials on racism and hate crime, and were featured guests on four nationally syndicated television talk shows. As pointed out in this research, excessive television coverage of the far right can have devastating effects. Mulugeta Seraw was murdered within hours of the November 11, 1988, skinhead brawl on the Geraldo Rivera show. Racist media images, be they mainstream or clandestine, figure prominently in the geometry of domestic terrorism.

It is often said that the media has become the fourth estate of American government; and in November of 1991, former KKK Grand Wizard and American Nazi Party activist David Ernest Duke transfixed the American media on his image (to the exclusion of his politics) to make a historically unprecedented bid to become the forty-second governor of the state of Louisiana. And then, remarkably, the media—not Duke—began to speculate on his bid for the 1992 presidential campaign. "For years," claimed Democratic presidential candidate Bob Kerry, "Republicans have watered the tree of racism, and that tree has grown full blown and dropped a nut called David Duke" (quoted in Fielder, 1991:4).

Duke's ascendancy into the national political arena was based on (and inspired by) media hyperbole about his ability to create a populist movement by tapping into working-class frustrations about welfare and affirmative action, violent crime, failing schools, lost jobs, and a stagnant economy. Without the media, in 1991 David Duke would have been just another southern politician who made an unsuccessful run at the governorship in a Baptist hinterland of relative poverty, fundamentalism, and disapproval. But David Duke became much more than this.

Ten days before Duke's defeat, President Bush stood before a nationally televised audience and said, "when someone has so recently endorsed Nazism, it is inconceivable that such a person can legitimately aspire to . . . a leadership role in a free society." In response, Duke appeared before nationally televised audiences and proclaimed: "I believe in equal rights for all, special privilege for none." Duke delivered his message to audiences of *Face the Nation, Nightline, This Week with David Brinkley, Larry King Live,* NBC News, CBS News, ABC News, CNN, *A Current Affair,* and virtually any nationally televised forum that would have him. Duke became the focus of exposés in the *New York Times,* the *Los Angeles Times,* the *Washington Post, Newsweek,* and the *Economist.* On November 4, 1991, *Time* magazine described Duke's neo-Nazism as a "thinly veiled appeal to frustrated whites who feel they are victims of reverse discrimination" (Riley, 1991:24).

Hence, American neo-Nazism had become respectable through the media's confirmation of the skinhead paranoia that working-class whites will have their self-respect, power, and economic well-being usurped by racial and ethnic minorities. And then, in December of 1991, David Duke—the former Grand Wizard of the Ku Klux Klan—became a candidate for the president of the United States.

FIVE RECOMMENDATIONS FOR PREVENTING DOMESTIC TERRORISM

On one hand, the cultural forces supporting neo-Nazism appear to be so immense and intractable that nothing can be done to retard its progress. The High Priest of Bigotry sits comfortably in his throne attended by the disciples of white power rock, beer, guns, bonding, vengeance, and working-class consciousness. In short, American neo-Nazism has achieved such momentum that nothing may slow it down, even if we improve the economy by offering more jobs and tax benefits for working-class families; improve the quality of higher education so that it appeals to more working-class youth; curb the national impulse to define self-worth in gross materialism; teach youth to treat the occult with contempt; and produce intelligent rock and roll and artistic movies that appeal to working-class youth of the day.

On the other hand, several strategies do offer hope for turning the tide. The hard-fought success of Morris Dees in bankrupting the leadership of W.A.R. promises to remove from the equation a primary source for transmitting terrorist values to an entire generation of American youth. Similarly, immediate legal remedies for prosecuting domestic terrorists are increasingly available under federal civil rights statutes (Dees, 1991; Padgett, 1984) and methods for their treatment and rehabilitation are available in the literature of correctional management (Hamm, 1991).

As important as they are, however, these strategies are based on controlling domestic terrorism after an incident of terrorism has taken place. Dees's incredible efforts in the Portland trial notwithstanding, they do not seek to prevent a new generation of American white kids from embroiling themselves in neo-Nazism with its attended forms of violence. Accordingly, five specific proposals provide a fitting end to this research.

1. *Boycotting White Power Rock:* The major obstacle associated with preventing domestic terrorism is that all of the forces promoting neo-Nazism are protected by the U.S. Constitution. White power rock, the primary transmitter of neo-Nazism among American skinheads, is safely protected by the First Amendment right to freedom of speech; perhaps the most sacred of all rights in the constitutional pantheon.

Yet the First Amendment also guarantees the right to protest messages that are deemed threatening to community standards of decency. Protesting the sale and distribution of white power records and tapes is, therefore, a legal and highly effective way to prevent the spread of American neo-Nazism in years to come.

For example, in 1987 the City of Minneapolis experienced a brief surge of police-reported incidences of racial assaults and gay bashing committed by a local group of neo-Nazi skinheads. In response, a small band of youth calling themselves SHARP (Skinheads Against Racial Prejudice) organized a boycott of the city's record stores that stocked recordings by Skrewdriver, Brutal Attack, No Remorse, Doc Marten, Vengeance, Skullhead, and other white power bands. The boycott effectively persuaded record store owners to remove these white power recordings from their shelves; and today, neo-Nazi skinheads do not have a visible street presence in Minneapolis.

Similarly, in 1989 antiracist activists in Louisville threatened an organized boycott of a local Electric Ladyland record store that stocked white power rock and Nazi regalia. Anticipating a widespread public backlash over the proposed boycott, Electric Ladyland removed these transmitters of ideology and morality. Today, neo-Nazi skinheads do not have an active street presence in Louisville and hate crimes are limited to occasional Klan-oriented cross burnings.

2. *Expanded Litigation Against Publishers of Racist Literature:* The dissemination of neo-Nazi propaganda is also protected by the First Amendment right to freedom of speech. Yet in the Portland trial, Morris Dees convinced a jury that such propaganda played an important role in inciting skinheads to provoke confrontations with minority groups. Similarly, the present research has shown that exposure to racist media images has an important bearing on the development of neo-Nazi ideology, group bonding, beer drinking, and terrorism.

These findings imply that future criminal and civil prosecutions of domestic terrorists may be strengthened by considering the publishers of neo-Nazi propaganda as conspirators in the act of terrorism. For example, a number of terrorists in the present study were regular readers of David Duke's *NAAWP News*. The

NAAWP News carries advertisements for *The White Man's Bible, The Holy Book of Adolf Hitler,* and *The Turner Diaries*—the holy trilogy of Nazi Occultism and its morality of vengeance.

3. *Conservative Gun Control Legislation:* Whereas the first two strategies rely on the activism of community groups and civil rights attorneys, the third strategy relies on actions taken by elected officials. Perhaps the most straightforward discovery of the present research is this: Exposure to guns is a direct consequence of neo-Nazism and a necessary antecedent of domestic terrorism. Therefore, the solution to this problem is equally as straightforward.

If, as President Bush has implored, "each one of us must work to eliminate racism and bigotry . . . right now!" then the chief executive of the United States can most responsibly fulfill his role in the struggle against neo-Nazism and domestic terrorism by proposing legislation to eliminate—not control, but eliminate—gun ownership in America.

Yet such a radical reform is not likely to receive much support in today's marketplace of political ideas. Americans have a long and deeply ingrained fascination with firearms, and gun ownership is protected by the Second Amendment to the Constitution. Therefore, a compromise legislation is necessary to prevent future acts of domestic terrorism in the United States. In this regard, public officials may take note of recent events in the Canadian House of Commons.

In December of 1989, a twenty-five-year-old white male named Marc Lepine committed the most heinous hate crime in Canadian history. Lepine, an avowed misogynist, entered the University of Montreal engineering school with a loaded assault rifle and massacred fourteen women enrolled in a feminist seminar. Persistent demands for gun control legislation intensified in the Canadian government following Lepine's rampage; and in November 1991, the House of Commons overwhelmingly passed a stringent seven-point compromise package hailed by the Canadian justice minister as "a very important contribution to public safety." "What this does," said the justice minister, "is make it a lot harder for the Marc Lepine's of this world to get firearms" (quoted in the *Miami Herald,* November 8, 1991:5A).

Based on the Canadian model, such a struggle against domestic terrorism in the United States would:

- Impose a permanent ban on automatic assault weapons and sawed-off shotguns.
- Raise the minimum age of gun ownership to twenty-one years old.
- Create a mandatory thirty-day waiting period for firearms acquisition certificates.
- Set the cost of firearms acquisition certificates at no less than $1,000 and earmark these tax revenues for research and education for primary targets of hate crime and domestic terrorism.
- Require gun owners to follow strict regulations for the safe storage of all weapons.
- Raise the maximum sentence for illegal possession of prohibited weapons to ten years in prison.

- Create a lifetime ban on gun ownership for anyone convicted of a hate crime or an act of domestic terrorism punishable by a prison term of one or more years.
- Set a ten-shot cartridge maximum for handguns, and a five-shot maximum for rifles.

4. *Standards for Responsible Media Coverage:* In many ways, domestic terrorism is nothing more than an exercise in high theater. "The media," writes Walter Laqueur, "are the terrorists' best friend" (quoted in Braungart and Braungart, 1983:326). The present research has shown that neo-Nazi leaders are well aware of television's influence. Indeed, they hunger for publicity as a means of promoting their beliefs. Thus, television coverage is a reward to neo-Nazis. However, this is not a one-way relationship.

Instead, it is a mutually beneficial association. As neo-Nazis use the television to promote their causes, television producers use the attraction of neo-Nazis to survive in the high-stakes ratings game. The most expedient way to remove the rewards received for coverage of neo-Nazi events is press censorship. Yet the right of free press and the public's right to know about the activities of the far right are valued features of our constitutional republic. Hence, there is no use trying to stop television from doing its job and reporting the news. Two essential strategies, however, can be employed to present a balanced and truthful depiction of neo-Nazism and its attendant forms of terrorism.

First, and most important, media reporters can endeavor to remove the sensationalism and demonology of neo-Nazism by focusing more on accuracy than emotionalism. This means that reporters must be careful not to provoke or exploit neo-Nazis and their behavior. The treatment of skinheads by Oprah Winfrey and Geraldo Rivera stand as testaments to bad television reporting. In Geraldo Rivera's case, his coverage of neo-Nazism borders on criminal. In fact, a case can be made that Oprah Winfrey, Geraldo Rivera, Phil Donahue, and Sally Jessy Raphael should not even attempt to provide responsible reporting on such complex issues as neo-Nazism and domestic terrorism. After all, their primary business is to sell largely worthless products to an unsuspecting public. Therefore, these programs do not offer the appropriate vehicle for explaining and interpreting ideas, a sense of history, and the subtleties and ironies of civilized discourse (Fussell, 1991). Within this context, mendacity and mediocrity naturally govern the complexities surrounding politics, youth subcultures, and violence.

Second, reporters can solicit the assistance of authorities to help them explain and analyze the events and activities of neo-Nazis. For example, on November 10, 1991, David Duke appeared on NBC's "Meet the Press" and boldly stated that "Through Jesus Christ, I have become more moderate . . . I now reject Nazism."

Duke could have then been asked to explain why, in a 1985 interview, he described the ultimate goal of his politics as being "like apartheid except . . . a complete separation [of races] on a volunteer basis" (quoted in Hughes, 1991:28). He could have been asked to explain why, as recently as 1989, he was still promoting an idea to divide America into ethnic nations. (Duke proposed to resettle all American Jews to New York and rename it West Israel.) If he was no longer a neo-Nazi, then why in 1989 as a member of the Louisiana State Legislature, was Duke still selling neo-Nazi pamphlets from his office? And why, from the same office, was he selling revisionistic accounts of history claiming that the Nazi Holocaust was a hoax? Why did he attempt to pass Louisiana legislation that would award government grants to encourage high-IQ white couples to breed? As a born-again Christian, why does Duke continue to offer a mail-order service for *The White Man's Bible* and *The Holy Book of Adolf Hitler*? As a self-described political moderate, why does he continue to sell copies of the terrorist manifesto known as *The Turner Diaries*?

Duke was not asked to explain any of this. Perhaps he was not asked these questions because the television reporters themselves were uninformed about David Duke and his long-standing commitment to neo-Nazism. Perhaps they were uninformed because of a paucity of research on the subject.

5. *Future Research:* Finally, the present study suggests a need for future research on American neo-Nazism and domestic terrorism. Such a research agenda may be implemented at three levels of analysis:

First, criminologists can examine the etiology of domestic terrorism by viewing the underlying character structure of such violence as having a moral and political basis, rather than being merely deviant, pathological, or simply an artifact of recalcitrant bonding to the dominant social order. Domestic terrorism has a strong ideological wind blowing through it, and to recognize this "requires a conception of man that is quite different from the one usually employed by criminologists" (Clinard and Quinney, 1973:163). This conceptualization requires that scholars recognize the existence of *principled deviance* and begin applying it to modern criminological theories of crime causation.

Second, political scientists and social psychologists can reinvigorate the research traditions of Theodor Adorno and Leo Srole by examining trends in neo-Nazism, occult religion, and alienation. Such a research agenda must be dedicated to monitoring the continuity and change in these trends.

Third, criminal justice scholars can begin to examine the effectiveness and efficiency of public policies to control domestic terrorism. Yet when they do, they must be mindful of the causes of neo-Nazism and domestic terrorism, and realize that significant changes through conventional routes of public administration will come to little avail. Moreover, the system is often a coconspirator in the problem.

Such a widespread academic interest in deconstructing neo-Nazism and domestic terrorism could provide the basis for transpraxis—or an intellectual pursuit wherein scholars with a variety of skills descend on these problems and collaboratively study them until they produce a coherent body of knowledge on causality and control. Such a collaboration, itself, could potentially serve as a natural prophylactic against hostility and violence within contemporary youth subcultures. This alone, it seems, would make a meaningful contribution to the character of American culture and public administration in the years ahead.

References

ADL (Anti-Defamation League). 1989a. *1988 ADL Audit of Anti-Semitic Incidents.* New York: ADL.
———. 1989b. *Skinheads Target the Schools.* New York: ADL.
———. 1988a. *Hate Groups in America: A Record of Bigotry and Violence:* New York: ADL.
———. 1988b. *Law Enforcement Bulletin.* New York: ADL.
———. 1988c. *Young and Violent: The Growing Menace of America's Neo-Nazi Skinheads.* New York: ADL.
———. 1987a. *The Hate Movement Today: A Chronicle of Violence and Disarray.* New York: ADL.
———. 1987b. *"Shaved for Battle": Skinheads Target America's Youth.* New York: ADL.
———. 1987c. *Special Edition.* New York: ADL.
———. 1983. *The "Identity Churches": A Theology of Hate.* New York: ADL.
Adler, Patricia A. 1985. *Wheeling and Dealing: An Ethnography of an Upper-Level Drug Dealing and Smuggling Community.* New York: Columbia University Press.
Adorno, T. W., Else Frenkel-Brunswik, Daniel J. Levinson, and R. Nevitt Sanford. 1950. *The Authoritarian Personality.* New York: Harper & Brothers.
Akers, Ronald L. 1985. *Deviant Behavior: A Social Learning Approach.* Belmont, CA: Wadsworth.
Akers, Ronald L., Marvin Krohn, Lonn Lanza-Kaduce, and Marcia Radosevich. 1979. "Social Learning and Deviant Behavior: A Specific Test of a General Theory." *American Sociological Review,* 44: 635–55.
Akiyama, Yoshio. 1991. "The Role of the FBI's Uniform Crime Reporting Program in the Implementation of the Hate Crimes Statistics Act." Paper presented at the annual meeting of the American Society of Criminology, San Francisco.
Albrecht, Stan L., Bruce A. Chadwick, and Daniel S. Alcorn. 1977. "Religiosity and Deviance: Application of an Attitude-Behavior Contingent Consistency Model." *Journal for the Scientific Study of Religion,* 16: 263–74.
Anderson, Jack. 1990. "Profile of a Skinhead." *Terre Haute Tribune/Star,* January 10: 12.
Arendt, Hannah. 1963. *Eichmann in Jerusalem: A Report on the Banality of Evil.* New York: Viking Press.

Babbie, Earl. 1989. *The Practice of Social Research.* Belmont, CA: Wadsworth.

Baird, Jay. 1990. *To Die for Germany: Heroes in the Nazi Pantheon.* Bloomington: Indiana University Press.

Baron, Stephen W. 1989. "The Canadian West Coast Punk Subculture: A Field Study." *Canadian Journal of Sociology,* 14: 289–316.

Barrett, Paul M. 1989. "Hate Crimes Increase and Become More Violent; U.S. Prosecutors Focus on 'Skinhead' Movement." *Wall Street Journal,* July 14: 12.

Becker, Howard S. 1978. "Practitioners of Vice and Crime." In Norman K. Denzin, ed., *Sociological Methods: A Sourcebook.* New York: McGraw-Hill.

Beirne, Piers, and James Messerschmidt. 1991. *Criminology.* San Diego: Harcourt Brace Jovanovich.

Bensinger, Gad J. 1991. "Hate Crimes: A New/Old Problem." Paper presented at the annual meeting of the American Society of Criminology, San Francisco.

Berrill, Kevin. 1990. "Anti-Gay Violence: Cause, Consequences, and Responses." Address before the Office of International Criminal Justice, Chicago.

Bishop, Katherine. 1988. "Neo-Nazi Activity Is Arising among U.S. Youth." *New York Times,* June 13: 17.

Bloomington Herald Tribune. 1991. "Semi-Automatic Guns Being Imported." *Bloomington Herald Tribune,* October 21: A2.

Blumberg, Abraham S. 1974. "Crime and the Social Order." In Abraham S. Blumberg, ed., *Current Perspectives on Criminal Behavior: Original Essays on Criminology.* New York: Knopf.

Bookin-Weiner, Hedy, and Ruth Horowitz. 1983. "The End of the Youth Gang: Fad or Fact?" *Criminology,* 21: 585–602.

Bowling, Benjamin. 1990. "Racist Harassment and the Process of Victimization: Conceptual and Methodological Implications for Crime Surveys." Paper presented at the Realist Criminology Conference, Vancouver, B.C.

Bracher, Karl Dietrich. 1976. "The Role of Hitler: Perspectives of Interpretation." In Walter Laqueur, ed., *Fascism: A Reader's Guide.* Hants, England: Wildwood House.

Brake, Mike. 1985. *Comparative Youth Culture.* London: Routledge & Kegan Paul.

Braungart, Richard G., and Margaret M. Braungart. 1983. "Terrorism." In Arnold Goldstein and Leonard Kraser, eds., *Prevention and Control of Aggression.* New York: Pergamon Press.

Bromberg, Craig. 1989. *The Wicked Ways of Malcolm McLaren.* New York: Harper & Row.

Brown, C. 1984. *Black and White Britain: The Third PSI Survey.* London: Heinemann.

Brown, Owen. 1989. "Know Your Enemy . . . Tom Metzger an American Fascist." *No KKK! No Facist USA!,* Spring/Summer: 5–6.

Brownstein, Henry H., and Paul J. Goldstein. 1990. "A Typology of Drug-Related Homicides." In Ralph Weisheit, ed., *Drugs, Crime and the Criminal Justice System.* Cincinnati: Anderson Publishing.

Burgess, Robert L., and Ronald L. Akers. 1966. "A Differential Association-Reinforcement Theory of Criminal Behavior." *Social Problems,* 14: 128–47.

Burkett, Steven, and Melvin White. 1977. "Hellfire and Delinquency: Another Look." *Journal for the Scientific Study of Religion,* 13: 445–62.

Buursma, Bruce. 1988. "Neo-Nazi Skinheads Throw Shadow over Northwest." *Chicago Tribune,* December 18: 25.

Cable Street Beat review. n.d. "Blood & Honour." *Cable Street Beat review,* 1–4.

Came, Barry 1989. "A Growing Menace: Violent Skinheads Are Raising Urban Fears." *Maclean's,* January 23: 43–44.

Cameron, Mary Owen. 1964. *The Booster and the Snitch: Department Store Shoplifting.* Glencoe, IL: Free Press.

Carr, William. 1976. "National Socialism — Foreign Policy and Wehrmacht." In Walter Laqueur, ed., *Fascism: A Reader's Guide.* Hants, England: Wildwood House.

Center for Democratic Renewal. n.d. *Skinhead Nazis and Youth Information Packet.* Atlanta: Center for Democratic Renewal.

Chambliss, William J. 1988. *Exploring Criminology.* New York: Macmillan.

———. 1986. "The Curious Career of the Rehabilitative Ethic." Address before the Conference on Reaffirming Rehabilitation at Arlington, Virginia, in July.

———. 1978. *On the Take.* Bloomington: Indiana University Press.

———. 1975. *Box Man: A Professional Thief's Journal,* by Harry King. New York: Harper and Row.

———. 1973. "The Saints and the Roughnecks." *Society,* November/December: 24–31.

———. 1962. "The Selection of Friends." Ph.D. diss., Indiana University.

Chambliss, William J., and Robert B. Seidman. 1971. *Law, Order, & Power.* Reading, MA: Addison-Wesley.

Chin, Ko-Lin. 1986. "Chinese Tiead Societies, Tongs, Organized Crime, and Street Gangs in Asia and the United States." Ph.D. diss., University of Pennsylvania.

Clarke, Floyd I. 1991. "Hate Violence in the United States." *FBI Law Enforcement Bulletin,* January: 14–17.

Clarke, James W. 1989. "Identifying Potential Assassins: Some Situational Correlates of Dangerousness." In Ted Robert Gurr, ed., *Violence in America.* Newbury Park, CA: Sage.

Clarke, John. 1976a. "The Skinheads and the Magical Recovery of Community." In Stuart Hall and Tony Jefferson, eds., *Resistance through Rituals.* London: Hutchinson.

———. 1976b. "Style." In Stuart Hall and Tony Jefferson, eds., *Resistance through Rituals.* London: Hutchinson.

Clarke, John, Stuart Hall, Tony Jefferson, and Brian Roberts. 1976. "Subcultures, Cultures and Class: A Theoretical Overview." In Stuart Hall and Tony Jefferson, eds., *Resistance through Rituals.* London: Hutchinson.

Cleaver, Eldridge. 1967. *Soul on Ice.* New York: McGraw-Hill.

Clinard, Marshall B., and Richard Quinney. 1973. *Criminal Behavior Systems.* New York: Holt, Rinehart and Winston.

Cloward, Richard A., and Lloyd E. Ohlin. 1960. *Delinquency and Opportunity.* Glencoe, IL: Free Press.

Coates, James. 1987. *Armed and Dangerous: The Rise of the Survivalist Right.* New York: Noonday Press.

Cohen, Albert K. 1976. "Prison Violence: A Sociological Perspective." In Albert K. Cohen, George F. Cole, and Robert G. Bailey, eds., *Prison Violence.* Lexington, MA: D.C. Heath.

———. 1955. *Delinquent Boys.* Glencoe, IL: Free Press.

Cohen, Phil. 1972. "Sub-Cultural Conflict and Working Class Community." *W.P.C.S.* 2. Birmingham: University of Birmingham.

Cohen, Stanley. 1980. *Folk Devils and Moral Panics.* London: Macgibbon and Kee.

Collier, Peter, and David Horowitz. 1989. *Destructive Generation: Second Thoughts About the Sixties.* New York: Summit Books.

Conklin, John E. 1989. *Criminology.* New York: Macmillan.

Cooper, Mary H. 1989. "The Growing Danger of Hate Groups." *Editorial Research Reports,* 18: 262–75.

Coplon, Jeff. 1989. "The Skinhead Reich." *Utne Reader,* May/June: 80–89.

Corrigan, Paul. 1979. *Schooling the Smash Street Kids.* London: Macmillan Press.

Cressey, Donald R. 1960. "The Theory of Differential Association: An Introduction." *Social Problems,* 8: 2–6.

Cronbach, Lee J. 1951. "Coefficient Alpha and the Internal Structure of Tests." *Psychometrika,* 16: 297–334.

Cullen, Francis T. 1988. "Were Cloward and Ohlin Strain Theorists?" *Journal of Research in Crime and Delinquency,* 24: 214–41.

Curry, G. David, and Irving A. Spergel. 1988. "Gang Homicide, Delinquency, and Community." *Criminology,* 26: 381–405.

Dalleck, Robert. 1984. *Ronald Reagan: The Politics of Symbolism.* Cambridge, MA; Harvard University Press.

Dancis, Bruce. 1978. "Safety-Pins and Class Struggle: Punk Rock and the Left." *Socialist Review,* 8: 58–83.

Davis, Stephen. 1985. *Hammer of the Gods: The Led Zeppelin Saga.* New York: Ballantine Books.

Dees, Morris. 1990. Personal communication, letter.

Dees, Morris, with Steve Fiffer. 1991. *A Season for Justice: The Life and Times of Civil Rights Lawyer Morris Dees.* New York: Charles Scribner's Sons.

Degrelle, Leon. 1938. *Revolution Des Ames* (Cited in Zeev Sternhell, 1976, "Fascist Ideology." In Walter Laqueur, ed., *Fascism: A Reader's Guide.* Hants, England: Wildwood House).

Dentler, Robert A., and Lawrence J. Monroe. 1961. "Social Correlates of Early Adolescent Theft." *American Sociological Review,* 26: 733–43.

Dillehay, Ronald C. 1978. "Authoritarianism." In Harvey London and John Exner, Jr., eds., *Dimensions of Personality.* New York: John Wiley & Sons.

Dinges, John. 1989. *Our Man in Panama: How General Noriega Used the United States — And Made Millions in Drugs and Arms.* New York: Random House.

Donovan, Frank. 1964. *The Vikings.* New York: American Heritage Press.

Downes, D. 1966. *The Delinquent Solution.* London: Routledge & Kegan Paul.

Doyle, Kirby. 1970. *Happiness Bastard.* San Francisco: City Lights Books.

Duke, Paul (ed.) 1986. *Beyond Reagan: The Politics of Upheaval.* New York: Warner Books.

Durkheim, Emile. 1893/1984. *The Division of Labour in Society.* W. D. Halls, trans. New York: Free Press.

———. 1894/1982. *The Rules of Sociological Method.* W. D. Halls, trans. London: Macmillan.

———. 1897/1951. *Suicide. A Study in Sociology.* John A. Spaulding and George Simpson, trans. New York: Free Press.

Dylan, Bob. 1971. *Tarantula.* New York: Macmillan.

Eddy, Chuck. 1985. "Heavy Metal." In Dave Marsh et al., eds., *Rock & Roll Confidential.* New York: Pantheon Books.

Elifson, Kirk W., David M. Peterson, and C. Kirk Hadaway. 1983. "Religiosity and Delinquency: A Contextual Analysis." *Criminology,* 21: 505–28.

Elliott, Delbert S., and Suzanne Ageton. 1980. "Reconciling Race and Class Differences in Self-Reported and Official Estimates of Delinquency." *American Sociological Review,* 45: 95–110.

Elliott, Delbert S., David H. Huizinga, and Suzanne Ageton. 1985. *Explaining Delinquency and Drug Use.* Beverly Hills: Sage.

Elliott, Delbert S., David H. Huizinga, and Scott Menard. 1989. *Multiple Problem Youth: Delinquency, Substance Use and Mental Problems.* New York: Springer-Verlag.

Ellis, Desmond. 1987. *The Wrong Stuff: An Introduction to the Sociological Study of Deviance.* Toronto: Collier Macmillan.

Erickson, Maynard, and LaMar T. Empey. 1963. "Court Records, Undetected Delinquency and Decision-Making." *Journal of Criminal Law, Criminology and Police Science,* 54: 456–69.

Erlanger, Howard S. 1979. "Estrangement, Machismo and Gang Violence." *Social Science Quarterly,* 60: 235–48.

Esposito, John C., and Larry J. Silverman. 1970. *Vanishing Air: Ralph Nader's Study Group Report on Air Pollution.* New York: Grossman.

Fact Sheet Five. 1990. "Getting Zines." *Fact Sheet Five,* January: 4.

Fagan, Jeffrey. 1990a. "Intoxication and Aggression." In Michael Tonry and James Q. Wilson, eds., *Drugs and Crime.* Chicago: University of Chicago Press.

———. 1990b. "Social Processes of Delinquency and Drug Use among Urban Gangs." In C. Ronald Huff, ed., *Gangs in America.* Newbury Park, CA: Sage.

———. 1989. "The Social Organization of Drug Use and Drug Dealing among Urban Gangs." *Criminology,* 27: 633–69.

Falk, Gene. 1987. "1987 Budget Perspectives: Federal Spending for Human Resource Programs." *Report No. 86-46 EPW.* Washington, D.C.: Congressional Research Service.

Fielder, Tom. 1991. "Democrats Rail at Bush Over Recession." *Miami Herald,* November 4: 4.

Finn, Peter, and Taylor McNeil. 1988. *Bias Crime and the Criminal Justice Response.* Washington, D.C.: U.S. Department of Justice.

Flynn, Kevin, and Gary Gerhardt. 1989. *The Silent Brotherhood: Inside America's Racist Underground.* New York: Free Press.

Frith, Simon. 1985. "Britbeat." In Dave Marsh et al., eds., *Rock & Roll Confidential.* New York: Pantheon Books.

———. 1978. *The Sociology of Rock.* London: Constable.

Fromm, Eric. 1941. *Escape from Freedom.* New York: Rinehart & Company.

Fussell, Paul. 1991. *Bad or, The Dumbing of America.* New York: Summit Books.

Gatewood, Rex. 1989. "America's Nazi Children." *No KKK—No Fascist USA,* Spring/Summer: 1–4.

Gibson, Michael. 1972. *The Vikings.* London: Wayland Publishers.

Ginsberg, Allen. 1968. *Planet News: 1961–1967.* San Francisco: City Lights Books.

Glaser, Daniel. 1956. "Criminality Theories and Behavioral Images." *American Journal of Sociology,* 61: 433–44.

Goldstein, Jeffrey H. 1986. *Aggression and Crimes of Violence.* New York: Oxford University Press.

Goleman, Daniel. 1986. "Researchers Dispute Pornography Report on Its Use of Data." *New York Times,* May 17: 1.

Gordon, Paul. 1990. *Racial Violence and Harassment* 2nd ed. London: Runnymede Trust.

Gottfredson, Michael R., and Travis Hirschi. 1990. *A General Theory of Crime*. Stanford, CA: Stanford University Press.

Gottschalk, Peter T. 1988. "Retrenchment in Antipoverty Programs in the United States: Lessons for the Future." In B. B. Kymlicka and Jean V. Matthews, eds., *The Reagan Revolution?* Chicago: Dorsey Press.

Grogan, Emmett. 1972. *Ringolevio: A Life Played for Keeps*. Boston: Little, Brown.

Gurr, Ted Robert. 1989. "Political Terrorism: Historical Antecedents and Contemporary Trends." In Ted Robert Gurr, ed., *Violence in America*, Vol. 2. Newbury Park, CA: Sage.

Hackett, George. 1987. "Skinheads on the Rampage." *Newsweek*, September 7: 22.

Hagan, Frank E. 1989, 1990. *Research Methods in Criminology and Criminal Justice*. New York: Macmillan.

Hagedorn, John. 1990. "Back in the Field Again: Gang Research in the Nineties." In C. Ronald Huff, ed., *Gangs in America*. Newbury Park, CA: Sage.

———. 1988. *People and Folks: Gangs, Crime and the Underclass in a Rustbelt City*. Chicago: Lakeview Press.

Hamm, Mark S. 1991. "Confronting the Appeal of White Extremism through Correctional Education." In Stephen Duguid, ed., *The 1991 Yearbook of Correctional Education*. Burnaby, B.C.: Simon Fraser University.

———. 1986. *Heroin Addiction, Anomie, and Social Policy in the United States and Britain*. Washington, D.C.: Academy of Higher Education.

Hardt, Robert H., and Sandra Peterson Hardt. 1977. "On Determining the Quality of the Delinquency Self-Report Method." *Journal of Research in Crime and Delinquency*, 14: 247–61.

Hebdige, Dick. 1979. *Subculture: The Meaning of Style*. London: Methuen.

———. 1976. "Reggae, Rastas, and Rudies." In Stuart Hall and Tony Jefferson, eds., *Resistance through Rituals*. London: Hutchinson.

Hershey, Robert D., Jr. 1991. "Jobless Rate 6.8%, Reflecting Stalled Rebound." *New York Times*, November 2: 1.

Hexham, I. 1984. "British Israelitism." In W. Elwell, ed., *Evangelical Dictionary of Theology*. Grand Rapids, MI: Baker Book House.

Hindelang, Michael J., Travis Hirschi, and Joseph G. Weis. 1981. *Measuring Delinquency*. Beverly Hills: Sage.

Hiro, Dilip. 1991. *Black British White British: A History of Race Relations in Britain*. London: Grafton Books.

Hirschi, Travis. 1969. *Causes of Delinquency*. Berkeley: University of California Press.

Hirschi, Travis, and Rodney Stark. 1969. "Hellfire and Delinquency." *Social Problems*, 17: 202–13.

Hofstadter, Richard. 1967. *The Paranoid Style in American Politics and Other Essays*. New York: Vintage Books.

Horowitz, Ruth. 1990. "Sociological Perspectives on Gangs: Conflicting Definitions and Concepts." In C. Ronald Huff, ed., *Gangs in America*. Newbury Park, CA: Sage.

———. 1987. "Community Tolerance of Gang Violence." *Social Problems*, 34: 437–50.

Horowitz, Ruth, and Gary Schwartz. 1974. "Honor, Normative Ambiguity and Gang Violence." *American Sociological Review*, 39: 238–51.

Hotchner, A. E. 1990. *Blown Away*. New York: Fireside.

Huff, C. Ronald (ed.) 1990. *Gangs in America*. Newbury Park, CA: Sage.

———. 1989. "Youth Gangs and Public Policy." *Crime & Delinquency*, 35: 524–37.

Hughes, Sallie. 1991. " 'Duke Factor' Has All Eyes on Louisiana." *Miami Herald,* November 10: 1–28.

Hynes, Charles J., and Bob Drury. 1990. *Incident at Howard Beach: The Case for Murder.* New York: G. P. Putnam's Sons.

Inciardi, James. 1988. "Narcoterrorism." Paper presented at the annual meeting of the Academy of Criminal Justice Sciences, San Francisco.

Irwin, John. 1980. *Prisons in Turmoil.* Boston: Little, Brown.

———. 1970. *The Felon.* Englewood Cliffs, NJ: Prentice Hall.

Irwin, John, and Donald Cressey. 1964. "Thieves, Convicts, and the Inmate Culture." *Social Problems,* Fall: 145–48.

Jackson, James O. 1991. "Unity's Shadows." *Time,* July 1: 6–14.

Jacobs, James B. 1977. *Stateville.* Chicago: University of Chicago Press.

Jefferson, Tony. 1976. "Cultural Responses of the Teds: The Defense of Space and Status." In Stuart Hall and Tony Jefferson, eds., *Resistance through Rituals.* London: Hutchinson.

Jensen, Gary F. 1972. "Parents, Peers and Delinquency Action: A Test of the Differential Association Perspective." *American Journal of Sociology,* 78: 562–75.

Jensen, Gary F., and Maynard L. Erickson. 1979. "The Religious Factor and Delinquency: Another Look at the Hellfire Hypothesis." In Robert Wuthnow, eds., *The Religious Dimension: New Directions in Quantitative Research.* New York: Academic Press.

Jewell, John. n.d. "Skinhead Rock 'n' Roll." *WAR,* 8: 4–7.

John Brown Anti-Klan Committee. 1990a. "New York: Racism Increasing." *No KKK—No Fascist USA,* Winter/Spring: 2.

———. 1990b. "Rich Kid Skinheads Bash Gays," *No KKK—No Fascist USA,* Winter/Spring: 2.

———. 1990c. "$3 Million in Stolen Loot Linked to Nazi Skinheads." *No KKK—No Fascist USA,* Winter/Spring: 2.

———. 1989. "Anti-Racist Skins Form the 'Syndicate.' " *No KKK—No Fascist USA,* Spring/Summer: 6.

———. 1986. "Law and the Order." *Death to the Klan!* Summer: 1–7.

———. 1985. "What's Behind the White American Bastion." *Death to the Klan!* June: 1–12.

Johnson, Bruce D., Mitchell A. Kaplan, and James Schmeidler. 1990. "Days with Drug Distribution: Which Drugs? How Many Transactions?" In Ralph Weisheit, ed., *Drugs, Crime and the Criminal Justice System,* Cincinnati: Anderson Publishing.

Johnson, Richard E., Anastasios C. Marcos, and Stephen J. Bahr. 1987. "The Role of Peers in the Complex Etiology of Adolescent Drug Use." *Criminology,* 25: 323–40.

Joint Committee Against Racialism. 1981. *Racial Violence in Britain.* London: JCAR.

Kahaner, Larry. 1988. *Cults that Kill.* New York: Warner Books.

Katz, Jack. 1988. *Seductions of Crime.* New York: Basic Books.

Keiser, R. Lincoln. 1969. *The Vice Lords: Warriors of the Streets.* New York: Holt.

Kelman, H. C., and J. Barclay. 1963. "The F Scale as a Measure of Breadth of Perspective." *Journal of Abnormal and Social Psychology,* 67: 608–15.

Kerouac, Jack. 1955. *On the Road.* New York: Viking Press.

King, Dennis. 1989. *Lyndon LaRouche and the New American Fascism.* New York: Doubleday.

Kingsman, Caroline. n.d. "High Theory . . . No Culture: Decolonizing Canadian Subcultural Studies." Unpublished manuscript. Ottawa, Ontario: Carleton University.

Klanwatch. 1991. *The Ku Klux Klan: A History of Racism and Violence.* Montgomery, AL: Southern Poverty Law Center.

————. 1989. *Intelligence Report.* Montgomery, AL: Southern Poverty Law Center.

Klein, Malcolm W. 1971. *Street Gangs and Street Workers.* Englewood Cliffs, NJ: Prentice Hall.

Knight, Nick. 1982. *Skinhead.* London: Omnibus Press.

Koch, Ron. 1990. "Activist Leaders Back 'Hate Crime' Legislation." *Terre Haute Tribune/ Star,* February 10: 1.

Kraemer, Helena Chmura, and Sue Thiemann. 1987. *How Many Subjects? Statistical Power Analysis in Research.* Newbury Park, CA: Sage.

Kushnick, Louis V. 1981. "Racism and Class Consciousness in Modern Capitalism." In Benjamin P. Bowser and Raymond G. Hunt, eds., *Impacts of Racism on White Americans.* Newbury Park, CA: Sage.

Kymlicka, B. B., and Jean V. Matthews (eds.) 1988. *The Reagan Revolution?* Chicago: Dorsey Press.

Laing, Dave. 1985. *One Chord Wonders: Power and Meaning in Punk Rock.* Milton Keynes, England: Open University Press.

————. 1969. *The Sound of Our Time.* London: Sheed & Ward.

Lane, Hana Umalauf (ed.). 1986. *The World Almanac and Book of Facts.* New York: Newspaper Enterprise Association.

Langer, Elinor. 1990. "The American Neo-Nazi Movement Today." *Nation,* July 16/23: 82–108.

LaVey, Anton Szandor. 1969. *The Satanic Bible.* New York: Avon Books.

Leo, John. 1988. "A Chilling Wave of Racism." *Time,* January 25: 57.

Levine, Harold, and Steven Stumpf. 1983. "Statements of Fear through Cultural Symbols: Punk Rock as a Reflective Subculture." *Youth and Society,* 14: 417–35.

Levi-Strauss, Claude. 1969. *The Elementary Structures of Kinship.* London: Eyre & Spottiswood.

Lillyquist, Michael J. 1980. *Understanding and Changing Criminal Behavior.* Englewood Cliffs, NJ: Prentice Hall.

Linedecker, Clifford E. 1989. *Hell Ranch: A Nightmare Tale of Drugs, Death and Voodoo in Matamoros.* Austin, TX: Diamond Books.

Linker, Alan N. 1989. "Neo-Nazi Skinheads." Address before the Congregation of Temple Beth El Israel, Louisville.

Linz, Juan J. 1976. "Some Notes toward a Comparative Study of Fascism in Sociological Historical Perspective." In Walter Laqueur, ed., *Fascism: A Reader's Guide.* Hants, England: Wildwood House.

Liska, Allen E. 1981. *Perspectives on Deviance.* Englewood Cliffs, NJ: Prentice Hall.

London Borough of Newham. 1986. *The Newham Crime Survey.* London: London Borough of Newham.

London, Robb. 1990. "Sending a $12.5 Million Message to Hate Group." *New York Times,* October 26: 1.

Lotz, Roy, Eric D. Poole, and Robert M. Regoli. 1985. *Juvenile Delinquency and Juvenile Justice.* New York: Random House.

Marcus, Greil. 1989. *Lipstick Traces: A Secret History of the Twentieth Century.* Cambridge, MA: Harvard University Press.

Marovitz, William A. 1991. "Hate or Bias Crime Legislation." In Nancy Taylor, ed., *Bias Crime: The Law Enforcement Response*. Chicago: Office of International Criminal Justice.

Marsh, Peter. 1977. "Dole Que Rock." *New Society,* 39: 112–15.

Martell, Clark. n.d. "Skinheads." *WAR,* 7: 14.

Martin, Randy, Robert J. Mutchnick, and W. Timothy Austin. 1990. *Criminological Thought: Pioneers Past and Present.* New York: Macmillan.

Matthews, Victor M. 1968. "Differential Identification: An Empirical Note." *Social Problems,* 15: 376–83.

Maximum Rock 'N' Roll. 1989. "Letters." *MRR,* September (unpaginated).

Maxson, Cheryl, and Malcolm W. Klein. 1990. "Street Gang Violence: Twice as Great, or Half as Great?" In C. Ronald Huff, ed., *Gangs in America.* Newbury Park, CA: Sage.

———. 1983. "Gangs: Why We Couldn't Stay Away." In James R. Kleugel, ed., *Evaluating Contemporary Juvenile Justice.* Beverly Hills: Sage.

McNiven, James D. 1988. " 'Ron, Reaganism, and Revolution': The Rise of the New American Political Economy." In B. B. Kymlicka and Jean V. Matthews, eds., *The Reagan Revolution?* Chicago: Dorsey Press.

McNulty, Jennifer. 1989. "Crowd of Protestors Jeers 100 Skinheads at Whites-Only Rally." *Indianapolis Star,* March 6: 1.

Merry, Sally. 1981. *Urban Danger.* Philadelphia: Temple University Press.

Merton, Robert K. 1957. *Social Theory and Social Structure.* Glencoe, IL: Free Press.

Metzger, Tom. 1990. Personal communication, letter.

Miami Herald. 1991. "Canada's House Backs Compromise on Tighter Gun Control." *Miami Herald,* November 8: 5A.

Mieczkowski, Thomas. 1986. "Geeking Up and Throwing Down: Heroin Street Life in Detroit." *Criminology,* 24: 645–66.

Miller, Walter B. 1980. "Gangs, Groups and Serious Youth Crime." In D. Shichor and D. Kelly, eds., *Critical Issues in Juvenile Delinquency.* Lexington, MA: Lexington.

———. 1958. "Lower-Class Culture as a Generating Milieu of Gang Delinquency." *Journal of Social Issues,* 15: 5–19.

Mills, James. 1986. *The Underground Empire: Where Crime and Government Embrace.* Garden City, NY: Doubleday.

Mommsen, Hans. 1976. "National Socialism – Continuity and Change." In Walter Laqueur, ed., *Fascism: A Reader's Guide.* Hants, England: Wildwood House.

Monitor. 1988. "Neo-Nazi Youth Gang Activity Builds Up." *Monitor,* April: 6.

———. 1987. "Far-Right Youth Recruitment Serious Long Term Threat." *Monitor,* September: 4–5.

Moore, Joan W. 1985. "Isolation and Stigmatization in the Development of an Underclass: The Case of Chicano Gangs in East Los Angeles." *Social Problems,* 33: 1–10.

———. 1978. *Homeboys.* Philadelphia: Temple University Press.

Morash, Mary. 1983. "Gangs, Groups, and Delinquency." *British Journal of Criminology,* 23: 309–31.

Mücke, Thomas. 1991. "Bericht uber das projeckt – Miteinander statt gegeneiandeer." *Jervental:* 38–47.

Muncie, John. 1981. *Politics, Ideology and Popular Culture.* Milton Keynes, England: Open University Press.

Nagin, Daniel S., and Raymond Paternoster. 1991. "On the Relationship of Past to Future Participation in Delinquency." *Criminology,* 29: 163–89.

Nash, Jeffrey. 1985. *Social Psychology: Society and Self.* St. Paul, MN: West Publishing.

National Gay & Lesbian Task Force Policy Institute. 1991. *Anti-Gay/Lesbian Violence, Victimization & Defamation in 1990.* Washington, D.C.: National Gay & Lesbian Task Force Policy Institute.

National Information Network. 1989. *General Information Manual with Respect to Satanism and the Occult.* St. Charles, MO: NIN.

National Institute of Mental Health. 1982. *Television and Behavior: Ten Years of Scientific Progress and Implications for the Eighties,* Vol. 1: Summary Report. Washington, D.C.: U.S. Department of Health and Human Services.

Neilsen, Robert C. 1990. "Videos Help Police Fight Campus Crime." *Forum,* 5: 2.

New York Times. 1990. "Five Texans Convicted of Plot Against Rights." *New York Times,* August 4: 17.

Orcutt, James D. 1983. *Analyzing Deviance.* Chicago: Dorsey Press.

Owens, Eric. n.d. "Eric Owens Interviews Ian Stuart of Skrewdriver." *WAR,* 8: 8–9.

Padgett, Gregory L. 1984. "Racially Motivated Violence and Intimidation: Inadequate State Enforcement and Federal Civil Remedies." *Journal of Criminal Law and Criminology,* 26: 591–625.

Page, Joseph, and Mary Win O'Brien. 1973. *Bitter Wages: Ralph Nader's Study Group Report on Disease and Injury on the Job.* New York: Grossman.

Pelz, Mary E., James W. Marquart, and C. Terry Pelz. 1991. "Right-Wing Extremism in the Texas Prisons: The Rise and Fall of the Aryan Brotherhood." Paper presented at the annual meeting of the American Society of Criminology, San Francisco.

Peterson, Iver. 1991. "Americans See Dimmer Prospects." *Miami Herald,* November 4: 5.

Pettigrew, Thomas S. 1981. "The Mental Health Impact." In Benjamin P. Bowser and Raymond G. Hunt, eds., *Impacts of Racism on White Americans.* Newbury Park, CA: Sage.

Poertner, Rudolf. 1971. *The Vikings.* London: St. James Press.

Polenberg, Richard. 1988. "Roosevelt Revolution; Reagan Counter-Revolution." In B. B. Kymlicka and Jean V. Matthews, eds., *The Reagan Revolution?* Chicago: Dorsey Press.

Reckless, Walter, and Simon Dinitz. 1967. "Pioneering with Self-Concept as a Vulnerability Factor in Delinquency." *Journal of Criminal Law, Criminology and Police Science,* 58: 515–23.

Reed, Bruce. 1989. "Nazi Retreat." *The New Republic,* April 3: 10–11.

Regoli, Robert M., and John D. Hewitt. 1991. *Delinquency in Society: A Child-Centered Approach.* New York: Macmillan.

Reiss, Albert, and Lewis Rhodes. 1964. "An Empirical Test of Differential Association Theory." *Journal of Research in Crime and Delinquency,* 1: 5–18.

Ridgeway, James. 1990. *Blood in the Face.* New York: Thunder's Mouth Press.

Riley, Michael. 1991. "The Duke of Louisiana." *Time,* November 4: 23–25.

Robinson, John P., and Phillip R. Shaver. 1973. *Measures of Social Psychological Attitudes.* Ann Arbor: Survey Research Center, University of Michigan.

Rosenthal, Robert, and Ralph L. Rosnow. 1984. *Essentials of Behavioral Research: Methods and Data Analysis.* New York: McGraw-Hill.

Sanchez-Jankowski, Martin. 1991. *Islands in the Street: Gangs in American Urban Society.* Berkeley: University of California Press.

Sandberg, Michael. 1990. "What Happens After the Bias Crime?" Address before the Office of International Criminal Justice, Chicago.

Sapp, Allen D. 1991. "Value and Belief Systems of Right-Wing Extremists: Rationale and Motivation for Bias-Motivated Crimes." In Nancy Taylor, ed., *Bias Crime: The Law Enforcement Response*. Chicago: Office of International Criminal Justice.

Schafer, Steven. 1974. *The Political Criminal: The Problem of Morality and Crime*. New York: Free Press.

Schwendinger, Herman, and Julia Siegel Schwendinger. 1985. *Adolescent Subcultures and Delinquency*. New York: Praeger.

Sears, Eva. 1989. "Skinheads: A New Generation of Hate-Mongers." *USA Today*, May 24: 24–26.

Seidelpielen, Eberhardt. 1991. *Krieg im den Stadten*. Berlin: Rotbuch, 34.

Shapiro, Lena. 1990. "Tom Metzger and White Aryan Resistance Sued for Murder." *No KKK—No Facist USA!*, Winter/Spring: 1–6.

Shaw, Clifford R. 1930. *The Jack Roller*. Chicago: University of Chicago Press.

Shaw, E. Clay Jr. 1991. "Bill Seeks to Toughen Gun-Crime Penalties." *Miami Herald*, November 3: 14.

Shepard, Charles E. 1989. *Forgiven: The Rise and Fall of Jim Bakker and the PTL Ministry*. New York: Atlantic Monthly Press.

Short, James F. 1990. "New Wine in Old Bottles? Change and Continuity in American Gangs." In C. Ronald Huff, ed., *Gangs in America*. Newbury Park, CA: Sage.

———. 1957. "Differential Association and Delinquency." *Social Problems*, 4: 233–39.

Short, James F., and Fred L. Strodtbeck. 1965. *Group Process and Gang Delinquency*. Chicago: University of Chicago Press.

Siegel, Larry J., and Joseph J. Senna. 1981. *Juvenile Delinquency: Theory, Practice, & Law*. St. Paul: West Publishing.

Singular, Stephen. 1987. *Talked to Death: The Murder of Alan Berg and the Rise of the Neo-Nazis*. New York: Berkley Books.

Smith, Hedrick. 1986. "Congress: Will There Be Realignment?" In Paul Duke, ed., *Beyond Reagan: The Politics of Upheaval*. New York: Warner Books.

Snydor, Charles. 1977. *Soldiers of Destruction: The SS Death's Head Division, 1933–1945*. Princeton, NJ: Princeton University Press.

Social Education. 1988. "Skinheads Target America's Youth." *Social Education*, April/May: 290.

Spergel, Irving A. 1990. "Youth Gangs: Continuity and Change." In Michael Tonry and Norval Morris, eds., *Crime and Justice: A Review of Research*. Chicago: University of Chicago Press.

———. 1984. "Violent Gangs in Chicago: In Search of Social Policy." *Social Service Review*, 58: 199–225.

———. 1964. *Racketville Slumtown Haulberg*. Chicago: University of Chicago Press.

Spitz, Bob. 1989. *Dylan*. New York: McGraw-Hill.

Srole, Leo. 1989. "The Origins of Anomia." In Earl Babbie's *The Practice of Social Research*. Belmont, CA: Wadsworth Publishing.

———. 1986. "The Origins of Anomia." In Earl Babbie's *The Practice of Social Research*. Belmont, CA: Wadsworth Publishing.

———. 1956. "Social Integration and Certain Corollaries: An Exploratory Study." *American Sociological Review*, 21: 709–16.

Sternberg, William, and Matthew C. Harrison, Jr. 1989. *Feeding Frenzy: The Gang Who*

Stole Wedtech. New York: Henry Holt.

Sternhell, Zeev. 1976. "Fascist Ideology." In Walter Laqueur, ed., *Fascism: A Reader's Guide.* Hants, England: Wildwood House.

Stevens, Sayre. 1988. "The Star War Challenge." In B. B. Kymlicka and Jean V. Matthews, eds., *The Reagan Revolution?* Chicago: Dorsey Press.

Stills, Peter. 1989. "Dark Contagion: Bigotry and Violence Online." *PC Computing,* December: 144–49.

Stokes, Randall, and John Hewitt. 1976. "Aligning Actions." *American Sociological Review,* 41: 838–49.

Sutherland, Edwin H. 1949. *White Collar Crime.* New York: Dryden.

———. 1947. *Principles of Criminology,* 4th ed. Philadelphia: J. B. Lippincott.

———. 1937. *The Professional Thief.* Chicago: University of Chicago Press.

Sutherland, Edwin H., and Donald R. Cressey. 1970, 1978. *Principles of Criminology.* New York: J. B. Lippincott.

Suttles, Gerald D. 1968. *The Social Order of the Slum.* Chicago: University of Chicago Press.

Sykes, Gresham M., and David Matza. 1957. "Techniques of Neutralization: A Theory of Delinquency." *American Sociological Review,* December: 664–70.

Tafoya, William. 1990. "Rioting in the Streets: Deja Vu?" Address before the Office of International Criminal Justice, Chicago.

Talese, Gay. *Honor Thy Father.* 1971. Greenwich, CN: Fawcett.

Tamayo, Juan O. 1991. "Germany Faces Financial Slump." *Miami Herald.* November 4: 11.

Taylor, Carl S. 1990. *Dangerous Society.* East Lansing: Michigan State University Press.

Taylor, Ian, Paul Walton, and Jock Young. 1973. *The New Criminology: For a Social Theory of Deviance.* London: Routledge & Kegan Paul.

Terre Haute Tribune-Star. 1989. "Racism: Foes March in Protest of Neo-Nazis." *Terre Haute Tribune-Star,* April 23: B4.

Terrell, Adele Dutton. 1989. "Racial Violence and the Underclass." *Forum,* 4: 3–6.

Thompson, Hunter S. 1967. *Hell's Angels.* New York: Ballantine Books.

Thornburgh, Dick. 1990. Address before the Simon Wiesenthal Center, Chicago, on March 6.

Thrasher, Fredric. 1927, 1963. *The Gang.* Chicago: University of Chicago Press.

Tobin, James. 1988. "Reaganomics in Retrospect." In B. B. Kymlicka and Jean V. Matthews, eds., *The Reagan Revolution?* Chicago: Dorsey Press.

Tomaso, Al. 1990. "Hate Crimes – State's Attorney's Office Criminal Prosecution." Address before the Office of International Criminal Justice, Chicago.

Tomb, Geoffrey. 1991. "Retirees Get Offer to Roll Out Big Guns." *Miami Herald,* November 7: 1.

Toy, Eckard V., Jr. 1989. "Right-Wing Extremism from the Ku Klux Klan to the Order, 1915 to 1988." In Ted Robert Gurr, ed., *Violence in America.* Newbury Park, CA: Sage.

Trebach, Arnold S. 1982. *The Heroin Solution.* New Haven, CN: Yale University Press.

Tricarice, Christopher. 1987. "Outraged Crowd Clashes with White Supremacists." *Los Angeles Herald Examiner,* December 7: 1.

Turk, Austin T. 1982. *Political Criminality: The Defiance and Defense of Authority.* Beverly Hills, Sage.

Turner, James S. 1970. *The Chemical Feast. Ralph Nader's Study Group Report on the Food and Drug Administration.* New York: Grossman's.

U.S. Department of Justice. 1991. *Research Plan: 1991*. Washington, D.C.: U.S. Department of Justice.

———. 1985. *Prison Gangs: Their Extent, Nature and Impact on Prisons*. Washington, D.C.: U.S. Department of Justice.

Vigil, James Diego. 1990. "Cholos and Gangs: Culture Change and Street Youth in Los Angeles." In C. Ronald Huff, ed., *Gangs in America*. Newbury Park, CA: Sage.

———. 1988. *Barrio Gangs: Street Life and Identity in Southern California*. Austin: University of Texas Press.

Von Maltitz, Horst. 1973. *The Evolution of Hitler's Germany*. New York: McGraw-Hill.

Voss, Harwin. 1964. "Differential Association and Delinquent Behavior." *Social Problems*, 12: 78–85.

Wallace, Bill. 1985. "Racist Group Using Computers and TV to Recruit in Bay Area." *San Francisco Chronicle*, March 5: 1–2.

WAR. n.d. "Little Hoto Nose War." *WAR* 7(6): 2–3.

———. n.d. "Reich 'N Roll." *WAR* 8(3): 8–12.

Ward, Dick. 1991. "Hate Groups Increase in Wake of Change." *CJ Europe*, 1: 1–4.

Weaver, R. Kent. 1988. "Social Policy in the Reagan Era." In B. B. Kymlicka and Jean V. Matthews, eds., *The Reagan Revolution?* Chicago: Dorsey Press.

Wegner, Bernd. 1982. *The Waffen SS*. Cambridge, MA: Basil Blackwell.

Weiss, Joan C. 1989. "Prejudice, Conflict, and Ethnoviolence: A National Dilemma." *USA Today*, May 24: 27–29.

White, Helene Raskin. 1990. "The Drug Use-Delinquency Connection in Adolescence." In Ralph Weisheit, ed., *Drugs, Crime and the Criminal Justice System*. Cincinnati: Anderson Publishing.

White, Jonathan R. 1991. *Terrorism: An Introduction*. Pacific Grove, CA: Brooks/Cole.

Whyte, William Foote. 1943. *Street Corner Society*. Chicago: University of Chicago Press.

Willis, Paul. 1978. *Profane Culture*. London: Routledge & Kegan Paul.

Wilson, James Q. "Drugs and Crime." In Michael Tonry and James Q. Wilson, eds., *Drugs and Crime*. Chicago: University of Chicago Press.

Wilson, James Q., and Richard J. Herrnstein. 1985. *Crime and Human Nature*. New York: Simon and Schuster.

Wilson, L. A. II. 1981. "Measurement Issues in Public Administration." In Nicholas L. Henry, ed., *Doing Public Administration*. Boston: Allyn and Bacon.

Wilson, William J. 1987. *The Truly Disadvantaged: The Inner City, The Underclass, and Public Policy*. Chicago: University of Chicago Press.

Wooden, Wayne S. 1991. "Profiles of Teenage Skinheads and Satanists in Southern California." Paper presented at the annual meeting of the American Society of Criminology, San Francisco.

Yablonsky, Lewis. 1990. *Criminology: Crime and Criminality*. New York: Harper & Row.

———. 1983. *The Violent Gang*. New York: Irvington Publishers.

———. 1962. *The Violent Gang*. New York: Macmillan.

Zatarain, Michael. 1990. *David Duke: Evolution of a Klansman*. Gretna, LA: Pelican Publishing.

Zatz, Marjorie S. 1987. "Chicano Gangs and Crime: The Creation of a Moral Panic." *Contemporary Crises*, 11: 129–58.

———. 1985. "Los Cholos: Legal Processing of Chicano Gang Members." *Social Problems*, 33: 11–30.

Index

About the Author

MARK S. HAMM is Professor of Criminology at Indiana State University. He has published widely on crime and corrections.